# Śāradā and Ṭākarī Alphabets
Origin and Development

# Śāradā and Ṭākarī Alphabets
## Origin and Development

**Bhushan Kumar Kaul Deambi**

Foreword by
Prof. Walter Slaje
University of Halle

Tables redrawn through computer graphics
by
Dr. Prakash Pandey

INDIRA GANDHI NATIONAL CENTRE FOR THE ARTS, NEW DELHI

D.K. PRINTWORLD (P) LTD., NEW DELHI

**Cataloging in Publication Data — DK**
Courtesy: D.K. Agencies (P) Ltd. <docinfo@dkagencies.com>

**Deambi, Bhushan Kumar Kaul, 1937-**
Śāradā and Ṭākarī alphabets : origin and development / by Bhushan Kumar Kaul Deambi.
p. 29 cm.
Includes bibliographical references.
Includes index.
ISBN 8124604126

1. Sarada alphabet – History. 2. Himachali language – Alphabet – History. I. Title.

DDC 491.211 22

ISBN 81-246-0412-6
First published in India in 2008

*Published by:*
**Indira Gandhi National Centre for the Arts**
Central Vista, Janpath
New Delhi - 110 001
*Phone:* (011) 2338 1303; *Fax:* 2338 8280
*E-mail:* kalakosa_ed@yahoo.co.in
*Website:* www.ignca.org

*and*

**D.K. Printworld (P) Ltd.**
*Regd. Office:* 'Sri Kunj,' F-52, Bali Nagar
Ramesh Nagar Metro Station
New Delhi-110 015
*Phones:* (011) 2545 3975; 2546 6019; *Fax:* (011) 2546 5926
*E-mail:* dkprintworld@vsnl.net
*Website:* www.dkprintworld.com

*Printed by:* D.K. Printworld (P) Ltd., New Delhi.

To

*NIRJA*

*My Guiding Spirit, Inspiration and Better Half*

# Foreword

It was not until George Bühler's groundbreaking "Report of a Tour in Search of Sanskrit MSS made in Kaśmir, Rajputana, and Central India" had appeared in 1877 that the attention of scholars was directed towards the treasure of manuscripts preserved in Kashmir and to the local script in which the majority of these had been written, going by the name of "Śāradā." Well versed in epigraphy, palaeography and manuscripts, Bühler was in a position to judge the situation right. On the spot in Kashmir, he immediately recognized the importance of the Kashmiri manuscripts in terms of textual criticism and — to the best of his abilities — took measures to preserve them. Wherever physical preservation seemed to be a hopeless enterprise, he arranged for apographs prepared from the manuscripts on-site. Bühler's pioneering activities were supported and continued by the eminent archaeologist and Sanskrit scholar Sir Marcus Aurel Stein, who himself utilized a unique Śāradā manuscript for his unsurpassed edition of Kalhaṇa's *Rājataraṅgiṇī*. Moreover, Stein not only catalogued an enormous number of Sanskrit (Śāradā) manuscripts belonging to the Jammu Raghunātha Temple Library (1894), but also purchased manuscripts of Kashmiri origin and entrusted them to the care of distinguished libraries in Budapest, Oxford, Paris and Vienna. The accessibility of these manuscripts ensured, they soon attracted Indologists, whose research benefited greatly from consulting fresh and unexpectedly weighty source material. On account of the increased interest scholars were taking in these manuscripts, the Śāradā script as such also received attention to a greater extent. As early as 1884 Karl Burkhard reproduced the first charts ever of Śāradā characters (Vienna).[1] He had prepared them from a manuscript transmitting the Kashmiri Śakuntalā recension.[2] A few years later (1901), a high-quality, extraordinarily costly Śāradā facsimile edition in three volumes of the Tübingen Kashmiri (Paippalāda) Atharva Veda, which is the only one of its kind, saw the light of its publication.[3] Despite its undisputed importance for historical research, the

1. Karl Burkhard, *Die Kaçmīrer Çakuntalā-Handschrift*. Wien 1884.
2. Edited and translated by S. Vasudeva as: The Recognition of Shakúntala (Kashmir Recension). New York 2006 (Clay Sanskrit Library).
3. *The Kashmirian Atharvaveda (School of the Paippalādas)*. Reproduced by Chromatography from the MS in the Univ. Library at Tübingen. ed. by Maurice Bloomfield & Richard Garbe. Vol. 1-3. Baltimore 1901.

drawing up of Śāradā training aids seems to have been considered dispensable. In consequence thereof each scholar wishing to consult Śāradā manuscripts was bound to acquaint himself anew with the script all by himself. What holds true for this early disregard for synchronic depictions of Śāradā is equally true for diachronic — and in the strict sense palaeographic — explorations of the historic development of Kashmiri local handwriting. A number of Śāradā characters were published by Jean Philippe Vogel in 1911, but he dealt with inscriptional forms of the alphabet only.[4] And although George Grierson's laudable article "On the Śāradā Alphabet" (1916)[5] was indeed of help, it had its limits, too: the characters reproduced there represent the late 19th century mode of writing.

We may mark up as a considerable improvement on the unsatisfactory situation the appearance of Lore Sander's palaeographic investigation into Central Asian (Turfan) Sanskrit manuscripts, which resulted in a classification of proto-Śāradā characters and in the derivation of the fully-developed Śāradā script from what she had determined as "Gilgit-Bamiyan-Type II."[6] A subsequent, unquestionable milestone in the history of Śāradā-related studies was Dr Deambi's well-known *Corpus of Śāradā Inscriptions of Kashmir* (Delhi 1982), giving particular emphasis to their palaeographic stratification. Equipped with exhaustive tables, his book has served Indologists extremely well over the years. Among those benefiting from Dr Deambi's thorough study is also the writer of this foreword, who — in utilizing one of the Kashmiri manuscripts Stein had bought in 1894 and presented to the Viennese Imperial Library — published a Śāradā Primer in German.[7] To two papers of Michael Witzel (1994) we owe penetrating insights into the essentials of Kashmiri manuscript culture.[8] Another important reproduction-cum-transliteration edition was brought to the public in 1995. This famous mathematical treatise, known as the "Bakhshāli Manuscript," is considered the oldest extant manuscript written in Śāradā characters.[9]

The past decades have seen a gigantic progress in the cataloguing and microfilming of Sanskrit manuscripts, of which the early pioneers in Indology could not even have dreamt. Mention must be made of the microfilming and cataloguing campaigns of the IGNCA,

---

4. Jean Philippe Vogel, Antiquities of Chamba State. Vol. 1. Calcutta 1911.
5. George A. Grierson, *On the Sarada Alphabet.* JRAS 1916: 677-708.
6. Lore Sander, *Paläographisches zu den Sanskrithandschriften der Berliner Turfansammlung.* Wiesbaden 1968.
7. *Śāradā. Deskriptiv-synchrone Schriftkunde zur Bearbeitung kaschmirischer Sanskrit-Manuskripte.* Reinbek/Hamburg 1993.
8. Michael Witzel, Kashmiri Manuscripts and Pronunciation. In: *A Study of the Nīlamata. Aspects of Hinduism in Ancient Kashmir.* ed. by Yasuke Ikari. Kyoto 1994, pp. 1-53. Michael Witzel, *The Brahmins of Kashmir.* Ibid., pp. 237-294.
9. Takao Hayashi, *The Bakhshālī Manuscript.* Groningen 1995.

a vibrant, highly esteemed centre for manuscript research, and of the reputed Nepal-German Manuscript Preservation (and Cataloguing) Project (NGMP[/C]P), another inexhaustible mine of manuscripts. Under such favourable circumstances of easily accessible materials it was inevitable that the study of the wide range of the different scripts in use in South Asia had also made significant steps forward. The year 2005 saw the launch of a German Internet palaeography (IndoSkript).[10] As a database containing hundreds of thousands of single characters drawn from inscriptions and manuscripts, it can also be used as an electronic tool for analyzing their palaeography.

From the above, the importance of Dr Deambi's present publication will easily be gauged. The author has made every effort to select all the data relevant for carrying out a comprehensive study of a separable palaeographic subject, definable as the Śāradā and Ṭākarī spheres of writing. To be sure, their historical "cultural boundaries" extended far beyond the political borders and administrative districts of today. As a result of Dr Deambi's endeavours, scholars can now conveniently utilize the vast material he has collected and which he presents in a meticulous historico-systematic arrangement. The first chapters of his book treat the Śāradā alphabets arranged according to their developmental stages with special attention not only to their epigraphic and manuscript varieties, but also to the manner of writing numerals. It must be emphasized that Dr Deambi has also thoroughly treated the much neglected Ṭākarī alphabets, as they are the results of a transition from the Śāradā script to its descendent known as Devāśeṣa, to which the subsequent chapters are devoted. On this meritorious achievement Dr Deambi deserves to be congratulated in particular. It is for the first time that scholars will gain easy access to reading and interpreting numberless Ṭākarī inscribed artefacts and paintings, mainly from the region of Himachal Pradesh. It is the first comprehensive Ṭākarī study of its kind.

From the palaeographic point of view, Dr Deambi has manifestly recorded the Śāradā letters and their changes, and thus has rendered developments in the mode of their writing comprehensible. The exhaustive charts included in his book with carefully drawn *akṣaras* involve another, evidently practical, purpose: scholars consulting Śāradā and Ṭākarī documents cannot but welcome these tables as reliable guides and perfect reference points for decoding the characters of their sources.

In the realm of basic research in the humanities, the 16th century humanists' Latin motto *ad fontes* ("To the sources!") will ever retain its justification. There can be no knowledge without sources of knowledge. There can be no knowledge of the past without sources of knowledge of the past. The ultimate precondition for working with sources of the past handed down in writing is, incontrovertibly, a correct interpretation of their letters. Is there anything better one can say of Dr Deambi's ambitious book than that he has given

10. http://userpage.fu-berlin.de/falk/index.htm (ed. by H. Falk / W. Slaje)

scholars direct access to primary sources of knowledge as are the preserved treasures[11] of Kashmiri Sanskrit culture?

May this successful study of Dr Deambi, doyen of Śāradā palaeographers, receive a warm and friendly reception.

**Dr Walter Slaje**
Professor of Indology
Martin-Luther-University Halle Wittenberg
Director, Centre for Research in the
Historiography and Intellectual Culture of Kashmir,
Akademie der Wissenschaften und der Literatur zu Mainz

Halle (Germany)
March 12, 2007

11. For a significant collection of Śāradā manuscripts recently acquired by the Staatsbibliothek Berlin see Gerhard Ehlers, *Die Śāradā Handschriften der Sammlung Janert der Staatsbibliothek zu Berlin-Preussischer Kulturbesitz*. Stuttgart 2006.

# Preface

THE value of the epigraphic records as the most authentic and dependable source of history and culture in India has long been recognized. Ancient India did not produce any Herodotus, Strabo or Pliny, and in the absence of genuine and authentic written records of history, epigraphic records form the chief original source for the study of the history and culture of India's glorious past. Their value was recognized long ago by the sole historian, worth the name Kalhaṇa, of ancient India, who for writing his history of Kashmir consulted the extant epigraphic records of all types and was thus able "to overcome many errors" arising from other sources.

The study of the Indian epigraphic records presupposes the knowledge of the Indian scripts in which they are written. These scripts have been a subject of study of scholars now for more than a hundred years and many a mystery associated with their decipherment has been unravelled. However, some important regional scripts have not received the attention they deserve. Among these may be cited the examples of Śāradā and the Ṭākarī scripts.

The Śāradā script has a pride of place among the Indian scripts. Though evolved from Western Brāhmī about a millennium ago in the 9th century, it continues to be in use even today though its use is confined to the older generation of the Paṇḍit community of Kashmir. Though an alphabet of Kashmir *par excellence*, it remained for several centuries a popular script in an extensive area of north-western India including Afghanistan, Gandhāra or north-western Pakistan, the Darad territories of Gilgit, Chilas and Chitral, Ladakh, Jammu, Himachal Pradesh, Punjab and Delhi. The epigraphic records written in Śāradā script that have surfaced in these regions have thrown welcome light on many facets of the history and culture of the area of their provenance. Nearly the entire extant manuscripts of Sanskrit and old Kashmiri texts and historical works of Kashmir are written in this script, which in fact considerably enhances the value of the study of this important alphabet for the critical study and analysis of these priceless manuscripts.

The Śāradā alphabet continued to be used in Himachal Pradesh up to the 13th century when it was replaced by its descendant the Devāśeṣa which in turn gave rise to the modern alphabet of Ṭākarī.

The extant epigraphic records of Himachal Pradesh numbering over several hundred are written in Devāśeṣa and Ṭākarī, and only a part of these have been edited so far.

Besides, the captions of majority of paintings belonging to the famous schools of Basohli, Kangra and Chamba have been written in Ṭākarī. There is hardly any image of immense artistic value enshrined in any temple of Himachal Pradesh which does not contain an inscription in Ṭākarī. Thus, the importance of the study of Ṭākarī for the decipherment and critical analysis of early medieval records, paintings and art pieces of Himachal Pradesh can hardly be exaggerated.

The Śāradā and the Ṭākarī though very important regional scripts have not been taken up so far for critical study and analysis. A very brief account of Śāradā alphabet has been given by George Bühler in his *Indian Palaeography* (English edn. p.78 f.); by George Grierson in the *Journal of Royal Asiatic Society*, (p. 1916, p. 677 ff.); and a somewhat detailed treatment, but based only on the inscriptions of Chamba, has been given by J. Ph. Vogel in his *Antiquities of Chamba State*, Part I. More comprehensive study of the script has been attempted by the present investigator in Section I of his *Corpus of the Śāradā Inscriptions of Kashmir*. Since the publication of the latter work in 1982, lot more epigraphic records and manuscripts written in this script have come to light which have necessitated the revised treatment of the subject in a more comprehensive and detailed manner.

As far as Ṭākarī is concerned, first noteworthy study of the script is available in the introduction of the *Antiquities of Chamba State*, Part II, by B. Ch. Chabra.

The present work aims at fulfilling this desideratum. Besides, a detailed and scientific study of the origin and development of the Śāradā script, a systematic account of the evolution of the Ṭākarī script and its relationship with the Śāradā alphabet has been attempted. There is ample scope for further research on the Ṭākarī script provided one is well conversant with Chamiali and allied hill dialects.

As pointed out above, while almost all subjects pertaining to Indian history and culture have received comprehensive treatment at the hands of the scholars and palaeographers, the scientific study of the Indian scripts have remained neglected subjects. The result has been that the knowledge of ancient and medieval regional scripts of India has been consigned to oblivion. The Śāradā and Ṭākarī scripts are no exception. The number of scholars having a sound knowledge of these scripts is extremely small. There is every apprehension of the complete annihilation of the scripts unless timely measures are taken to disseminate the knowledge of the two scripts among the younger generation of the scholars. The knowledge of the Śāradā script is all the more necessary since a number of important and valuable manuscripts on medicine, architecture, mathematics, astronomy, linguistics, grammar, philosophy, etc. written in this script and preserved in the important museums and libraries in India and abroad, are in long wait for publication by the experts.

Though Ṭākarī is the alphabet of Himachal Pradesh *par excellence*, there are very few scholars in the state possessing a sound knowledge of the script and ability to decipher and analyse the records written in this script. Of late my enterprising student Dr Rita Devi Sharma, presently Curator, Epigraphy Section, National Museum, New Delhi has evinced some interest in the subject and has published Primer Part I and II of Modern Ṭākarī.

The present writer has been approached a number of times by scholars in India and abroad who are interested in the study of unpublished texts of Kashmir on scientific subjects written in the Śāradā script and in the study of medieval culture, arts and paintings of Himachal Pradesh. They wish a comprehensive treatise on the two scripts of Śāradā and Ṭākarī be prepared so that the same would serve as a guide and a valuable aid in their respective fields of study.

The entire study presented here is based on original records and is comprehensively illustrated by palaeographic tables and charts prepared from published facsimilies, photographs and original inscriptions and manuscripts.

The writer is profoundly grateful to the Department of Culture, Ministry of Art, Culture and Tourism, Government of India, for awarding him a Senior Fellowship to complete the project. He is equally grateful to the Indira Gandhi National Centre for the Arts, New Delhi, specially to its Member Secretary Dr K.K. Chakravarty and Professor G.C. Tripathi, Head of the Kalakośa Division for considering the publication of the completed project. Last but not the least he is thankful to his student Dr Mrs Advaitavadini Kaul, Editor, Kalākośa, IGNCA for editing and supervising the printing of this book.

The writer would be failing in his duty if he does not express his profound gratitude to all those epigraphic stalwarts whose most valuable works, plates and facsimilies he has ulitized in writing this monograph. But for these (cited in references in this work) and other eminent scholars, the study of Indian Epigraphy and Palaeography would have never received the attention it deserved. He is also highly grateful to Prof. Walter Slaje, Professor of Indology, Martin-Luther-University, Halle — Wittenberg, for the highly learned foreword he has written for this publication.

*Haldwani (Nainital)* **Bhushan Kumar Kaul Deambi**
*May 14, 2007*

# Contents

# List of Tables

# List of Plates

*Pl. 15* : Thunḍhu copper plate inscription of Āsaṭavarman, Chamba, H.P., 11th Century. (Source: J.Ph. Vogel, *Antiquities of Chamba State,* Part I)

*Pl. 16* : The S. P. S. Museum, Srinagar, stone slab inscription of the reign of Jayasimha (*Laukika* '25) CE 1149. (Courtesy: Chief Epigraphist, Archaeological Survey of India, Mysore)

*Pl. 17* : Tapar, Kashmir, stone lintel inscription of Parmāṇḍadeva, 12th Century. (Source: B.K. Kaul Deambi, *Corpus of Śāradā Inscriptions of Kashmir*)

*Pl. 18* : Devi-ri-kothi, Chamba, H.P., fountain inscription of Rājānaka Nāgapāla and Nānapāla, 12th Century. (Source: J.Ph. Vogel, *Antiquities of Chamba State* Part I)

*Pl. 19* : Devi-rī-kothi, Chamba, H.P., fountain inscription of Sri Raṇapāladeva, 12th Century. (Source: J. Ph. Vogel, *Antiquities of Chamba State* Part I)

*Pl. 20* : Salhi, Chamba, H.P., Fountain inscription of Rājānaka Ludrapāla, 12th Century. (Source: J. Ph. Vogel, *Antiquities of Chamba State* Part I)

*Pl. 21* : Arigom, Kashmir, stone slab inscription (*Laukika* '73) CE 1197. (Source: Chief Epigraphist, Archaeological Survey of India, Mysore)

*Pl. 22* : Baijnāth, Kangra, H.P., Siva Temple inscriptions, *Praśasti,* 1204 CE. (Source: J.N. Agrawal, Inscriptions of Haryana, Punjab, Himachal Pradesh, etc.)

*Pl. 23* : Bijbehara (Vejebror), Kashmir, stone inscription of the reign of Rājadeva (*Śaka* 58 ?), CE 1235-36 (?). (Source: B.K. Kaul Deambi, *Corpus of Śāradā Inscriptions of Kashmir*)

*Pl. 24* : Bijbehara, Kashmir, stone inscription of the reign of Yaskaradeva, 13th Century. (Source: B.K. Kaul Deambi, *Corpus of Sāradā Inscriptions of Kashmir*)

*Pl. 25* : Kotiher, Kashmir, stone slab inscription of the reign of Shāhabadena (Shihabud-din) dated CE 1369 (*Laukika* '44 or 45). (Source: B.K. Kaul Deambi, *Corpus of Śāradā Inscriptions of Kashmir*)

*Pl. 26* : The Bhuvaneshvarī, Khonamuh, Kashmir, stone inscription of the reign of Jayanolabadena (Zain-ul-ābidin) dated *Kali* 4530 (CE 1428). (Source: B.K. Kaul Deambi, *Corpus of Śāradā Inscriptions of Kashmir*)

*Pl. 27* : Peshawar, NWFP Pakistan, Musuem inscription of Vaṇhaḍaka (*Laukika saṁ* (4) 538), CE 1462. (Source: *Epigraphia India,* vol. X, p. 79ff and plate)

*Pl. 28* : Hariparbat, Srinagar, Kashmir, grave stone inscription of the reign of Mohammad Shāh (*Laukika saṁ* (45) 60), CE 1484. (Source: B.K. Kaul Deambi, *Corpus of Śāradā Inscriptions of Kashmir*)

*Pl. 29* : Wularhama Bijbehara, Kashmir, bathroom gate inscription, 15th-16th Century. (Source: B.K. Kaul Deambi, *Corpus of Śāradā Inscriptions of Kashmir*)

**Ṭākarī Inscriptions**

**Manuscripts**

# Key to Transliteration

## VOWELS

| | | | | | | | |
|---|---|---|---|---|---|---|---|
| अ *a* | आ *ā* | इ *i* | ई *ī* | उ *u* | ऊ *ū* | ऋ *ṛ* | ॠ *ṝ*[1] |
| (Roman) | (palm) | (it) | (police) | (put) | (rule) | (rig) | |
| ऌ *ḷ* | ॡ *ḹ*[1] | ए *e* | ऐ *ai* | ओ *o* | औ *au* | | |
| (able) | | (there) | (aisle) | (no) | (loud) | | |

## CONSONANTS

| | | | | | |
|---|---|---|---|---|---|
| **Guttural** | क *ka* | ख *kha*[2] | ग *ga* | घ *gha*[2] | ङ *ṅa* |
| | (skate) | (blockhead) | (gate) | (ghost) | (sing) |
| **Palatal** | च *ca* | छ *cha*[2] | ज *ja* | झ *jha*[2] | ञ *ña* |
| | (chunk) | (catch him) | (john) | (hedgehog) | (bunch) |
| **Cerebral** | ट *ṭa* | ठ *ṭha*[2] | ड *ḍa* | ढ *ḍha*[2] | ण *ṇa* |
| | (start) | (anthill) | (dart) | (godhead) | (under) |
| **Dental** | त *ta* | थ *tha*[2] | द *da* | ध *dha*[2] | न *na* |
| | (path) | (thunder) | (that) | (this) | (numb) |
| **Labial** | प *pa* | फ *pha*[2] | ब *ba* | भ *bha*[2] | म *ma* |
| | (spin) | (philosophy) | (bin) | (abhor) | (much) |
| **Semi-** | य *ya* | र *ra* | ल *la*[3] | व *va*[4] | |
| **vowels** | (young) | (drama) | (luck) | (vile) | |
| **Sibilants** | श *śa*[5] | ष *ṣa*[5] | स *sa* | ह *ha* | |
| | (shove) | (bushel) | (so) | (hum) | |
| **Others** | क्ष *kṣa* | त्र *tra* | ज्ञ *jña* | | |
| | (*kṣatriya*) | (*triśūla*) | (*jñānī*) | | |

अं ( ं ) *ṁ anusvāra* is a nasal off-glide that immediately follows the pronunciation of a vowel as in *saṁskṛti.*

अः *visarga* = *ḥ* consists in abrupt release of breath after a vowel as in *prātaḥ*.

ऽ *Avagraha* shows non-pronunciation, that is, deletion of "a" after "e" or "o" as in *ime 'vasthitāḥ*. In Vedic Sanskrit, it can also show word division.

## HINDI LETTERS (extras)

| | | | |
|---|---|---|---|
| ँ = *m̐* | ं = ṅ | ड़ = *ṛa* | ढ़ = *ṛha* |
| (*candrabindu*) | (*anusvāra*) | | |

1 Longer form of the preceding vowel.

2 Aspirated forms of the preceding consonants. The compound words given as examples should be pronounced without a syllabic break at the underlined places. "tha" and "pha" should not be pronounced as fricatives.

3 retroflexed and written as "L *la*" in certain phonetic contexts.

4 Pronounced like "w," without aspiration.

5 "śa" is palatal; "ṣa" cerebral or retroflex.

# 1

# Origin of Śāradā Script

THE use of the Śāradā script was confined to the north-western part of the Indian subcontinent. Earlier in this region the two well-known scripts of ancient India, viz. the Brāhmī and the Kharoṣṭhī were both fairly in use. But it is only the Brāhmī which survived and led to the development of the later Indian alphabets. The Kharoṣṭhī script went out of use after the 3rd century. So in this chapter we shall study the development of the Brāhmī alphabet of north-western India from the earliest known period of its use till the appearance of the Śāradā, its descendant in the 9th century.

## I. Brāhmī Alphabet of North-Western India

**(*c.* 300 BCE to *c.* CE 300)**

### A. Maurya Period (c. 300 to 200 BCE)

The earliest definitely datable records of north-western India written in the Brāhmī script are the edicts of the Maurya emperor Aśoka engraved on a rock situated at the village of Kalsi in the Dehra Dun district in Uttaranchal state,[1] and on a pillar which originally stood at village Topra in the Ambala district of Haryana and now stands in the Ferozeshah Kotla Grounds in Delhi.[2] The other record of the region assignable to the same period is a small inscription engraved on a rock lying in the village of Paṭhyar in the Kangra district of Himachal Pradesh.[3] The upper limit of the Brāhmī alphabet used in these records cannot be fixed with certainty and the lower limit according to George Bühler[4] cannot be far distant from Aśoka's reign and must fall about 200 BCE.

The Brāhmī alphabet of the Maurya period has been discussed at length by the palaeographists, both Indian and European, and for our purpose it would be sufficient to examine the peculiarities of the Brāhmī script used in our records which have a bearing on the development of the script in the subsequent periods.

---

1. Hultzsch, E., *Corpus Inscriptionum Indicarum,* vol. I (Inscriptions of Aśoka) p. 27 ff. and plates facing pp. 44, 50.
2. Ibid., p. 119 ff. and plates facing pp. 122-23, 128 and 134.
3. Vogel, J. Ph., *Epigraphia Indica,* vol. VII, p. 116 ff. and plate.
4. Bühler, George, *Indian Palaeography* (English edn.), p. 50.

THE KALSI ROCK EDICTS

The letters in the Kalsi edicts are hurriedly written and mostly show cursive forms. The following peculiarities deserve notice (see Table No. 1, col. I):

1. The initial *a* shows several forms but most of these are the variants of the most common form consisting of two curves placed one below the other and attached to a vertical on the right.
2. *k* has a dagger-like form but also sometimes shows a highly cursive form.
3. *kh* has a big round loop at the bottom.
4. *ch* has sometimes a peculiar shape. It consists of two circles with a small vertical line standing on the point of contact and bearing a serif at the upper end.
5. *j* which is mostly cursive possesses a loop in the middle.
6. *t* and *y* are mostly written with only two strokes instead of the usual three.
7. Among the Aśokan inscriptions, only in these edicts do we find the forms of *ś* and *ṣ*. In *ś* the inner stroke issues sometimes from the top and sometimes from the middle of the left curve.
8. No signs for *r* and *ṇ* can be traced in this version.

MEDIAL VOWELS

The following peculiarities of medial vowels leading to later forms may be noticed:

1. Medial *ā* is occasionally represented by a stroke slanting downwards.
2. Medial *e* is sometimes marked by a slanting stroke placed over the top of the letter.

THE DELHI-TOPRA PILLAR EDICTS (see Table no. 1, col. II)

In contrast to the Kalsi edicts, the Delhi-Topra pillar edicts have been beautifully executed with care and attention and the letters mostly show angular forms. The first six edicts display the following peculiarities:

1. Unlike *kh* of Kalsi these edicts show the letter with a dot instead of a loop at the foot of the vertical.
2. *j* does not show a loop as in Kalsi.
3. A rare *ḷ* consisting of *ḍ* with a dot below is first seen in these edicts.

The seventh edict has been comparatively engraved hurriedly and the letters show cursive forms.

The following features deserve notice:

1. The curves at the left end of *a* show sometimes greater bend.
2. *kh* shows a dot at the bottom of a bent vertical.
3. *ḍh* has a spiral form.

THE PATHYAR INSCRIPTION (see Table 1, col. III)

The Pathyar inscription consists of two lines cut into one stone. The letters are of considerable size, the last one being not less than 1½" high. The characters of the inscription correspond entirely to those of the Aśokan edicts and do not display any significant peculiarities except that the lower parts of the letters are much smaller in size as compared to their very long verticals.

The last phase of the Brāhmī alphabet of the Maurya period is represented by an inscription discovered from Kaṅkālī Ṭīlā in Mathurā by George Bühler and assigned by him on palaeographic grounds to 2nd century BCE.[5] The letters show forms which are later than those of the Aśokan inscriptions but decidedly earlier than those used in the records of the post-Maurya period. The following developments are noteworthy (see Table 1, col. IV):

1. The letters are more rounded in shape.
2. The verticals of the letters are smaller in size.
3. The curves of medial *i* and *ī* are elongated.
4. Small triangles replace usual circles in *m* and *v*.
5. In *s* the hooked curve on the left is drawn further down towards the right.

**B. Post-Maurya Period**
**(c. 200 BCE to the beginning of the Christian Era)**

The Brāhmī alphabet of north-western India in the post-Maurya period is represented among others by the following records:

1. Coins of the Indo-Grecian kings Agathocles and Pantaleon.[6]
2. The Mathurā inscriptions of the Kshatrap king Śoḍāsa.[7]
3. The Mora (Mathurā district) inscriptions.[8]

---

5. Bühler, George, *Epigraphia Indica,* vol. II, p. 195 ff., No. 1 and plate.
6. Gardener, Percy, *The Coins of the Greek and Seythic Kings of Bactria and India*, London, Plates 3-4.
7. *Epigraphia Indica,* vol. II, p. 199, Nos. 2, 5 and plates; Alexander Cunningham, *Archaeological Survey Report,* vol. III, p. 30, No. 1, plate XIII.
8. Cunningham, *Archaeological Survey Report,* vol. XX, p. 48, plate V, figure 4.

4. The Kanhiara (district Kangra) rock inscriptions.[9]

The alphabet of these records display two remarkable tendencies (see Table No. 1, cols. V-VIII):

1. Shortening and the equalization of the upper vertical lines.
2. Development of the top marks represented by serifs, nail heads or triangular wedges.

Besides we notice the following developments:

1. The lower curve of *a* shows sometimes greater bend towards the left.
2. The horizontal bar for initial *ā* is attached lower down near the foot of the vertical in an inscription from Mathurā.
3. The rare initial *ī* consisting of four dots placed in the position of a square is noticed in an inscription of Śoḍāsa.
4. *k* occurs in a developed form with bent bars in an inscription of Śoḍāsa.
5. The letter *d* shows a remarkable development with its direction changed from right to left and is mostly cursive in form.
6. The lower limb of *m* is mostly represented by a small triangle in place of a circle. We have already noticed this practice in an earlier inscription from Mathurā noted above.
7. *r* sometimes occurs with a curve at the foot of the vertical.
8. The letter *ś* which is cursive in form shows advanced form in the inscriptions of Śoḍāsa and in the Kanhiara inscription.
9. *ṣ* which is now mostly angular in shape displays marked development and may be regarded as the precursor of the form of the letter in the subsequent Kuṣāṇa period.

MEDIAL VOWELS

1. The curves of medial *i* and *ī* are further elongated
2. Medial *o* shows an advance form in the inscriptions of Śoḍāsa; and
3. Medial *ṛ* consisting of a downward stroke slanting towards the left is found for the first time in the Kanhiara and Mora inscriptions.

---

9. Vogel, *Epigraphia India*, vol. VII, p. 116, No. 16 and plate. Vogel assigns this inscription to 2nd and 3rd centuries CE. But the forms of most of the letters, e.g. *d, ś, s* agree more with those of 1st century BCE than those of the 2nd and 3rd centuries CE.

### C. Kuṣāṇa Period (1st-3rd century CE)

The Brāhmī alphabet of the Kuṣāṇa period which marks the next important stage of the development of the script is represented by several records both epigraphic and numismatic belonging to this period. The present study is based on the dated and well-preserved inscriptions of the Kuṣāṇa kings Kaniṣka, Huviṣka and Vāsudeva discovered from north-western part of the country mostly from Mathurā and its vicinity.[10]

The Brāhmī alphabet of this period displays the following developments (see Table 1, cols. IX-IX):

1. The left limb of *a* is occasionally represented by a wavy line.
2. The bar expressing the length of the vowel in *ā* is attached slightly above the foot of the vertical.
3. In *i*, the earlier three dots are replaced by three strokes one of which is sometimes placed vertically.
4. *u* shows a curve at the right end of the base stroke.
5. The base of *e* is mostly at the top.
6. The earlier straight bar in *k* becomes sometimes a curved line.
7. In *kh*, the triangle at the bottom replaces the earlier circle.
8. *ṇ* shows several peculiar forms.
9. *d* displays larger bulge on the right and its lower end is drawn further to the right.
10. In *n*, the base line is curved, or looped or made angular.
11. In *m*, the triangle uniformly replaces the earlier circle.
12. *y* mostly shows a hook, occasionally a loop in the left limb.
13. In *ś*, the two side limbs come closer and the earlier slanting stroke becomes a horizontal bar connecting the interior of the two limbs.
14. In *ṣ*, the central bar is sometimes drawn further to the right and touches the right vertical.
15. *s* shows occasionally a loop in the left limb.

MEDIAL VOWELS

The following developments are noticeable in the treatment of medial vowels:

1. Medial *ā* is sometimes expressed by a downward stroke attached to the top of the letter on the right side.

---

10. *Epigraphia Indica*, vol. I, p. 371 ff.; vol. II, 195 ff. and plates.

2. Medial *i* is generally expressed by sickle-shaped curve placed over the consonant.
3. Medial *u* is expressed occasionally by a curve drawn to the left and attached to the lower end of the consonant.
4. Medial *ṛ* is expressed occasionally by a curve open to the right.
5. Medial *e* is expressed by a slanting stroke placed over the top of the letter.
6. Medial *o* sometimes consists of two strokes placed over the consonant and rising upwards to the right and left, respectively.

LIGATURES

1. The letters forming a ligature are usually written one below the other.
2. The subscript *y* differs from the initial form and is bipartite in form. Its curve on the right is sometimes drawn to the level of the top of the letter in legends on some seals belonging to this period.[11]
3. The superscript *r* is represented by a short vertical placed at the top of the left vertical.
4. The subscript *r* is expressed by a curve or stroke drawn to the left.

## II. Brāhmī Alphabet of North-Western India

**(4th-5th centuries CE)**

The Brāhmī alphabet of north-western India of 4th and 5th centuries represented by the following records illustrates the next stage of the development of the alphabet.

1. The Abbottabad (Dist. Peshawar) inscription of the time of Kadambeśvaradāsa of the year 25.[12]
2. The Mathurā inscription of Candragupta II GE 61 = CE 380.[13]
3. The Mathurā stone inscription of Candragupta II.[14]
4. The Shorkot (Salt Range) inscription of the year 83.[15]
5. The Tusam (dist. Hissar) rock inscription.[16]
6. The Bower Manuscript.[17]

---

11. Handa, Devendra, *Studies in Indian Coins and Seals,* plate XIX, No. 5.
12. *Epigraphia Indica,* vol. XXX, p. 59 and plate.
13. Ibid., vol. XXI, pp. 8-9 and plate.
14. Fleet, *Corpus Inscriptionum Indicarum,* vol. III, pp. 25-27, plate IIA.
15. *Epigraphia Indica,* vol. XVI, p.15 and plate.
16. Fleet, *Corpus Inscriptionum Indicarum,* vol. III, pp. 269-70, plate XLA.
17. Hoernle (ed.), *The Bower Manuscript,* Archaeological Survey of India (New Imperical Series), vol. XXII.

7. Chilas (dist. Gilgit) inscriptions.[18]

INITIAL VOWELS (see Table 1 B)

1. The initial *a* shows at the lower end of the left limb a curve open to the left in the Tusam inscription (col. IV) and the Bower manuscript (col. VI).
2. In the initial *ā*, the length of the vowel is marked by a curve open to the left in the Mathurā inscription of GE 61 (col. II) and the Bower manuscript (col. VI). In the Chilas inscription number 61 (col. VII) the letter has a peculiar form with the left limb represented by a big curve open to the left and a small slanting stroke attached to its lower end. The length of the vowel is marked by a horizontal stroke attached to the middle of the vertical.
3. In initial *i*, the lower dot in the Bower Manuscript (col. VI) has been provided with a curve.
4. In the initial *ī* in the same record, the upper and the lower dots of the ancient sign which consisted of the four dots in the position of a square have been converted into a vertical stroke with a wedge at each end.
5. In initial *u*, the curve at the lower end is drawn further to the left (Bower Manuscript col. VI).
6. The Initial *ū* is formed like *u* with the addition of a small slanting stroke attached to the back of *u* near the top (Bower Manuscript. col. VI).
7. The initial *ṛ* shows a peculiar form in the Bower Manuscript.
8. In *e*, the base of the triangle is mostly at the top.
9. In *ai*, in the Bower Manuscript (col. VI), the flag-like line marking the length of the vowel has been attached to the vertex of triangular *e* with base below.
10. *o* is formed like *u* with the addition of a wedge at the left top end (Bower Manuscript col. VI).
11. *au* is formed like *o* with the addition of a hook at the back (col. VI).

CONSONANTS

1. In *k*, the earlier straight crossbar becomes a cursive bar. Occasionally the end of cursive stroke on the left is brought down to meet the foot of the central vertical resulting in the formation of a loop as in the Bower Manuscript (col. VI).
2. In *kh*, the loop on the left becomes a triangle as in the Tusam inscription (col. IV) and the Chilas inscription (col VII).

---

18. Dani, Ahmad Hasan, *CHILAS*, p. 75, plate 55; p. 79, plates 60-61.

3. *g* shows both cursive and flat top with right-hand vertically elongated downwards. The letter also develops small horizontal bar or a wedge or loop at the end of the left vertical.
4. *gh* in the Shorkot inscription (col. V) has a peculiar form with all the three verticals provided with hollow triangles at the top. The top mark represented by a hollow triangle is a peculiar feature of the inscription.
5. *ṅ* shows a wedge or a button at the right top end (cols. II, IV).
6. *c* is mostly beaked in form.
7. *ch* consists of two circles attached to the top bar with a small vertical as in the past.
8. *j* which is very conservative in development shows a slanting central bar in Tusam inscription (col. IV) and Bower Manuscript (col. VI). In all cases the upper-most horizontal bar merges with the top bar. In the Chilas inscription (col. VII) the lowermost horizontal bar ends in a curve.
9. *jh* occurs only in the Bower Manuscript (col. VI) and is characterized by a top bar with a vertical attached to its left end and an angular hook attached to the vertical in the middle.
10. *ñ* occurs only in conjunction with *c* and *j*, and is represented by a cursive downward stroke with another small cursive stroke attached to it at the back (cols. II, VI).
11. *ṭ* is sometimes flattened at the top as in Mathurā inscription (col. II) and the Bower Manuscript (col. VI).
12. *ṭh* has likewise been flattened on the right in the Mathurā inscription (col. II).
13. In *ḍ*, the lower straight stroke has been converted into a curve into the Tusam inscription (col. IV) and the Bower Manuscript (col. VI).
14. In *ḍh*, the loop is missing in the Chilas inscription No. 60 (col. VII).
15. In *ṇ*, the curves at either end of the base stroke are turned sharply round. A peculiar form is found in Chilas inscription No. 61 (col. VII).
16. In *t*, the earlier sloping stroke now becomes cursive.
17. In *th*, the earlier dot now becomes regularly a straight bar.
18. In *d*, the bulge is now more pronounced.
19. *dh* is regularly flattened on the right.
20. *n* consisting of two strokes of unequal length attached to the top bar with a small vertical is now more angular in shape.

21. The development in *p* is marked by the elongation of the right-hand vertical in the Bower manuscript (col. VI).

22. *ph* has a peculiar angular shape in the Mathurā inscription of GE 61 (col. II). In the Bower Manuscript (col. VI), the loop marking the aspirate is sometimes attached on the right instead of inside. In a few cases we have only the open curve on the right.

23. *b* shows a bend in the left arm in the Shorkot inscription (col. V).

24. *bh* shows angular form in the Mathurā inscription (col. II). In other examples it is cursive. A developed form is found in the Bower Manuscript (col. VI) with a wedge (solid or open) on the left.

25. In *m*, the development is marked by the twisted left limb. The later form with straight left limb is found sometimes in the Bower Manuscript (col. VI). The Mathurā inscription (col. II) retains the earlier form. The letter has been provided with a flat top in the Abbottabad inscription (col. I).

26. *y* occurs regularly with a loop on the left caused by the contact of the left hand stroke with the horizontal base. The intervening form is found in the Mathurā inscription (col. II). In the Chilas inscriptions (col. VII), we sometimes find the older form and the form where the curve on the left is turned round instead of inside to form the loop.

27. *r* which generally retains the archaic form shows an upward slant at the foot of the vertical in the Tusam inscription (col. IV) and a small wedge in the Bower Manuscript (col. VI). The two features signify an important development. In Shorkot (col. V) the letter shows a small triangle at the foot as at the top.

28. In *l*, the curve on the left is turned more sharply round and the right-hand stroke shows sometimes downward elongation as in the Mathurā inscription (col. II), the Shorkot inscription (col. V) and the Bower Manuscript (col. VI).

29. *v* is both cursive and angular in shape.

30. In *ś*, the top is sometimes flattened as in the Mathurā inscription (col. II), the Shorkot inscription (col. V), and the Bower Manuscript (col. VI). The development is marked throughout by the elongation of the right-hand vertical.

31. *ṣ* is universally angular in shape. The earlier cursive form becomes rare.

32. *s* shows a hooked left limb considered a mark distinguishing the western form of the letter from its eastern variety. In the Bower Manuscript (col. VI), a significant development is noticed in the conversion of the hook into a triangle or a wedge.

33. *h* shows downward elongation of the right-hand curve.

34. Example of *jihvāmūlīya* and *upadmānīya* are found only in the Bower Manuscript (col. VI).

MEDIAL VOWELS

1. The medial *ā* is expressed by a curve (cols. I, VI) or a button (col. VI), or an upward stroke (cols. III, IV, VII) or a small downward stroke (cols. IV, VI, VII) attached to the right top end of the consonant. In case of *j* (cols. III, V, VI, VII), the stroke is attached to the end of the middle bar. In some cases, the sign is expressed by a button attached to the right top end in the Bower Manuscript. In *thā,* in the Chilas inscription No. 61 (col. VII), the downward curve expressing the length of the vowel has been attached to the middle of the letter.
2. The curve of medial *i* is sometimes inordinately lengthened and drawn to the level of the bottom of the letter (cols. II, III, VII) or below (col. VI).
3. The medial *ī* is marked as earlier by a sickle-shape curve.
4. The medial *u* is rendered either by the lengthening of the right-hand vertical of the letter (cols. I, II, III, IV, V), or by a curve open to the left attached to the bottom of the letter (cols. II, IV, V, VI, VII). In the Bower Manuscript, the sign is also expressed by a wedge attached to the bottom of the letter. In case of *tu,* in the Chilas inscription No. 61 (col. VII), the vowel has been marked by a downward stroke attached to the end of the base curve.
5. The medial *ū* is rendered either by a cursive horizontal line attached to the bottom of the consonant on the left side (cols. VI, VII) or by the subscribed sign for initial *ū* (col. VI). In case of *pū,* in the Mathurā inscription (col. II), the sign has been expressed as in the case of *pu.*
6. The medial *ṛ* is expressed by a curve open to the left and attached to the lower end of the consonant.
7. The medial *e* is expressed by a cursive upward stroke placed over the top of the letter (cols. II, VI, VII) or by a knob attached to the left top end of the consonant. In case of *r* the vowel has been marked by a horizontal bar attached to the top end of the letter in the Mathurā inscription (col. II) and the Abbottabad inscription (col. I).
8. The medial *ai* is expressed either by two superscribed strokes (col. VI) or by a single stroke combined with a knob at the left top end. In the Mathurā inscription of GE 61 (col. II), the sign has been rendered by a superscribed stroke combined with two small downward strokes at either end of the top.
9. The medial *o* is expressed either by two small downward strokes or buttons attached to both sides of the top of the letter (cols. IV, VI) or by the two superscribed

strokes (cols. I, II, IV, V, VI, VII). In one case in *do* in the Tusam inscription (col. IV), it has been expressed by a superscribed stroke combined with a small downward stroke attached to the right end of the top bar.

10. The medial *au* is formed by two superscribed strokes combined with the small downward stroke or button at the left top end (cols. III, IV, VI) or by a single superscribed stroke combined with the sign for medial *o* (cols. II, III, VI).

LIGATURES

1. The superscribed *r* is marked by a small vertical attached to the top of the letter.
2. The subscribed *r* is marked by a straight, slanting or upward stroke attached to the bottom of the letter on the left.
3. *y* as the final element in ligatures is always bipartite in form. Its right end is drawn sometimes as high as the top of the letter (col. III).
4. Other noteworthy ligatures have been illustrated in the table.

## III. Brāhmī Alphabet of North-Western India

**(6th-8th centuries CE)**

In the following representative records of the 6th-8th centuries found in the north-western India, we find further development of the forms of 4th-5th centuries leading to those of the Śāradā in the 9th century.

1. The Kura (Salt Range) inscription of Toramāṇa.[19]
2. The Nirmand (dist. Kulu) copper-plate inscription of Mahāsāmanta Mahārāja Samudrasena.[20]
3. The Gilgit Manuscripts.[21]
4. Brahmor and Chittrahi (dist. Chamba) inscriptions of Meruvarma.[22]
5. The Gum (dist. Chamba) stone inscription of Sāmanta Āṣāḍhadeva.[23]
6. The Hatun (dist. Gilgit) inscription of Paṭoladeva.[24]

The development and the peculiarities of forms displayed by these records are discussed in detail below: (see Table 1C).

---

19. *Epigraphia Indica,* vol. I, p. 239 and plate.
20. Fleet, p. 286 ff., plate XLIV.
21. Facsimilies edited by Dr. Raghuvir and Dr. Lokesh Chandra. The forms of letters have been taken from the facsimilies, the *Śatapiṭaka,* vol. 10, parts I and II.
22. Vogel, J. Ph., *Antiquities of Chamba State,* Part I, Nos. 5-8, pp. 138 ff., plates VII-X.
23. Ibid., No. 9, pp. 145-47, plate XI.
24. *Epigraphia Indica,* vol. XXX, p. 226 ff., plate XXIV.

VOWELS

1. *a* shows a curve open to the left in the lower portion of the left limb similar to one found in the Tusam inscription and Bower manuscript above. In the Gilgit Manuscripts (col. III), the upper portion of the left limb is sometimes suppressed and the curve attached direct to the top represented by a triangular wedge. In the Hatun inscription (col. VI), the upper portion of the left-half consists of a cursive stroke than the usual vertical downward stroke. In the Kura inscription (col. I), the letter has an uncommon form.
2. The curve marking the length of the vowel in *ā*, noticed above in the Mathurā inscription of GE 61 and the Bower manuscript, is regularly found in the Kura inscription (col. I), the Nirmand plate (col. II), the Gilgit Manuscripts (col. III) and the Brahmor inscription (col. IV). In the Lakṣaṇā Devī image inscription of Brahmor (col. IV), it is marked by a downward stroke attached to the top of the vertical on the right side as in the Nāgarī. In the Śakti image inscription (col. IV), the curve signifying the length of the vowel slopes downwards instead of moving to the left. The vowel shows a peculiar form in the Kura inscription (col. I).
3. The initial *i* occurs in the Nirmand plate (col. II) both in the ancient triangular form and the later form of the Bower manuscript with the lower third dot furnished with a tail. In the Gilgit Manuscripts (col. III), the latter form alone is used.
4. The initial *ī* occurring in the Śakti image inscription (col. IV), differs from the earlier form of the Bower manuscript by a cursive stroke with a curve at the lower end and moving upwards on the right.
5. In the initial *u* and *ū*, the development is marked by the prolongation of the base curve which sometimes reaches up to the level of the top of the letter, e.g. Gilgit Manuscripts (col. III) and Nirmand plate (col. II).
6. The initial *o*, which amongst our records occurs only in the Gilgit Manuscripts (col. III), shows a slight development from that of the Bower manuscript noted above. The development consists in the prolongation of the base curve and the use of a wedge at the left top end.

CONSONANTS

1. *k* invariably shows, except in the Kura inscription, a loop on the left and a downward prolongation of the earlier bent bar on the right, e.g. in Nirmand plate (col. II), Gilgit Manuscripts (col. III), Gum inscription of Āṣāḍhadeva (col. V).
2. *kh* displays a significant development in the Gilgit Manuscripts (col. III). It shows a flat top, a vertical (occasionally provided with a footmark) on the left and the ancient loop flattened on the right side, to the right.

3. *g* is generally flat at the top. In the Hatun inscription (col. VI), it shows an upward stroke, while in the Gilgit Manuscripts (col. III), a triangular wedge or a small stroke at the foot of the left vertical is seen. In the Kura inscription (col. I), the letter has a cursive top and a left downward stroke showing a curve at the lower end.
4. *gh* retains its archaic form.
5. *ṅ* which occurs only in ligatures, shows a small upward stroke at the right top end in the Gilgit Manuscripts (col. III) and a small downward stroke in the Gum inscription (col. V).
6. *c* occurs throughout in beaked form.
7. *j* in the Kura inscription (col. I), retains the ancient form. In other records, it is cursive in form and has a slanting base and middle bar in Gilgit Manuscripts, Brahmor inscriptions and the Gum inscription. In the later record, the top bar is missing and is replaced by a wedge.
8. *ñ* which occurs only in combination with *c* or *j*, retains its earlier form in the Kura inscription. The curve at the back is converted into another curve joined to the base and the letter is written in one continuous stroke, facing right or left or laid upside down (cols. II, III).
9. The cerebrals *ṭ, ṭh, ḍ, ḍh, ṇ* retain their earlier forms and do not present anything remarkable.
10. *t* shows an important development in the Gilgit Manuscripts (col. III) and the Hatun inscription (col. VI). The left limb has been suppressed and the right one converted into a curve. The same form is met with later in the Śāradā.
11. *th* is flattened at the top and on the right in the Nirmand plate (col. II) and the Gilgit Manuscripts (col. III).
12. *d* is mostly angular in form.
13. *dh* with a vertical on the right does not present anything noticeable.
14. *n* occurs in a developed form in the Gilgit Manuscripts (col. III) and the Hatun inscription (col. VI). Its right stout limb has been converted into a vertical and the letter thus closely agrees with that of the Nāgarī and Śāradā. It has a unique form resembling Nāgarī *m* in the Brahmor inscriptions.
15. *p* shows a slight downward prolongation of the right-hand vertical in the Gilgit Manuscripts (col. III) and the Hatun inscription (col. VI).
16. No noticeable change is seen in *ph* and *b* except that in the Gilgit Manuscripts (col. III), it is hardly distinguishable from the letter *v*.

17. In *bh,* the right-hand curve noticed above in the Bower Manuscript is more pronounced in the Gilgit Manuscripts (col. III). In the Brahmor inscription (col. IV), it is represented by a cursive downward stroke with a curve at the end. The left limb is represented by a wedge in the Gilgit Manuscripts (col. III), by a triangle in the Brahmor inscriptions (col. IV) and by a small downward stroke with a serif or fork or a curve at the lower end in the Nirmand Plate (col. II), Kura inscription (col. I) and the Hatun inscription (col. VI).

18. *m* shows generally a straight left limb and a slightly slanting base stroke in the Nirmand plate (col. II), Gilgit Manuscripts (col. III) and Hatun inscription (col. VI). In the Kura inscription (col. I), the letter retains its earlier form with a curved left limb. The letter shows occasionally a small button in the Nirmand plate (col. II) and a small circle in the Brahmor inscription (col. V).

19. *y* shows earlier tripartite form with curved or looped left limb in the Kura inscription (col. I) and the Nirmand plate (col. II). It occurs in the later bipartite form in our other records. The transitional form leading to the bipartite one is noticed in the Gilgit Manuscripts (col. III).

20. *r* shows a small upward stroke at the lower end in the Gilgit Manuscripts (col. III) and a loop in the middle in the Brahmor inscriptions (col. IV). In other records, it retains its archaic form.

21. In *l,* the horizontal stroke has been converted into another curve in the Brahmor inscriptions (col. IV) and the letter with two curves resembles the later forms of the letter in Nāgarī and Śāradā. The downward prolongation of the right vertical is seen in the Gilgit Manuscripts (col. III), Brahmor inscriptions (col. IV) and the Gum inscription (col. V).

22. *v* shows a flat top and a vertical on the right in the Gilgit Manuscripts (col. III) and the Hatun inscription (col. VI). Its left limb is cursive in the Gilgit Manuscripts and angular in the Hatun inscription.

23. The squarish form of *ś* occurring in the Bower Manuscript (Table No. 1B, col. III), as noted above, is also found sometimes in the Gilgit Manuscripts (col. III) but with a difference, i.e. in the latter we find a wedge in place of the loop at the lower end of the left vertical. Among the Brahmor inscriptions, the squarish form is found only in the Shakti image inscription (col. IV).

24. *ṣ* does not present anything remarkable except that it occurs in a unique form in the Gum inscription (col. V).

25. *s* shows marked development in the Gilgit Manuscripts (col. III), the Brahmor inscriptions (col. III) and the Hatun inscription (col. VI). It differs from the earlier form by the conversion of the hook on the left into an open triangle in the Hatun

inscription (col. VI) and into a wedge in the Gilgit Manuscripts (col. III). The letter also shows the downward elongation of the right vertical in these records making a peculiar angular form in the Kura inscription (col. I) and a big loop to the left in the Gum inscription (col. V).

26. The *jihvāmūlīya* has a rounded form in the Nirmand plate (col. II) and a triangular one in the Gilgit Manuscripts (col. III).

27. The *upadhmānīya* occurs in the earlier circular form in the Nirmand plate (col. II) but shows significant change in the Gilgit Manuscripts (col. III) and the Gum inscription (col. V). Its form resembles *n* without base stroke with a horizontal line below. The same form is later seen in the Śāradā.

MEDIAL VOWELS

The system of marking the medial vowels continues to be the same as in the earlier periods. However, there are more and more attempts at ornamentation as seen significantly in the Brahmor and Chattrahi inscriptions (col. IV) showing high ornamental forms of medials *e* and *ai* with a loop in the middle. In the Gum inscription (col. V), the curves of medial *i* and *ī* are drawn below the consonants.

LIGATURES

1. The Gum inscription (col. V), shows a unique form of *kṣ* where the upper portion of the right limb of subscribed *s* is missing.
2. In the ligature *ry* in the Nirmand plate (col. I), the superscript *r* retains its full form.
3. The subscript *r* has a high ornamental form in the ligature *śrī* in the Brahmor inscription (col. V) and the Gum inscription of Āṣāḍhadeva (col. V).
4. In the ligature *tm* in the Gilgit inscription (col. III) and the Brahmor inscription (col. IV), the right limb of superscribed *t* gets merged with the left vertical of the subscribed *m*.
5. In the Brahmor inscription No. 7 (col. IV), the subscribed *ḍ* in ligature *ṇḍ* consists of a mere loop.
6. The noteworthy ligatures are shown in the table.

A link between the last phase of the Brāhmī alphabet of north-western India and the Śāradā alphabet is furnished by the Svaim (Chamba) inscription of Rājānaka Bhogata which on palaeographic grounds may be assigned to the last quarter of the 8th century CE. The characters of this inscription are closely related to those of the Śāradā alphabet as is shown by the forms *ṇ*, *y*, *ś* and *ṣ* which occur with very slight modifications in the Śāradā of the following period. We may discuss the forms of these letters in detail below (see Table 1C, col. VII):

1. The letter *ṇ* occurs with a suppressed base stroke and is found in exactly the same form in the Śāradā. Though this form of *ṇ* has already been noted above in the Gilgit Manuscripts yet our record provides the earliest illustration of its use in the inscriptions.
2. *y* differs from its earlier bipartite form by the downward elongation of the right-hand vertical and occurs in exactly the same form in the Śāradā.
3. The letter *ś* occurs regularly in a squarish form and shows a loop on the left though not so well defined as in the Śāradā.
4. *ṣ* also exhibits a later stage of development and comes very close to Śāradā *s*. Its right-hand vertical is prolonged downwards and regularly shows a wedge or a serif in the left limb.
5. This brief epigraph, however, shows an earlier form of *t* as found in the Brahmor and the Chattrahi inscriptions above. The characteristic form of Śāradā, the earlier instances of which we noted above in the Gilgit Manuscripts and the Hatun inscription, is not found in this record.

Mention may be made here of the coin legends of the Lalitāditya Muktāpīḍa of Kashmir where also *t* occurs in earlier form with two strokes.[25]

We have studied above, in a broad outline, the development of the Brāhmī alphabet of north-western India from 3rd century BCE to the end of the 8th century CE. The results of our study have been illustrated in the accompanying tables which illustrate the various stages of the development of this alphabet from its first appearance in the 3rd century BCE up to the advent of the Śāradā alphabet. The detailed description of this we shall study in the next chapter.

25. *Journal of the Numismatic Society of India*, vol. X, p. 31 ff.

# 2

## The Śāradā Alphabet

In the 9th century we witness in the Brāhmī alphabet of north-western India a development of a new script which, though agreeing largely with the Brāhmī alphabet of the immediately preceding centuries, shows essential differences in the forms of several characters. This alphabet is known as the Śāradā alphabet.

### Name

It is not definitely known as to how and when the alphabet received the appellation Śāradā. Śāradā, the Goddess of Learning, has been the tutelary deity of Kashmir. The famed centre of learning from ancient times and named after her as *Śāradā deśa* or *Śāradā maṇḍala,* Kashmir is also the only region in the north-western part of the subcontinent where the alphabet has been in use to this day since its appearance in the 9th century. Hence, it is not unlikely that the name of the alphabet owes its origin to Kashmir or the land of Śāradā. However, the name does not seem to have become very popular even in the time of Alberuni (11th century) who calls the alphabet used in his time in Kashmir as *Siddhamātṛkā.*[1] Alberuni has given a realistic and comprehensive account of contemporary Kashmir. It is unlikely that he would have failed to mention Śāradā as the name of the alphabet then prevalent in Kashmir had this name gained sufficient currency.

Thus, while it is certain that the name of the alphabet known as the Śāradā alphabet originated in Kashmir as also suggested by George Bühler[2] and George Greirson,[3] the exact time of its origination remains obscure.

### The Area of its Use

The epigraphic and written records in the Śāradā, discovered so far, hail from Jammu and Kashmir, Himachal Pradesh, Delhi, Pak-occupied Kashmir (POK) and north-western Pakistan.

---

1. *Alberuni's India,* E.C. Sachau, (tr.), vol. I, p. 173.
2. Bühler, George, *Tour Report,* 1877, p. 31.
3. *Journal of the Royal Asiatic Society,* 1926, p. 677.

## JAMMU AND KASHMIR

### *Kashmir*

Considering the fact that the Śāradā alphabet has been in use in Kashmir from the 9th century CE to this day and also taking into account the explicit statement of Kalhaṇa[4] that he studied and made use of all types of inscriptions including the land grants for writing his *Rājataraṅgiṇī,* the number of Śāradā epigraphic records discovered so far in the Valley is by no means large. Surprisingly not a single copper-plate inscription registering the grant of land has been discovered so far. The earliest specimens are the legends on the coins of the Utpala (Varman) dynasty[5] besides a brief inscription incised on the fragment of a broken jar discovered from the precincts of the Avantīswāmī temple containing the name of Avantivarman (CE 855-83), the founder of the temple.[6] Next in date are the two dedicatory inscriptions of the reign of queen Diddā (CE 980-1030) — one incised on the pedestal of an image of *bodhisattva* Padmapāṇi, dated *Laukika* 65 or CE 989 preserved in the S.P.S. Museum, Srinagar[7]; and the other engraved on a stone slab discovered from a private house in Srinagar, dated *Laukika* 68 or CE 992, and now preserved in Lahore Museum.[8] The other important inscriptions are: the Tapar stone lintel inscriptions of the reign of Parmāṇḍadeva dated *Laukika* 233 or CE 1157[9]; the Arigom stone slab inscription of the *Laukika* year 273 or CE 1197[10]; the Kotiher inscription of the reign of Shahabadena (Shihāb-u-Din) dated *Laukika* 445 or CE 1369[11]; the Khonamuh stone slab inscription of the reign of Jayanolabadenashaha (Zain-ul-ābidin) dated *Kali* 4530 or CE 1428[12]; and the Srinagar bilingual grave stone inscription of the reign of Muhammad Shāh, *Laukika* year 560 or CE 1484.[13]

The last-known Śāradā inscription from Kashmir belongs to the end of the 18th century. It has been discovered at Digom or Kapālamocana in the Pulwama district and is dated, *Vikram Saṁvat* 1846 or CE 1789.[14]

The Śāradā inscriptions mostly preserved in part do not add much to our information regarding the history and culture of Kashmir. But they are usually dated and help us

4. Kalhaṇa, *Rājataraṅgiṇī,* I. 15.
5. Cunningham, *Coins of Medieval India,* plates 4, 5; Rodgers, *Journal of the Asiatic Society of Bengal,* XLVIII, p. 18.
6. Deambi, B.K. Kaul, *Corpus of Śāradā Inscriptions of Kashmir,* No. 14, p. 133 ff., plate 1.
7. Ibid., No. 1, p. 97 ff., plate 1.
8. Ibid., No. 2, p. 100 ff., plate 2; *Epigraphia Indica,* vol. XXVII, p.153 ff., plate 81.
9. Deambi, B.K. Kaul, *Corpus of Śāradā Inscriptions of Kashmir,* No. 4, p. 103 f., plate 5.
10. Ibid., No. 6, p. 107 f., plate 6.
11. Ibid., No. 8, p. 113 ff., plate 9.
12. Ibid., No. 9, p. 119 ff., plate 10.
13. Ibid., No. 11, p. 128 ff., plate 12.
14. *Journal of the Asiatic Society of Bengal,* vol. VII, pp. 87-89.

verify the correctness of the chronology as given by Kalhaṇa and his successors. They also contain at times very useful information about the contemporary culture of ancient and medieval Kashmir not known from other sources.

### *Jammu*

In the Jammu province of the J&K state, a few inscriptions in Śāradā characters have come to light. Two of them were discovered at Dacchan[15] and Zaji-nai[16] in the Ḍoḍā district. Dacchan inscription is dated in the reign of Shri Nantadeva who may be identified with the king Ananta of Kashmir (CE 1028-63). It is dated in the year 112 presumably the *Laukika* era and corresponds to CE 1036. The other is comparatively of a late period and on palaeographic grounds can be assigned to the 16th century. Two more inscriptions were noticed by J. Ph. Vogel — one in a ruined temple at the ancient site of Babor, the ancient Babapura 25 km east of Jammu[17]; and the other on a stone *liṅga* in Kishtwar.[18] Both the inscriptions are now too much defaced to be deciphered.

### *Ladakh*

A few inscriptions in Śāradā characters were noticed in the Ladakh area by Vigne, Cunningham and Francke.[19] The more noteworthy are two inscriptions found at Dras in the Kargil district. One is incised on the back of a pillar lying on the Srinagar-Leh Road between the hamlet of Styalbo and the village of Dras. Consisting of seven short lines, the epigraph records the installation of an image of Maitreya by Ārya Tharanya-kula.[20] The other is incised on the pedestal of an image of *bodhisattva* Maitreya. Dated in the 7th year, it consists of fifteen lines nearly obliterated. Another inscription of five lines mostly defaced was found by Francke incised on the north wall of the Chigtan Monastery near Zanskar.[21]

## HIMACHAL PRADESH

### *Chamba*

In the Himachal Pradesh district of Chamba, formerly an old hill state, has yielded a pretty large number of Śāradā inscriptions of diverse types consisting of rock and

---

15. Ibid., p. 148 f.; R.C. Kak, *Antiquities of Marew Wadwan*, p. 24 f. & plate.
16. *Journal of the Asiatic Society of Bengal*, vol. VII, p. 151 f.
17. Ibid., p. 159; Vogel, *JRAS*, 1907, p. 415.
18. Vogel, *Journal of the Royal Asiatic Society*, 1907, p. 415.
19. Cunningham, *Ladakh*, p. 381, plate XXX; Vigne, *Travels in Kashmir, Ladakh, Iskardo*, vol. II, p. 393; Francke, *History of Western Tibet*, p. 52.
20. Deambi, B.K. Kaul, *Corpus of Śāradā Inscriptions of Kashmir*, p. 153 f.; P.S. Jina (ed.) *Pillar Inscription at Dras in Ladakh, Recent Researches on the Himalaya*.
21. Francke, *History of Western Tibet*, p. 52.

stone inscriptions, image inscriptions, copper-plate inscriptions and fountain stone inscriptions. The earliest Śāradā record is a beautifully executed inscription from Sarahan which contains a lovely poem in praise of the beauty of Somaprabhā, the wife of Sātyaki, a hill chieftain, in an elegant and well-embellished *kāvya* style.[22] The most important and well-preserved inscriptions are the copper-plate charters issued by the rulers of Chamba like Yugākaravarman,[23] Vidagdhadeva,[24] Somavarman[25] and Āsaṭavarman.[26] These charters are not only important for constituting an important source of information regarding the ancient and early medieval history of Chamba but are important for their geographical content as well.[27] They contain mention of some ancient districts and villages of Chamba and thus throw light on the ancient geography of the state. Their value is still more enhanced by the fact that they constitute the only specimen of this type of epigraphs that have come to light in the entire north-western hill region of the country so far.

A very important and unique group of Śāradā records is formed by those engraved on the elegantly carved fountain slabs discovered from different parts of Chamba and now preserved in the Bhuri Singh Museum in Chamba. These slabs were erected at springs by the pious donors for earning religious merit. The inscriptions on these slabs are particularly important from a historical point of view. While the copper-plate inscriptions are dated only in the regnal years of the kings, these often contain dates both in the regnal years of the kings and in the *Śāstra* era, the local designation of the *Laukika* or *Saptarṣi* era commonly used in Kashmir and the hills. This, no doubt, has helped build-up the chronology of the ancient rulers of Chamba on a more or less sound basis.[28]

### *Kangra*

Only a limited number of Śāradā records has come to light in Kangra, another old hill state, so far. The most important and the well-preserved inscriptions are the well-known Baijnāth *praśastis* incised on two large stone slabs in the famous temple of Baijnāth at Baijnāth (ancient Kīragrāma) in the Kangra district.[29] The *praśasti* I is dated in the year 80 of the reign of Jayacandra, the Lord of Trigarta, to whom the ruling chief of Kīragrāma Lakṣmaṇacandra owed allegiance. The date of the *praśasti saṁvat* 80 *Jyeṣṭha Śukla Pratipat*

22. Vogel, J. Ph., *Antiquities of Chamba State,* Part I, p. 152 ff., plate XV.
23. Ibid., p. 159 ff., plate XVI.
24. Ibid., p. 164 ff., plate XVII.
25. Ibid., p. 182 ff., plate XXIV.
26. Ibid., p. 187 ff., plate XXV; p. 197 ff., plate XXVI.
27. For incisive study of the inscriptions, see Deambi, B.K. Kaul, *History and Culture of Ancient Gandhara and Western Himalayas.*
28. Vogel, *Catalogue of Bhuri Singh Museum.*
29. Bühler, *Epigraphia Indica,* vol. I, p. 97 ff.

corresponds to May 2, CE 1204. The *praśasti* II is dated in the Śaka year 1126 corresponding to CE 1204. The *praśasti* I gives an account of the construction of a temple in honour of Lord Vaidyanātha by two merchant brothers Manyuka and Āhuka, and *praśasti* II contains a brief account of the baronial house of Kīragrāma to which Lakṣmaṇacandra belonged.

Another record worthy of note from Kangra is a brief inscription engraved on the pedestal of a statuette of Jain *tīrthaṅkara* Pārśvanātha dated *Laukika Saṁvat* 330 corresponding to CE 1254.[30]

DELHI

*Palam*

An inscription engraved on a stone slab was discovered from a spring (*bāolī*) at the village of Palam, 20 km south-west of Delhi. Only the concluding portion of the inscription is in Śāradā, the rest is in Nāgarī. It records the sinking of a small tank (*bāolī*) by a certain *uddhara*. It is dated *Vikram Saṁvat* 1337 *Śrāvaṇa va ti* 13 *Budhavāre* corresponding either to Wednesday, the 26th June 1280 or Wednesday, the 13th August 1281 in the reign of Sultan Ghiyāthud-din (Giyas-u-din) Balban.[31]

PAK-OCCUPIED KASHMIR

*Chilas*

A few inscriptions were noticed by A.H. Dani incised on a boulder and on the base of an old *stūpa* at Chilas, the famous town of what is known as Dardistan.[32] The latter inscription mentions a Shāhī chief named Vajrasūra.

Dani names the script on the inscriptions as proto-Nāgarī but it is Śāradā, the direct descendant of the script used in the Hatun inscription and the Gilgit manuscripts found in this region and discussed in detail above.

NORTH-WESTERN PAKISTAN

A number of Śāradā inscriptions have been discovered in north-western Pakistan but most of them are either fragmentary or defaced and are now lying in the Lahore and Peshawar museums. The earliest known Śāradā inscription from the region is the Dewai inscription of the Shāhī king Bhīmadeva (10th century).[33] The other important inscriptions

30. Ibid., p. 120.
31. Agarwal, J.N., *Inscriptions of Haryana, Himachal Pradesh, Punjab, Kashmir and Adjoining Hilly Tracts*, No. 14, p. 124 ff.
32. Dani, A.H., *CHILAS*, p. 80 ff., plates 63, 65.
33. *Epigraphia Indica*, vol. XXI, p. 298, & plate; Agarwal, op. cit., No. 103, plate LXXXVIII.

are those of the Shāhī king Jayapāla discovered from Barikoṭ in upper Swāt[34] and Hund (ancient Udabhāṇḍapura) dated 146;[35] and of queen Kāmeśvarīdevī dated 154, 157.[36] Other important inscriptions belong to the reigns of Vijayapāla[37] and Anantadeva.[38] The last known inscription from the region is the stone inscription of a certain Vaṇhadaka now preserved in the Peshawar Museum and dated *Laukika* 538 or CE 1461.[39] The Śāradā inscription from north-west Pakistan, though very brief and fragmentary, constitutes an important source of information regarding the Hindu Shāhī rulers of Kabul and Gandhāra who were previously known to us only from their account given by Alberuni in his *Kitāb-ul-Hind* or *Tehquiq-e-Hind.*[40]

It is worthwhile to note that the earliest known manuscript written in Śāradā characters also hails from north-west Pakistan. It was discovered from the village Bakshali in the Peshawar district of north-west Pakistan. The title of the manuscript is lost but it is known as Bakshali Manuscript from the place of its origin. Assigned on palaeographic grounds to the 12th century, the manuscript contains an important mathematical work dealing with a variety of subjects.[41]

### The Period of Use

Till recently it was not possible to arrive at any definite conclusion with regard to the upper limit of the date of the use of Śāradā alphabet. The paucity of material obliged the learned epigraphists like Bühler and Hoernle to make tentative suggestions which in the light of the latest discoveries are not wholly tenable. Thus Hoernle's suggestion[42] that the "elaboration of the so-called Śāradā alphabet may be placed about CE 500" is far from fact since the script used at this time in north-western India was, as seen above, the so-called Gupta script, and Śāradā had not yet appeared on the scene. Again Bühler's observation[43] that the Śāradā script appeared from about CE 800 is based on the erroneous reading of the dates of the two Baijnāth *praśasti*s as Śaka 726 or CE 804. As first pointed out by Kielhorn[44] and Vogel[45] the correct reading of the date is Śaka 1126 or CE 1204. As

34. *Epigraphia Indica,* vol. XXI, p. 30 ff.; Agarwal, op. cit., No. 107.
35. *Journal of Central Asia,* Peshawar, vol. II, no. 1, p. 71 ff., plate.
36. *Epigraphia Indica,* vol. XXII, p. 97 ff., plate.
37. Agarwal, J.N., op. cit., no. 105, plate XC.
38. *Epigraphia Indica,* vol. XXXVIII, p. 94 ff., Agarwal, op. cit., No. 109.
39. *Epigraphia Indica,* vol. X, p. 80 ff., and plate.
40. *Alberuni's India,* E.C. Sachau, (tr.) vol. II, p. 10 ff.
41. Kaye, G.R., *Archaeological Survey of India,* New Imperial Series, vol. XLIII, Parts I & II.
42. *Journal of the Asiatic Society of Bengal,* vol. LX, p. 90.
43. Bühler, George, *Indian Palaeography,* p. 76.
44. *Indian Antiquary,* vol. XX, p. 154
45. Vogel, *Antiquities of Chamba State,* Part I, pp. 43-44.

such, the Baijnāth *praśasti*s cannot be regarded as the earliest known Śāradā inscriptions[46] as suggested by Bühler nor can the inscriptions discovered from Hund (Pakistan) written in Śāradā characters dated *Saṁvat* 168 and 169 considered to be the earliest-known Śāradā inscriptions. As previously believed, the years 168, 169 as mentioned in the inscription, cannot be assigned to the Harṣa era as suggested by Daya Ram Sāhni[47] who first edited the record. The dates of this inscription mentioning queen Kāmeśvarīdevī as also of a number of other Śāradā records discovered from Hund belonging to the Shāhī rulers of Kabul and Udabhāṇḍapura (now Hund), are to be assigned to the Shāhī era of CE 843 or 850 as suggested by A. Rehman[48] and Prof. Jagan Nath Agarwal[49] and earlier postulated by Elliot.[50] Palaeographically also the above record cannot be assigned to the 9th century as suggested by Sahni.

This much is also certain that the Śāradā had not appeared on the scenes in Kashmir and Chamba, the two main seats of Śāradā alphabet in the 8th century. The records discovered from these states and assignable to the 8th century, for example, the coin legends of Lalitāditya Pratāpaditya of Kashmir[51] and the inscriptions of Meruvarman of Chamba,[52] are written in the Kuṭila or acute angled script and not Śāradā. The earliest known specimens in which the Śāradā characters appear for the first time are, as suggested by Bühler, the coin legends of the Utpala rulers of Kashmir (9th century CE) and the Avantipura Ghaṭa inscription of Avantivarman (CE 855-83).[53] The earliest known Śāradā inscription from Chamba, the Sarahan *praśasti*, belongs to the period earlier than the foundation of the state of Chamba by Sahilavarman in the 10th century. On palaeographic grounds also the inscription as suggested by Vogel can be assigned to the 9th century.[54]

Thus, on the basis of the present state of our knowledge of the Śāradā alphabet, it can be suggested that the alphabet made its appearance first in the 9th century.

### Lower Limit

Nothing definite can be said about the lower limit of the use of the Śāradā script in north-western Pakistan. Its use in the 15th century is, however, attested by the evidence

46. Ibid.
47. Ibid.
48. Rehman, *Journal of Central Asia*, Peshawar, 1979, vol. IX, No. 1, p. 71 ff.,
49. Ibid., J.N. Agarwal, op. cit., p. 24.
50. Ibid.
51. *Journal of the Numismatic Society of India*, vol. X, pp. 30-32.
52. Ref. p. 11 f.n. 22
53. Ref. p. 18 f.n. 6
54. Ref. p. 20 f.n. 22

of the Peshawar Museum inscription of Vanhadaka dated *Laukika Saṁvat* 538 (CE 1461) which is written in the Śāradā characters.[55] Its use in Kashmir continues even to this day though it is confined only to the older generation of the priestly class. Its use in inscriptions even as late as the 18th century is testified by the Digom (Kapālamocana, district Shopian) inscription of (Vikram) 1846 (CE 1789).[56]

In Chamba and Kangra in Himachal Pradesh, it remained a popular script till the 13th century when it was replaced by its descendant, the Devāśeṣa which in turn gave rise to the modern alphabet of Tākarī.

### Details of Characters — in Early Phase (9th-10th centuries)

The early phase of the Śāradā alphabet is represented by the following records referred to above:

1. Avantipura (Kashmir) Ghaṭa inscription of Avantivarman of CE 855-83.
2. The Chilas (PoK) inscription nos. 63-65.
3. The Sarahan (Chamba, H.P.) stone inscription of a ruler called Sātyaki of *c.* 9th century.
4. The Dewai (Upper Swāt, Pakistan) stone inscription of the Shāhī king Bhīmadeva, of *c.* CE 940-60.
5. The Hund (Pakistan) inscription of Shāhī king Jayapāladeva of the year 146 (CE 996).
6. The Hund (Pakistan) inscription of Vijayapāla Shāhī of the year 120 (CE 970).
7. The Barikoṭ (Godun territory, Pakistan) inscription during the reign of Jayapāladeva.
8. S.P.S. Museum, Srinagar, bronze image inscription during the reign of queen Diddā, dated (*Laukika*) *Saṁvat* 65 or CE 989.
9. The Srinagar (now Lahore Museum) fragmentary stone inscription in the reign of queen Diddā (*Laukika*) *Saṁvat* 68 or CE 992.
10. The Brahmor (Chamba, H.P.) copper-plate inscription of Yugākaravarman (10th century).
11. The Sungal (Chamba, H.P.) copper-plate inscription of Vidagdhadeva (10th century).
12. Tur (Chamba, H.P.) inscription of Rājānaka Thathika during the reign of Vidagdhadeva (10th century).

---

55. Ref. p. 43 f.n. 3
56. Deambi, B.K. Kaul, *Corpus of Śāradā Inscriptions of Kashmir*, p. 131f.

VOWELS (see Table 2 a)

1. The initial *a* retains in Śāradā the same form as it has in the north-western Brāhmī alphabet of 6th and 7th centuries. It has an open top and a curve open towards the left in the lower portion of the left half of the letter. The earliest examples of the same form occur in Tusam inscription and the Bower manuscript (*supra* Table 1B, cols. IV and VI). The letter shows, except in the Chilas and Sarahan inscriptions (cols. II, III), a circle (Avantipura inscription col. I), a wedge or a small triangle at the foot of the right hand vertical towards its left. In the Brahmor copper-plate grant (col. X), it has a usual foot mark consisting of two small strokes forming a fork of an angle of about 45°. This fork is also seen at the top of almost all the letters in this inscription in place of the usual horizontal bar.

2. The initial *ā* is formed like *a* with the addition of a curve open towards the left and attached to the foot of the vertical on the right. This curve which marks the length of the vowel is already regularly found in the records of 6th, 7th and 8th centuries. Examples can be seen in the Nirmand copper-plate grant (Table 1C, col. II), the Gilgit manuscripts (Table 1C, col. III) and the Brahmor inscription No. 6 of Meruvarman (Table 1C, col. IV). It is also noticed in the Bower manuscruipt (Table 1B, col IV) and even earlier in the 4th century CE in the Mathurā inscription of Candragupta II (Table 1B, col. II).

3. The letter *i* consisting of two dots above and the curve below agrees with earlier forms of 5th, 6th and 7th centuries as seen in the Bower manuscript, the Nirmand grant and the Gilgit manuscripts. In one instance in the Sarahan *praśasti* letter shows a well-developed curve drawn towards the left as in the later Śāradā. In the Sungal grant (col. XI) we have small circles in place of the usual dots.

4. Amongst the early Śāradā records the initial *ī* occurs only in the Sarahan *praśasti* (col. III). It has exactly the same shape as in the Bower manuscript (Table 1B, col. IV). It consists of a vertical stroke with a dot on either side and a wedge at its upper and lower ends.

5. The initial *u* also perserves the earlier shape but the curve below is drawn further to the left.

6. The letter *ū* occurs only in the Sarahan (col. III) and the Hund inscriptions (col. V). It is formed like *u* with the addition of a downward stroke attached to the back of the letter near the top.

7. The initial *e* retains the ancient triangular form but shows a wedge (col. III) or a serif (col. XI) at the left top end of the top base. In the Brahmor inscription (col. X) it has an uncommon triangular shape.

8. The letter *o* occurs in the benediction *oṁ* in the Brahmor and the Sungal copper-plate inscriptions. It is formed like *u* with the addition of a wedge (col. XI) or a serif (col. X) at the left top end.
9. The initial vowels *ṛ*, *ai* and *au* do not occur in early Śāradā records.

CONSONANTS (see Tables 2 b, c, and d)

*Gutturals*

1. The letter *k* retains in early Śāradā the form of the preceding centuries as found in the Nirmand copper-plate (Table 1C, col. II), the Hatun inscription of Patoladeva (Table 1C, col. VI) and the Gilgit manuscripts (Table 1C, col. III). It consists of a loop on the left limb caused by the connection of the lower end of the left bent bar with the foot of the vertical. The loop is both rounded and angular. Vogel's contention that the left hand loop is more rounded in the older Śāradā inscriptions and more angular in later ones may be true in case of the Śāradā records from Chamba. But in general we find both the forms used side by side.
2. *kh* with a flat top, vertical on the left and a loop, reminiscent of the loop of the Aśoka's Kalsi edicts (Table 1A) attached to the vertical on the right, differs very little from the Gilgit manuscripts (Table 1C, col. III). In the Srinagar inscription of queen Diddā (col. IX), the letter is more cursive and has an archaic appearance. In the Brahmor copper-plate inscription (col. X) the right limb looks more like *v*.
3. *g* shows a flat top and a wedge, a small triangle, a serif or a small upward stroke at the lower end of the left vertical. In the Sungal copper-plate grant (col. XI), the letter shows sometimes a rounded top. The small triangle at the foot of the right vertical is also missing sometimes, e.g. in *bhogika* line nine.
4. The letter *gh* occuring in diverse forms — rounded, angular and cursive — preserves the shape of the Kuṣāṇa inscriptions (Table 1A). In the Tur inscription (col. XII), the right-hand vertical protrudes downwards.
5. The letter *ṅ*, which occurs in our records only in combination with other gutturals, preserves its earlier form as found in the Bower manuscript (Table 1B, col. III). It regularly shows a wedge, a serif or small downward stroke at the right end of the top horizontal-bar. In combination with medial *ā*, the letter has a loop in place of a wedge or serif as in the Tur inscription (col. XII).

*Palatals*

6. The letter *c* occurs in the early Śāradā records both in a rounded and a quadrangular form. The rounded form with a pointed projection to the left is more common while the quadrangular form occurs in Hund (col. VI), Brahmor

(col. X) and Tur (col. XII) inscriptions. Vogel[57] states that the quadrangular form of *c* regarded by Bühler as a characteristic peculiarity of the Śāradā is not found in the inscriptions from Chamba. This is, however, far from the truth as even in one of the earliest Śāradā inscriptions from Chamba, the Brahmor copper-plate grant (col. X), we find the quadrangular *c* occurring very frequently, e.g. in line three (*caṇpakā*), line eight (*caṇḍī*) and line sixteen (*carma).*

7. The letter *ch* occurs in the Brahmor and Sungal copper-plate inscriptions (cols. X, XI). It does not materially differ from its ancient shape as found in Kalsi edict V line 14.

8. The letter *j*, the most conservation letter in the Śāradā, differs from its earlier form as found in the Bower Manuscript (Table 1B, col. VI) by the development of a wedge or a serif at the right end of the top bar. It is mostly angular in shape though cursive forms also occur sometimes. The central bar issues also sometimes from the upper end of the left-hand vertical and occasionally from the middle of the upper horizontal bar. Examples can be seen in cols. II, III, V, XI, and XII.

9. *jh* occurs only once in Sarahan *praśasti* (col. III) in combination with *j* (in *resojjhitena* 1.11). Its form is similar to that of the Bower Manuscript (Table 1B, col. VI).

10. The palatal nasal occurs only in combination with *c* and *j*. In the Sarahan *praśasti* (col. III), it occurs in superscript form and shows a developed top bar with a wedge attached to it at the left end. In subscript form (cols. IX, X, XI), it completely changes its form.

*Cerebrals*

11. The letter *ṭ* mostly occurs in ancient semi-circular form. Occasionally it shows a serif (cols. VIII, X, XI) or a downward cursive stroke (col. XII). The letter also shows flat top in Brahmor (col. X) and Tur (col. XII) inscriptions.

12. *ṭh* preserves its ancient shape of a circle most faithfully and does not present anything remarkable.

13. Bühler[58] mentions *ḍ* as one of the Śāradā letters which exhibits a peculiar development. He describes it as showing a loop in the middle instead of an acute angle and a wedge at the lower end. However, it may be pointed out here that the loop which occurs frequently in the later Śāradā especially in the manuscripts is conspicuously absent in early Śāradā records where the letter occurs. The wedge at the lower end is missing in the letter in the Hund (col. V) and Tur

57. Vogel, *Antiquities of Chamba State,* Part I, p. 52.

58. Bühler, *Indian Palaeography,* p. 76.

(col. XII) inscriptions. In the Sungal grant (col. XI) as ususal we have a small triangle in place of the wedge and a fork in the Brahmor copper-plate (col. XI).

14. The letter *ḍh* which occurs only in the Hund inscription (col. V) agrees with the form of the Bower Manuscript (Table 1B, col. VI) and shows a thickening in the left limb.

15. The cerebral nasal as found in the Sarahan *praśasti* (col. III), the Hund inscription (col. V), the Srinagar inscription (col. IX), Sungal grant (col. XI) and Tur inscription (col. XII) retains the form of the Gilgit manuscripts (Table 1C, col. III). Its base stroke is suppressed and two curves thus united are sometimes supported by a small upward stroke on the right. The Sarahan *praśasti* (col. III) occasionally shows a transitional form of the letter with a small base stroke. In the Chilas (col. II), the Hund (col. V) and the Brahmor copper-plate inscription (col. X), the letter exhibits further development. It is provided with a downward stroke attached to its left end and slanting towards the right. This form of the letter with a tail occurs regularly in the later Śāradā. Vogel's[59] contention that the tailed *ṇ* occurs only after the 12th century cannot be upheld in the face of our earlier examples. The Hund inscription of Vijayapāla (col. VI) shows a peculiar angular form.

*Dentals*

16. The *akṣara t* with its ancient left half missing and the right converted into a curve closely resembles the form of Gilgit Manuscripts (Table 1C, col. III) and the Hatun inscription of Paṭoladeva (Table 1C, col. VI). Its form remains constant all through the Śāradā. In the Sarahan *praśasti* (col. III) the letter occasionally shows a loop in the middle (1.1 *satata)* and in the Tur inscription (col. XII) thickening in the middle as in the letter *bha.*

17. The letter *th* occurs both in the semi-circular and the rectangular forms called by Vogel[60] the crescent shape with the convex side turned to the left and the lozenge-shape. Vogel's contention that the lozenge shape of the letter occurs only in the 12th century is not vouchsafed by our records where we find both the forms used.

18. The letter *d* preserves its shape of the Gupta and the post-Gupta periods. In the Brahmor copper-plate grant (col. X), the letter is provided with a tail at the right end of the base stroke. In the Dewai inscription (col. IV), it has a circular loop in the middle and this form of the letter is the precursor of the looped *d* found in the Śāradā of the later periods.

19. The letter *dh* occurs both in old crescent-shaped form as also in the form where it has a flat top. The quadrangular form of the letter caused by the flattening of the

59. Vogel, *Antiquities of Chamba State,* Part I, p. 54.

60. Ibid.

top and the bottom is found in the Hund inscription of Vijayapāla (col. VI), the Srinagar inscription of queen Diddā (col. IX) and the Tur image inscription (col. XII).

20. The dental nasal resembling the modern Devanāgarī form of the letter retains the shape the letter has in the Hatun inscription of Paṭoladeva (Table 1C, col. VI) and the Gilgit Manuscripts (Table 1C, col. III).

*Labials*

21. *p* retains the shape of the earlier centuries except in a few cases where we find the downward elongation of the right-hand vertical, a feature already noticed above in the Hatun inscription of Paṭoladeva (Table 1C, col. VI) and the Gilgit Manuscripts (Table 1C, col. III).

22. *ph* occurs in looped form. The loop which marks the aspirate is caused by the contact of the older open curve with the base stroke. The letter thus differs from the form of the Bower Manuscript (Table 1B, col. VI) where the loop is attached to the right of *p* instead of inside. In the Brahmor grant (col. X), the letter retains its older form with an open curve turned sharply inside. The letter in this form closely resembles the letter *dh.*

23. The letter *b* in the early Śāradā is mostly represented by *v* and will be described subsequently.

24. *bh* occurs in two forms either with a wedge occasionally a knob or with an open triangle in the middle. The wedged form closely agrees with that found in the Bower Manuscript (Table 1B, col. VI) and the Gilgit Manuscripts (Table 1C, col. III). The uncommon forms with wide open triangles giving the letter the shape of *h* are found in the Dewai (col. IV) and Barikoṭ inscriptions (col. VII). In the Tur image inscription (col. XII), the letter shows two forms, with an incomplete triangle and with an upward stroke in the middle.

25. The letter *m* generally retains its earlier shape as found in the Nirmand copper-plate (Table 1C, col. II), the Hatun inscription of Paṭoladeva (Table 1C, col. VI) and the Gilgit Manuscripts (Table 1C, col. III). Sometimes, however, the right-hand vertical protrudes downwards and there appears a knob on the left as in the Sarahan (col. III), the Hund (col. V) and the Srinagar (col. IX) inscriptions. The letter retains its earlier twist in the left limb in the Barikoṭ inscription (col. VII).

SEMI-VOWELS

26. The letter *y* is exclusively bipartite. It differs from the earlier bipartite form of the Nirmand copper-plate, the Hatun inscription and the Gilgit Manuscripts (Table 1C, cols. II, III, VI) by a greater bulge on the left and by the occasional downward

prolongation of the right-hand vertical. A unique form more common in the later Śāradā occurs in the Tur inscription (col. XII) where the letter shows a closed top.

27. *r* shows generally a wedge at the lower end of the vertical on the left side. Sometimes the wedge is replaced by a small upward stroke and occasionally by a triangle as, for example, in the Dewai inscription (col. IV) and the Sungal grant (col. XI). In the Chilas inscription no. 63, the letter occurs in its archaic form without a wedge and in the Hund inscription of Vijayapāla (col. VI) the letter resembles the Nāgarī form of the letter as seen earlier in the Brahmor inscriptions of Meruvarman (Table 1C, col. IV).

28. The letter *l* with the right-hand vertical protruding the body of the letter and the left-hand curve attached to it by means of a small horizontal stroke which represents the original base stroke retains the form of the preceding centuries. In the Dewai stone inscription (col. IV) and sometimes in the Srinagar inscription (col. IX), the horizontal stroke connecting the left-hand curve and the right-hand vertical is converted into another curve and this form of the letter with two curves is regularly found in the Śāradā of the subsequent periods.

29. The letter *v* which mostly represents *b*, occurs in old cursive form and the angular forms. The unique uncommon forms are found in the Ghaṭa inscription (col. I). and the Dewai inscription (col. IV).

*Sibilants*

30. *ś* is squarish in shape and has generally a wedge on the left. The wedge is sometimes replaced by a triangular loop in the Dewai inscription (col. IV) and the Sungal grant (col. XI), and sometimes by a triangle left open on one side as in the Brahmor grant (col. X) or a knob as in the Chilas inscription (col. II). An older form of the letter with rounded top occurs occasionally in the Sungal copper-plate grant (col. XI), as for example in *Parameśvara* 1.1.

31. The letter *ṣ* preserves faithfully the form of the western Gupta character but sometimes the right-hand vertical is seen protruding downwards as in the Hund (col. V), the Brahmor (col. X) and the Sungal (col. XI) copper-plate grants and the Tur image inscription (col. XII).

32. *s* is similar to *ś* but open at the top. In the Sungal copper-plate grant (col. XI) it has an open triangular wedge on the left similar to that of *bh*. An uncommon form is seen in the Chilas inscription (col. II).

*Spirants*

33. The letter *h* does not present anything remarkable except that in the Dewai (col. IV) and Barikoṭ (col. VII) inscriptions and in the Sungal grant (col. XI), the lower curve is sometimes turned round and drawn further to left.

34. The *visarga* and the *anusvāra* do not present anything worthy of note.

35. The *jihvāmūlīya* and the *upadhmānīya* are frequently used in the inscriptions from Chamba. The former does not occur in any other of our early Śāradā records. The latter, however, also occurs in the Hund inscription of Jayapāladeva (col.V) and the Srinagar inscription of queen Diddā (col. IX). The shape of the *jihvāmūlīya* resembles the smaller version of the letter *v*. The *upadhmānīya* is described by Vogel[61] as resembling the figure 8 laid sideways. The Hund inscription (col. V), the Brahmor inscription (col. X) and Sungal (col. XI) copper-plate inscriptions show a form resembling the letter *ṇ* with a horizontal line below. This form occurs regularly in later Śāradā.

36. The *virāma* is characterized by a slanting stroke drawn over the head of the letter on the right. The letter to which the *virāma* is attached appears in a very changed form. Thus *t* becomes a mere curve as in the Sarahan *praśasti* (col. III) and *m* a mere dot or a small circle (see Table 2 d).

MEDIAL VOWELS (see Table 2 e)

1. Medial *ā* is expressed by means of a wedge, knob, serif or a downward stroke attached to the top of the consonant on the right side. However, in case of certain consonants with a double top, as for example, *p, y, ś* and *ṣ* either single or accompanied by a subscribed consonant we find the vowel sign expressed in the Sarahan *praśasti* (col. IV) and the Sungal copper-plate grant (col XI) and the Tur inscription (col. XII) by means of a horizontal top stroke with a wedge or a serif at its right end, attached to the left top end of the consonant. The vertical on the right is shortened above and remains free from the top bar. Occasionally in the Sungal copper-plate grant, the vowel sign in *pā* (ll. 7, 10, 21, 24) and *sā* (ll. 25, 26), is expressed in the usual manner, i.e. by a serif attached to the top of the right-hand vertical. In case of consonants like *ṅ, ṭ* and *ṇ*, the *a* sign is expressed by a hook or a semi-circle and in case of *j*, by a small vertical attached to the right end of the central stroke and forming a right angle with it. In the latter case, the letter drops the top bar and the wedge attached to it. A peculiar form of *jā* corresponding to the *ja* of the later periods is found in Tur inscription, 1.5 (col. XII).

2. The signs for medial *i* and *ī* are generally the same as in the preceding centuries and consists of curves drawn respectively to the left and right of the consonant reaching sometimes to the level of the bottom of the consonant. Old signs of marking the vowels by sickle-shaped curves are occasionally met with in the Sarahan *praśasti* (col. IV) and Brahmor and Sungal copper-plate grants (col. X, XI).

---

61. Ibid., p. 58.

3. Medial *u* is expressed in two ways:

   (i) by a curve representing the initial *u* and attached to the bottom of the letter, and

   (ii) by a wedge, small triangle, or a short upward stroke attached to the foot of the vertical on the left side. In case of consonants like *ṇ, ḍ, ph, y, h* where the vertical is absent the wedge is attached by means of a short vertical.

   In case of *ru,* the vowel sign is denoted by the usual curve below the vertical in the Sarahan *praśasti* (col. III) while in the Chilas inscription (col. II), the Srinagar inscription, Brahmor and Sungal copper-plate grants (cols. X, XI), the sign is expressed by attaching a downward steamer to the right of the letter.

4. Medial *ū* is also expressed like the medial *u* in two ways:

   (i) by the subscribed sign for initial *ū*, and

   (ii) by a horizontal, sometimes wavy flag-like line attached to the lower end of the vertical on the left side. Peculiar form is noticed in the Srinagar inscription (col. IX) where the sign in *nū* (1.1) has been marked by a triangle attached to the foot of the vertical on the left.

   Mention may be made of the groups *rū* and *brū* occurring in the Sarahan *praśasti* (col. III). Here *rū* has been formed by "the *mātṛkā* with the subscribed initial vowel mark." The right-hand streamer of the vowel, however, has been attached above the curve near the middle of the vertical of the superscribed *r*. In *brū* we find the vowel sign expressed by two curves attached to the middle of the letter, one slanting downwards and the other rising upwards.

5. According to Bühler,[62] the angular medial *ṛ* is a peculiar development of the Śāradā. But in our early Śāradā records the shape of the curve, representing the medial *r* is mostly rounded. The angular form occurs occasionally in the Sarahan *praśasti* (col. III), Hund inscription (col. VI) and the Brahmor copper-plate grant (col. X).

6. Medial *e* is expressed either by a stroke — horizontal or slanting — placed over the consonant or by the *pṛṣṭhamātrā,* i.e. by a wedge, serif, or a small downward stroke attached to the left end of the top bar.

7. Medial *ai* is expressed by the combination of two *e* symbols, i.e. by the superscribed slanting stroke accompanied by a *pṛṣṭhamātrā.* In one case in Brahmor copper-plate grant (in *vai* l. 19), the vowel has been rendered by two *e* strokes placed above the letter, (see col. X).

8. Medial *o* is expressed in three distinct ways:

62. Bühler, *Indian Palaeography,* p. 57.

(i) by two wedges, serifs or small knobs attached to both ends of the top bar or in case of letters with open top to two top ends,

(ii) by a superscribed slanting stroke accompanied by a wedge, serif or a downward stroke or a curve in case of *ṭ, ṇ* attached to the right end of the top bar, and

(iii) by a superscribed flourish.

A peculiar form of marking the vowel is found once in case of *lo* line seven in the Sarahan *praśasti* (col. III) where the left-hand wedge has been attached to the curve instead of to the top stroke.

9. Medial *au* is expressed by the superscribed *o* flourish combined with the wedge or a serif attached to the right end of the top bar. Occasionally it is marked in the Sarahan *praśasti* (col. III) and the Srinagar stone inscription (col. IX) by two wedges or small downward strokes attached to both ends of the top bar combined with the superscribed *e* stroke.

LIGATURES (see Table 2 f)

As regards the ligatures, the early Śāradā alphabet preserves faithfully the ancient method of writing the conjunct consonant one below the other:

1. *k* retains its ancient form without the loop when in combination with subscript vowels *u, r* or when forming the upper and the middle element of the ligature. As the final element, it retains its usual looped shape.
2. The subscript *ñ* occurs in a form absolutely distinct from the superscript *ñ*. Its shape resembles the figure 3 (see cols. IX, XI) and it occurs only in combination with *j*. A peculiar form of the subscript *ñ* is noticed in the word *rājñi* l. 12 in the Brahmor copper-plate grant (col. X).
3. The lingual *ṭ* as a second member of the ligature occurs in its normal form in the Sarahan *praśasti* (col. III). In our other records, it assumes a distinctive shape and consists of a semi-circular curve open to the right and a slanting stroke attached to the foot of the upper consonant on the right. Subscript *ṭh* is similarly formed except in the Sungal (col. XI) and Tur (col. XII) inscriptions where it has sometimes the shape of subscribed *v*.
4. The dental *th* as the second or the final element of a ligature considerably differs in shape from the *mātṛkā*. In the Sarahan *praśasti* (col. III), it is expressed by a spiral or an inward curve drawn from left to right. In the Brahmor copper-plate grant (col. X), it is rendered by long drawn curve open on the right with a hook at its lower end. In the Sungal copper-plate grant (col. XI), it consists of a spiral similar in shape to that of the Sarahan *praśasti* but sometimes the curve forming the spiral instead of turning inside turns sharply round and moves towards the

left. The same form of subscribed *th* is found in the Barikoṭ inscription (col. VII) with the difference that the curve turns further back towards the left.

5. The subscribed *y* preserves the form of the Kuṣāṇa and the Gupta inscriptions. Its right limb is not so much elongated as is seen in some of our records of the 6th and 7th centuries, e.g. the Hatun inscription and the Gilgit Manuscripts (Table 1C). A unique form of the subscribed *y* occurs in the Barikoṭ inscription (col. VII) in the ligature *jya* l. 1 where the right limb of *y* moving upwards forms a contact with the right end of the central bar of *j*.

6. Bühler[63] has drawn attention to one of the peculiar features of the Śāradā according to which *r* as the first part of the ligature is inserted into the left side of the second letter. In general, the superscript *r* retains its full form with the vertical slightly shortened. In ligatures *r̥ṇ, r̥th, r̥ḍh* it does not preserve its distinctive shape and usually loses its bottom part. In ligature *rv,* it is marked only by a "small excrescence on the left curve of the *v mātr̥kā*." In the group *ry,* it is expressed by a short vertical to which the curve of *y* is attached in one continuous stroke.

7. In ligatures where *r* forms the middle or final element, it is rendered by an upward stroke attached to the lower end of the upper consonant on the left. In the Sarahan *praśasti* (col. III), it is sometimes confused with the medial *u* but in the other records, its upwards elongation gives it a distinctive character.

8. The subscribed *v* in the ligature *sv* is generally triangular in shape. In the Brahmor copper-plate grant (col. X) it retains its original rounded form.

9. Attention may be drawn to the ligatures *nt* (col. I), *pur* (col. II), *kṣm* (col. III), *ṅś* (col. IV), *nty, ṅgu* (col. V), *tkha, st* (col. IX), *ddhy* (col. X), *tpr, ndrau* (col. XI).

63. Ibid., p. 76.

# 3

## Development of the Śāradā Alphabet

### (11th-13th Centuries)

WE have discussed above in detail the features of the Śāradā characters as they first appear in the epigraphic records of the 9th and the 10th centuries. We now proceed to discuss their development in the 11th, 12th and the 13th centuries on the basis of the following records:

1. Coins of the following rulers of Kashmir and NWFP: Ananta (CE 1028-63), Kalaśa (CE 1063-89), Harṣa (CE 1089-1101), Uccala (CE 1101-11), Sussala (CE 1112-20), Jayasiṁha (CE 1128-55) and Mahmūd of Ghazni.[1]
2. Hund (NWFP) inscription of Mahārānī Kāmeśvarīdevī (Shāhī). *Saṁvat* 169 (CE 1019).[2]
3. Bhakund (Chamba, Himachal Pradesh) fountain inscription of the reign of Trailokyadeva, *Śāstra* (410) 4 (CE 1028-29).[3]
4. Dacchan (district Ḍoḍā, Jammu) stone inscription of the reign of Shri (A)Nantadeva, (*Laukika*) *Saṁvat* (410) 12 (CE 1036).[4]
5. Kulait (Chamba, Himachal Pradesh) copper-plate inscription of Somavarman (11th century).[5]
6. Chamba copper-plate inscription of Somavarman and Āsaṭavarman (11th century).[6]
7. Thundu (Chamba, Himachal Pradesh) copper-plate inscription of Āsaṭavarman 11th century.[7]

---

1. Cunningham, A., *Coins of Medieval India*, plates IV, V, VII; Rodgers, *Journal of the Asiatic Society of Bengal*, vol. XLVIII, plate 18.
2. *Epigraphia Indica*, vol. XXII, p. 97 ff., and plate.
3. Vogel, J. Ph., *Antiquities of Chamba State*, Part I, p. 177 ff., and plate XX.
4. Deambi, B.K. Kaul, *Corpus of Śāradā Inscriptions of Kashmir*, p. 149 f.
5. Vogel, *Antiquities*, p. 182 ff., and plate XXIV.
6. Ibid., p. 187 ff., and plate XXV.
7. Ibid., p. 197 ff., and plate XXVI.

8. Luj (Chamba, Himachal Pradesh) fountain inscription of the 1st year of Jāsaṭa, *Śāstra* (41) 81 (CE 1105-06).[8]
9. S.P.S. Museum, Srinagar stone slab inscription of the reign of Jayasiṁha, (*Laukika*) *Saṁvat* (42) 25 (CE 1149).[9]
10. Tapar (Kashmir) stone lintel inscription of Parmāṇḍadeva, (*Laukika) Saṁvat* (42) 33 (CE 1157).[10]
11. Devī-rī-koṭhī (Chamba, Himachal Pradesh) fountain inscription of Rājānaka Nāgapāla (CE 1159-61) and Rājānaka Raṇapāla.[11]
12. Salhi (Chamba, Himachal Pradesh) fountain inscription of Rājānaka Ludrapāla of the 27th year of Lalitavarman, *Śāstra* (42) 46 (CE 1170).[12]
13. Arigom (Kashmir) stone slab inscription, (*Laukika*) *Saṁvat* (42) 73 (CE 1197).[13]
14. Baijnāth (district, Kangra, Himachal Pradesh) Śiva temple inscriptions, Śaka 1126 (CE 1204).[14]
15. Vejebror (Kashmir) stone inscription of the reign of Rājadeva (Śaka*) Saṁvat* 58 (CE 1236).[15]

### Details of the Forms

VOWELS (see Table 3 a)

1. The vowels *a* and *ā* retain their earlier forms and do not exhibit any significant change. Only in very rare cases do we find *a* with a closed top as, for example, in some coins of Mahmūd of Ghazni (col. I) and in one case in the Thundu copper-plate grant of Āsaṭavarman (col. VII), line 21 (*ati*). This form of the letter becomes common in the later Śāradā of Kashmir and in the Devāśeṣa of Chamba.
2. The initial *i* preserves its older shape consisting of two dots and a curve below. In the copper-plate inscription, the curve is small while in the stone inscriptions it turns round and moves further to the left. In the Bhakund fountain inscription (col. III) and the Thundu copper-plate grant (col. VII), the two dots are replaced by two small circles.

---

8. Ibid., p. 202 ff., and plate XXVIII.
9. Deambi, B.K. Kaul, op. cit., p. 102 and plate 4.
10. Ibid., p. 103 f. and plate 5.
11. Vogel, op. cit., p. 207 ff., plates XXIX, XXX.
12. Ibid., p. 216 ff. and plate XXXII.
13. Deambi, B.K. Kaul, op. cit., p. 197 ff., plate 6.
14. Bühler, *Epigraphia Indica*, p. 197 ff.; *Indian Palaeography*, plate V.
15. Deambi, B.K. Kaul, op. cit., p. 110 ff., plate 7.

3. The initial *ī,* the solitary instance of which we noticed in the Sarahan *praśasti* above shows a distinct development in the Baijnāth Śiva temple inscriptions (col. XIV) where the two dots which stood previously on the either side of the central vertical now appear above the top of the letter. The same form of *i* is regularly met with in the later Śāradā and the Devāśeṣa.
4. *u and ū* preserve their earlier forms except that in the Bhakund fountain inscription (col. III) *u* shows a loop in the middle.
5. No instance of initial *ṛ* is found in the Śāradā records of the period.
6. The initial *e* displays no significant change.
7. The initial *ai* also does not occur in the records of the period.
8. The initial *o* which occurs mostly in the syllable *oṁ* is formed like *u* with the addition of a wedge at the left top end. In the Bhakund inscription (col. III), the wedge is replaced by a small triangle. An uncommon form of *o* occurs in the Baijnāth Śiva temple inscription (col. XIV) where instead of a wedge we find a curve attached to the back of *u* and similar to that of initial *u.*
9. No instance of initial *au* is noticed in our records.

CONSONANTS (see Tables 3 b, c, d, e)

*Gutturals*

10. *k* generally preserves its earlier form with a loop to the left. In certain cases, however, it develops a second loop to the right evidently caused by the contact of the right-hand curve with the bottom of the central vertical. This double loop form of the letter is regularly found in the later Śāradā and the Devāśeṣa. In our records the example of the double loop *k* are found in the Dacchan (col. IV), Salhi (col. XII) and Arigom (col. XIII) inscriptions.
11. *kh* occurs regularly with a flat top and a vertical stroke to the left. The archaic form with rounded top and cursive stroke on the left as found in the Sungal copper-plate grant above becomes rare.
12. *g* with a serif, wedge or a small upward stroke at the foot of the left vertical demonstrates no change except sometimes a small triangle replaces the wedge. A unique form of the letter is noticed in the Dacchan inscription (col. IV) in the word *guptena* l. 3.
13. In *gh* the development is marked by the elongation of the right-hand stroke which henceforth becomes the regular feature of the letter.
14. *ṅ* which occurs only in ligature with *k* and *g* generally preserves its earlier shape. An uncommon form occurs in the Arigom inscription (col. XIII) where the wedge

at the right end is replaced by a small vertical which protrudes down and touches the lower slanting stroke, in Gaṅgeśvara, l. 2.

*Palatals*

15. *c* occurs mostly in quadrangular form. The ancient rounded form occurs only in one case in the Chamba grant of Somavarman and Āsaṭavarman. In the Dacchan inscription (col. IV) and the S.P.S. Museum inscription of Jayasiṁha (col. IX), the letter shows a circular loop to left. In the Vejebror inscription (col. XV), it occurs with open top.

16. The conservative letters *ch* and *j* occur in their ancient forms and hardly present anything remarkable.

17. No instance of *jh* is found either singly or in ligatures in the records of the period under review.

18. The palatal nasal which occurs only in ligatures retains its earlier form with minor variations here and there.

*Cerebrals*

19. *ṭ* occurs regularly with a flat top and generally with a wedge or a serif at the right top end. The archaic rounded form found in Dewai and Barikoṭ inscriptions above now becomes rare.

20. *ṭh* is as usual represented by a circle.

21. *ḍ* shows regularly a wedge or a serif at the lower end.

22. Of the three forms of cerebral *n*, one with connecting base stroke becomes rare and is found only in one case in the Bhakund fountain inscription (col. III). The other two forms continue to be used with equal regularity.

*Dentals*

23. *t*, a conservative character in Śāradā, remains un-changed. A peculiar form occurs in the Bhakund inscription (col. III) where the letter is provided with a loop in the middle.

24. *th* shows a flat top and is lozenge or rectangular in shape. Ancient crescent form becomes rare.

25. *d* does not exhibit any material change except that it shows a loop in the left limb in the Bhakund inscription (col. III) and a unique form resembling the rounded *c* in the Dacchan inscription (col. IV).

26. *dh* shows regularly a flat top and is usually angular in shape. The cursive forms occur only in the copper-plate inscriptions.

27. The dental nasal agrees closely with the modern *n* of the Devanāgarī. An uncommon looped form occurs in the Bhakund inscription (col. III).

*Labials*

28. The labials *p* and *ph* retain their earlier characteristics and exhibit no significant change.

29. *b* is usually represented by *v* and will be described subsequently.

30. *bh* generally shows a wedge in the middle. In some cases, the wedge is replaced by a triangular loop, as for example, in the S.P.S. Museum inscription of Jayasiṁha (col. IX) and in the Nārāyaṇa Image (Devī-rī-koṭhī) inscription of Rājānaka Nāgapāla (col. XI). The letter occurs with a less pronounced wedge or an open triangle in the Hund (col. II), Bhakund (col. III). and Luj (col. VIII) inscriptions.

31. *m* does not present anything remarkable except that the right-hand vertical more frequently protrudes downwards.

*Semi-Vowels*

32. *y* occurs in a developed form with a closed top in the Arigom stone slab inscription (col. XIII). This form of the letter is frequently met with in the later records of Kashmir. In all our other records the letter retains its earlier shape with open top.

33. *r* generally shows a wedge at the lower end of the vertical to the left. The wedge is occasionally replaced by a small triangle, for example, in Bhakund (col. III), Dacchan (col. IV), S.P.S. Museum (col. IX) and in one instance in the Devī-rī-koṭhī inscription of Nāgapāla (col. XI). In the copper-plate inscriptions (cols. V, VI, VII), we find in place of a wedge a small upward stroke attached to the vertical stroke on the left. In the Dacchan inscription (col. IV), the letter occurs with a big triangular loop on the left.

34. *l* displays no change except that the right-hand vertical is regularly elongated downwards.

35. *v* which also represents *b* has a flat top and is both angular and cursive in shape. In the S.P.S. Museum inscription (col. IX), it shows uncommon form resembling *y* with closed top. Another unique form occurs in the Dacchan inscription (col. IV) where the letter looks like *dh*.

36. *ś* occurs with a loop, wedge, open triangle (col. VII) or a triangular loop as in Bhakund (col. III), S.P.S. Museum (col. IX) and as in Devī-rī-koṭhī inscription of Nāgapāla (col. XI). The letter is regularly marked with a downward elongation of the right-hand vertical.

37. *ṣ* retains its conservative character.
38. *s* shares all the characteristics with *ś* but is distinguished from the latter by its open top.
39. *h* shows no material change except that the curve below often moves further towards the left.
40. *Jihvāmūlīya* generally retains its earlier form. In the Baijnāth inscription (col. XIV) it is more angular in shape.
41. *Upadhmānīya* occurs in a changed form and may be described as cerebral *ṇ* with a horizontal line below. Its shape resembles that of the Gilgit Manuscripts noted above.

*Virāma*

*Virāma* is expressed by a slanting stroke running through the right top end of the vowelless consonant. In the Vejebror inscription (col. XV) we, however, find the stroke running through the middle of the *akṣara*. The consonants, mostly *t* and *m* with which the *virāma* is attached, appear in modified forms in the copper-plate inscriptions (cols. V, VI, VII) and occasionally in the Bhakund inscription (col. III). In all other records, they retain their fuller and complete forms.

THE MEDIAL VOWELS (see Table 3 f)

The method for expressing medial *a* continues to be practically the same as in the preceding centuries. The following peculiarities, however, deserve notice:

1. The hook or semi-circle peculiar to *ṅā*, *ṭā* and *ṇā* has also been attached to *ñā (jñā)* in a Devī-rī-koṭhī inscription (col. XI), to *dā* and *yā* in the Salhi fountain inscription (col. XII) and to *jā* in the Baijnāth inscription (col. XIV).
2. The medial *i* and *ī* are rendered more frequently by the long curves drawn respectively to the left and right of the consonants. The small curves placed over the consonants occur only in the copper-plate inscriptions (cols. V, VI, VII). The sickle-shaped medial *ī* occurs only in one case in *nī* (l. 1) in the Thundu copper-plate inscription (col. VII).
3. The signs for expressing the medial *u* are the same as in the earlier records. These are indiscriminately used in one and the same line.
4. Medial *ū* is expressed in the older fashion, viz. by a wavy or slanting line attached to the foot of the vertical on the left side or by the subscribed initial *ū*.
5. Medial *ṛ* is both cursive and angular in shape.

6. Medial *e* continues to be expressed by a *pṛṣṭhamātrā* or a superscribed stroke either horizontal or slanting. The *pṛṣṭhamātrā* denoted by a small downward stroke becomes a full-fledged vertical in the Arigom inscription (col. XIII).
7. Only in two inscriptions, viz. Dacchan (col. IV) and Devī-rī-koṭhī (col. XI), we find medial *ai* expressed by two superscribed strokes. In all other inscriptions the sign is expressed as earlier, by a *pṛṣṭhamātrā* combined with the superscribed *e* stroke.
8. Medial *o* is expressed more often by superscribed flourish and less frequently by a wedge at the left top end combined with a superscribed *e* stroke. The ancient method of two wedges attached to both ends of the top of the letter becomes rare and is found only in the Arigom inscription (col. XIII) where, however, the wedges have been replaced by long downward strokes.
9. Medial *au* is rendered throughout by the combination of superscribed flourish and the *ā* mark. The method of expressing the vowel by two wedges attached to both ends of the top bar combined with the superscribed *e* stroke and used in the Sarahan *praśasti* above becomes obsolete.

LIGATURES (see Table 3 g)

1. As in the previous period, *k* as the first or the middle part of the ligature retains its archaic crossbar form. As a final part of the ligature its form remains intact.
2. Superscripts *ṅ* and *ñ* do not present any significant change.
3. The subscribed *ñ* in ligature *jñā* has, as in the earlier records, the shape of numeral 3 and is attached to the upper consonant in varied positions, sometimes lying, sometimes straight and sometimes half straight half lying. A peculiar form occurs in the Devī-rī-koṭhī inscription (col. XI) and the Salhi fountain inscription (col. XII) where the letter loses its upper portion and is represented just by a curve open to the left.
4. *t* as the final member of the ligature retains only its lower portion as in the earlier period.
5. The *s*-like form of the subscribed *th* which occurred occasionally in the earlier records now becomes more common. Spiral form occurs only in copper-plate inscriptions (cols. V, VI, VII). Peculiar forms are noticed in Hund inscription (col. II) in *sth* and in Luj inscription (col. VIII) in *rth*.
6. *y* as the final element of the ligature continues to be denoted by a curve which is now more pronounced and moves further to the right.
7. *r* as the first part of the ligature with *y* and *ṇ* loses its bottom part as noticed in the previous period.

8. *r* in ligature *rv* continues to be marked by a small excrescence on the left.
9. In ligatures where *r* forms the middle or the final element it is usually rendered as in the earlier period by an upward stroke attached to the lower end of the upper consonant on the left. In certain cases as in Salhi (col. XII) and the Arigom (col. XIII) inscriptions it is rendered by a slanting stroke drawn from left to the right. In ligature *tr* in the Thundu inscription (col. VII), the subscribed *r* is accompanied by a small downward stroke in the middle.
10. The ligature *ṣṭ* and *ṣṭh* usually have an identical shape with their true value ascertainable only by the content in which they occur in the inscription. Sometimes distinction is sought to be made by representing subscribed *ṭh* in its initial form with a tail, as for example in Arigom (col. XIII) and Hund inscriptions (col. II). In Arigom inscription *ṣṭ* is also rendered as *ṣṭh.*

# 4

## Development of the Śāradā Alphabet
### (14th-16th Centuries)

THE development of the Śāradā alphabet up to the 13th century CE has been discussed above. In the following periods the alphabet displays conspicuous development in the records of Chamba and adjoining hill tracts. Here, the shapes of a few letters appear in such an altered form that the alphabet has been given a separate name Devāśeṣa. The detailed treatment of the Devāśeṣa would be given in a separate section and here we shall discuss the development of the Śāradā alphabet in the 14th and the subsequent centuries on the basis of the following inscriptions of Kashmir and NWFP (Pakistan).

1. The Koṭiher (Kashmir) stone slab inscription of the reign of Shahabadena (Shihāb-ud-dīn), dated *Laukika Saṁvat* (44)45 (CE 1369).[1]
2. The Bhuwaneśvarī (Khonamuh, Kashmir) stone inscription of the reign of Jayanolabadena Śāha (Zain-ul-abidin), dated *Kali* 4530 (CE 1428).[2]
3. The Peshawar (NWFP, Pakistan) Museum inscription of Vaṇhaḍaka, dated *Laukika Saṁvat* (4) 538 (CE 1462).[3]
4. The Hariparbat (Srinagar, Kashmir) grave stone inscription of the reign of Muhammadushāha (Muhammad Shah) dated *Laukika Saṁvat* (45) 60 (CE 1484).[4]
5. The Wularhama (Vejebror, Kashmir) bathroom gate inscription.[5]
6. The Zajinai (dist Ḍoḍā, Jammu) stone inscription.[6]

---

1. Deambi, B.K. Kaul, *Corpus of Śāradā Inscriptions of Kashmir* p. 113 ff. and plate 9.
2. Ibid., p. 119 ff. and plate 10.
3. Konow, Sten, *Epigraphia Indica*, vol. X, p. 79 ff. and plate.
4. Deambi, B.K. Kaul, op. cit., p. 128 ff. and plate 12.
5. Ibid., p. 145 ff. and plate 14.
6. Ibid., pp. 151-52. The inscription originally found by R.C. Kak is preserved partly in fragments in S.P.S. Museum, Srinagar.

## Details of Forms

VOWELS (see Table 4 a)

1. The initial *a* is generally closed at the top except in one case in the Koṭiher inscription (col. I) and the Peshawar Museum inscription (col. III) where the letter occurs in its earlier form with an open top. In the Khonamuh inscription (col. II), the letter has only one curve attached directly to the top bar instead of the usual two.
2. The peculiar form of *ā* with a loop in the left limb is noticed in the Hariparbat inscription (col. IV). In the Zajinai inscription, the letter shows an upward stroke in place of the usual curve at the foot of the right-hand vertical. In both cases the letter occurs with a closed top.
3. The initial *i* occurs only in the Khonamuh inscription (col. II) and displays significant development. The earlier two dots above the curve are converted into a small angular curve facing downwards.
4. The initial *ī* is found only in the Peshawar Museum inscription (col. III) and has the same shape as in the Baijnāth Śiva Temple inscription noted above except that the letter has an unusual tail attached to it not found in the earlier record.
5. The initial *u* remains unchanged.
6. No instances of initial *ū* and *ṛ* are provided by our inscriptions.
7. The initial *e* occurs only in the Hariparbat grave stone inscription (col. IV) and shows marked development with the earlier wedge or small downward stroke converted into a full-fledged vertical.
8. The initial *ai* does not occur in our records.
9. The initial *o* occurs in the syllable *oṁ* in the Koṭiher inscription (col. I) and Peshawar Museum inscription (col. III) and shows the same development as the initial *e*, viz. the wedge at the left top end converted into a vertical stroke.
10. No example of initial *au* is found in our inscription.

CONSONANTS (see Tables 4 a, b, c, d)

*Gutturals*

11. The *akṣara k* occurs regularly in double loop form in all records except the Peshawar Museum inscription (col. III) where it still preserves its earlier form with a single loop.

12. The letter *kh* with a well-developed vertical on the left preserves its earlier shape and does not present anything remarkable.

13. *g* also occurs in its earlier forms and shows either a wedge or a small triangle or an upward stroke at the lower end of the left vertical. An uncommon form occurs in the Koṭiher inscription (col. I).

14. *gh* does not also present anything remarkable except that it shows a typical angular form in the Peshawar Museum inscription (col. III).

15. The guttural nasal which as usual occurs only in ligatures with other gutturals preserves its earlier form with a wedge, knob or a serif at the right end of the top bar.

*Palatals*

16. *c* occurs only in the quadrangular form and shows a circular loop in the left limb in the Wularhama (col. V) and Khonamuh inscriptions (col. II).

17. *ch* occurs in a typical angular form in the Khonamuh inscription (col. II).

18. *j* also occurs in its earlier forms.

19. *jh,* a rare character, does not occur in our inscriptions.

20. A developed form of *ñ* is found in the Khonamuh inscription (col. II) where the earlier wedge at the left top end has developed into a vertical stroke as in the case of *e* and *o* noted above.

*Cerebrals*

21. *ṭ* and *ṭh* display no change.

22. No significant change is noticed in *ḍ* as well.

23. *ḍh* occurs only in the Khonamuh inscription (col. II) and shows a loop in place of the more common kink at the right end of the base horizontal.

24. Of the two forms of *ṇ* noticed in the earlier records above, only one is more commonly found in our inscriptions, viz. that without the left-hand tail. In the Koṭiher (col. I) and Khonamuh (col. II) inscriptions, the letter occurs in a typical angular form where we have in place of the usual curves three downward strokes suspended from the top horizontal bar.

*Dentals*

25. *t* does not present anything remarkable except that in the Hariparbat (col. IV) and the Wularhama (col. V) inscriptions, the letter shows a loop in the middle as noticed earlier above in the Bhakund inscription (Table 3, col. III). An unknown form is

found in the Koṭiher inscription (col. I) line seven where the lower curve has been attached directly to the top bar.

26. *th* occurs only in quadrangular form. Its shape is similar to that of *ṣ* with the difference that it has its top closed by means of horizontal bar while the latter has its top open.

27. *d* develops a knob or a loop on the left in the Peshawar (col. III), Hariparbat (col. IV) and Wularhama (col. IV) inscriptions. The uncommon forms are seen in the Peshawar and Hariparbat inscriptions where the usual small upward stroke on the right of the base stroke has been developed into a vertical lengthened downward stroke.

28. *dh* shows regularly a well developed top bar.

29. *n* does not present anything remarkable except that the letter shows an unusually long vertical in the Hariparbat inscription (col. IV).

*Labials*

30. *p* retains its earlier form and shows no change.

31. *ph* occurs only in the Zajinai inscription (col. VI) where the curve instead of turning inside, turns sharply round.

32. *b* is usually represented by *v*. A distinction in their forms is, however, noticeable in the Hariparbat inscription (col. IV) where *b* is rounded in shape as compared to *v* which is angular.

33. The form of *bh* remains constant except that it shows a loop in the middle in the Wularhama inscription (col. V) in place of the wedge as in the Bhakund inscription above.

34. The form of *m* remains essentially the same but for a few peculiarities that it displays in some of our records. Thus, it shows a circular loop in the left limb in the Wularhama (col. V), a knob in the Peshawar Museum (col. III) and Hariparbat (col. IV) inscriptions.

*Semi-Vowels*

35. *y* occurs with a close top except in the Peshawar Museum inscription (col. III) where it retains its earlier form with an open top. In the Khonamuh inscription (col. II), it shows an inward stroke issuing from the left top end, similar to the one found in the early Śāradā manuscript. An uncommon cursive form occurs in the Koṭiher inscription (col. I).

36. *r* with a wedge or a triangular loop at the lower end of the left shows no marked change.

37. *l* also in essential features remains the same.

38. *v* which also represents *b*, occurs in both angular and cursive forms.

*Sibilants*

39. The form of *ś* does not differ materially from the earlier form. It shows as usual a wedge or a small triangle in the left limb. In the Koṭiher inscription (col. I), the wedge is sometimes less defined.

40. *ṣ* does not display any significant development. An uncommon form occurs in the Hariparbat inscription (col. IV).

41. *s* displays the same characteristics as *ś* but is open at the top.

*Spirants*

42. A somewhat developed form of *h* occurs in the Peshawar Museum inscription (col. III) which closely agrees with the modern *h* of the Devanāgarī. In our other records its form remains constant.

43. *Jihvāmūlīya* does not occur in the records under reference.

44. *Upadhmānīya* occurs in the Koṭiher (col. I) and Khonamuh (col. II) inscriptions and its shape is similar to that of angular *ṇ* described above with a horizontal bar below.

*Virāma*

45. *Virāma*, which usually occurs after *m* and *t*, shares the features of the earlier period. In the Khonamuh inscription (col. II), however, it consists of a long vertical stroke attached to the consonant on the right side. The final *m* with *virāma* appears in modified form in the Peshawar Museum inscription (col. III) while final *t* in the Khonamuh inscription (col. II) retains its complete form.

MEDIAL VOWELS (see Table 4 e)

1. The methods of expressing the medial *ā* continues to be the same as in the earlier records. In *jā* in the Koṭiher (col. I) and Wularhama (col. V) inscriptions, the small vertical denoting medial *ā* has been prolonged downwards to touch the central horizontal stroke. A small circle denotes the medial *a* in *nā* and *ṇā* in the Koṭiher (col. I) and the Khonamuh (col. II) inscriptions, respectively.

2. Medial *i* and *ī* are rendered as usual by curves drawn respectively to the left and right of the consonant. The curve of medial *i* in the Wularhama inscription (col. V) is comparatively shorter and presents an archaic appearance.

3. Medial *u* is expressed in the older fashion, viz. by a wedge, a small triangle or by a curve at the lower end of the consonant.

4. Medial *ū* is rendered as usual by the subscript initial *u* or by a horizontal stroke attached to the bottom of the consonant on the left side.
5. Medial *ṛ* occurs mostly in angular form. A form resembling subscript *p* is noticed in *ghr*, 1.2, in the Peshawar Museum inscription (col. III).
6. Except in the Peshawar Museum inscription (col. III), medial *e* is rendered throughout by a horizontal stroke placed above the consonant. The *pṛṣṭhamātrā* has been used in only one case in *ke* (l. 3) in the Peshawar Museum inscription. In this inscription the stroke of medial *e* continues to be a slanting one as in the earlier records.
7. Medial *ai* is rendered throughout by two horizontal *e* strokes placed above the consonant.
8. Medial *o* is rendered more often by the superscribed flourish. In the Khonamuh inscription (col. II) it has also been rendered in earlier fashion by a small downward stroke (in place of the usual wedge) at the right top end combined with a superscribed *e* stroke in *Khonamoshe* l. 2.
9. Medial *au* is rendered throughout by the combination of superscribed flourish and the *ā* mark.

LIGATURES (see Table 4 f)

1. Superscript and subscript *k* continues to have earlier forms, the former with the ancient crossbar form and the latter retaining its complete shape.
2. *ṅ* which occurs only in combination with *k* and *g* has an uncommon form in the Peshawar Museum inscription (col. III) line six (*ṅga*), where the base stroke of *ṅ* and the top of *g* have been merged into one.
3. The subscript *ñ* occurs in a developed looped form in the ligatures *jñā* (l. 5) and *jñ* (l. 9) in the Khonamuh inscription (col. II).
4. The subscript *th* is rendered throughout by the *S* like form with a steamer on the right. An uncommon form occurs in the ligature *rth* in the Khonamuh inscription where the sign consists of a *t* with a steamer attached to it on the right side.
5. *r* as usual loses its bottom part when forming the first member of the ligature. Sometimes it retains its full form as, for example, in *rtra* in Peshawar Museum inscription (col. III) and *rma* in Wularhama inscription (col. V). In *rva* in the Khonamuh inscription (col. II), the letter is not inserted in the left limb of *v* but forms a separate component.
6. Subscript *r* is rendered in the earlier fashions. In ligatures *dra* and *bra* in the Hariparbat inscription (col. IV), it shows uncommon looped form similar to that of subscript *ṭ* or *ṭh*.

7. The subscript *ṭ* and *ṭh* in the ligatures *sta* and *stha* is rendered by a loop with a tail attached to it on the right side. A peculiar form occurs in ligature *grṣṭa* in the Peshawar inscription (col. III) where the subscribed *ṭ* has been written as subscript *ṭh*.

This brings our study of the development of the Śāradā alphabet to a close so far as its use in the inscription is concerned. No doubt, the use of this alphabet in the inscription in Kashmir continued even up to as late as the 18th century as is proved by the discovery of a Śāradā inscription dated *Vikram* 1846 (CE 1789) by Pt. Anand Kaul.[7] But since we do not possess the facsimile of the inscription, nor is the original traceable now, we are not in a position to say what further developments of the alphabet displayed in the inscription took after the 16th century. This much is, however, clear that even in the inscriptions of the 15th and the 16th centuries, the development of the Śāradā script is almost complete with the exception of a few letters, the final changes of which are noticed in the Śāradā manuscripts. A detailed account will follow in the next chapter, titled "Śāradā Alphabet in Manuscripts."

---

7. Deambi, B.K. Kaul, op. cit., pp. 131f.

# 5

## Śāradā Alphabet in Manuscripts

We have discussed above the use of the Śāradā alphabet in inscriptions. In this chapter we shall study the use of this alphabet in manuscripts. The earliest known manuscript written in Śāradā characters is the Bakshali Manuscript written on birch bark and preserved in the Bodleian Library. The title of the manuscript is lost and it has been named after the name of the place of its discovery Bakshali, a village in Peshawar district of West Pakistan. The manuscript bears no date but on palaeographic and other considerations has been assigned to $12^{th}$ century CE.[1] The manuscript contains an important work on mathematics dealing with a variety of topics on mathematics. It contains the earliest treatment of certain topics on algebra, such as simple algebraic equations, linear equations involving several unknown and simultaneously indeterminate quadratic equations.[2] The manuscript is written in incorrect Sanskrit and the rules of grammar have not been followed very strictly.

The manuscript is written in clear and bold Śāradā characters. Now follows a discussion in detail on the palaeographic features of this manuscript.

**Details of the Forms** (see Table 5 col . I)

VOWELS

1. The initial *a* regularly shows a wedge, occasionally a triangle at the foot of the right vertical. It usually occurs with an open top but in certain cases the top has been closed by the extension of the top bar to the right top end.[3]
2. In initial *ā*, the wedge at the lower end has been replaced by a small curve drawn to the left. The letter occurs like initial *a*, occasionally with its top closed.
3. The initial *i* shows early Śāradā form with two dots above and a curve below drawn to the left.

---

1. The manuscript has been edited by G.R. Kaye in *Archaeological Survey of India's New Imperial Series*, vol. XLIII, part I and II.
2. Datta, B., and A.N. Singh, *History of Hindu Mathematics*, Part 2, pp. 36, 47, 258.
3. The examples of this form may be seen in folio 9 Recto L-6, 10; Verso L-8, 11; Recto L-5; Verso L-7, 12; Verso, L-7, etc.

4. The initial *ī* does not occur in the manuscript.
5. The initial *u* has its curve drawn to the level of the top of the letter and occasionally even beyond the top level.
6. The initial *ū* is formed like *u* with the addition of a streamer hanging down from near the top of the letter on the right.
7. Only one example of initial *ṛ* is found in the manuscript.[4] Unlike the form found in the inscriptions it is less cursive in shape.
8. The initial *e* occurs in both archaic and developed forms sometimes in the same folio. In the latter form, the left end stroke of triangle is drawn further below to give the letter a shape resembling the Devanāgarī *e*.
9. The initial *ai, o* and *au* are not noticed in the manuscript.

CONSONANTS

10. *k* occurs with a single loop but there are instances where the right-hand curve draws closer to the vertical, giving rise to a second loop on the right.[5]
11. *kh, g,* and *gh* have the same forms as found in the Śāradā inscriptions of 11th and 12th centuries. Occasionally, *g* shows a rounded top similar to one found in the Sungal copper-plate grant above (Table 2, col. XI).
12. *ṅ* which occurs only in combination with other consonants has a knob or a button at the right end of the top horizontal.
13. *c* is semi-quadrangular in shape, though old rounded form, as found in early Śāradā, also occurs occasionally.
14. *ch,* a conservative character, retains its form but is more cursive in shape.
15. *j* occurs with a pronounced knob on the right end of the top horizontal.
16. The rare character *jh* occurs only in combination with *j* on a couple of occasions and its shape does not materially differ from that found in the Sarahan *praśasti* above (Table 2, col. III).
17. The palatal nasal *ñ,* which is found only in combination with *c* and *j,* retains the form as found in the early Śāradā inscriptions.
18. *ṭ* has a well developed knob at the right top end.
19. *ṭh* does not occur independently.

---

4. Folio 63 Recto.
5. Folio 42 Recto Plate XXVIII.

20. *ḍ*, with a wedge at the lower end, does not differ from the letter found in the inscriptions.
21. In *ḍh*, the lower curve is turned round to form a kink.
22. *ṇ* occurs mostly without left-hand tail, though the examples of the form with thin tail are also found occasionally.
23. The dentals *t* and *d* have the same form as found in the inscriptions.
24. *th* and *dh* occur both in cursive and angular forms.
25. *n* does not differ from the modern Devanāgarī *n*.
26. *p* has its right-hand vertical drawn further down.
27. *ph* occurs in two forms with a kink and with a well developed loop. In the form with kink, it is hardly distinguishable from *ḍh*.
28. *b* also represents *v* and has the same form as in the inscriptions.
29. *bh* and *m* occur in the same form as found above in the inscriptions of 12th and the subsequent centuries.
30. *y* occurs both with open top and the top closed. Besides, in certain examples, we find an inward stroke similar to the one found in the Khonamuh inscription of the reign of Zain-ul-abidin above (Table 4, col. II).
31. *r* has a well developed wedge at the bottom on the left.
32. *l* and *v* do not differ much from their corresponding forms in the inscriptions.
33. *ś* shows a well developed wedge or a knob at the left lower end.
34. *ṣ*, a conservative character, occurs in both ancient and a later form with right-hand vertically extended downwards.
35. The form of *s* and *h* are also the same as found in the inscriptions above.
36. *Jihvāmūlīya* with *v* like form and *upadhmānīya* with the form of a cerebral *ṇ* with a horizontal below, have the same shape as in the inscriptions.
37. *Virāma* is characterized by a long drawn streamer. Letters except *m* usually retain their complete form even when the *virāma* is attached to them.
38. *Visarga* consists of two dots written one below the other after the consonant.

MEDIAL VOWELS

1. Medial *ā* is marked as in the inscriptions noted above by a wedge, button or a serif attached to the right end of the top. In case of *ṇa* and *ṭa*, it is rendered by a curve and in case of *jā* by a short vertical attached to the right end of the central

bar. In this case the upper bar is shortened or suppressed. Occasionally it is also marked by a loop attached to the right end of the top bar.

2. Medial *i* and *ī* are represented as usual by straight strokes with curves at the upper end and drawn to the left and right of the consonant, respectively.
3. The methods of expressing medial *u* are the same as noticed in the inscriptions above, viz. by a triangular wedge attached to the bottom of the vertical on the left. Where the vertical is absent, the wedge is attached by means of a short vertical or by a curve representing the initial *u*. In case of *ru*, it is also expressed by a downward streamer attached to the right of the letter near the top.
4. Medial *ū* is expressed by a horizontal streamer attached to the lower end of the vertical on the left. It is also expressed sometimes by the sign for initial *u*. In case of *brū*, it is expressed by an angular hook attached to the vertical on the right.
5. Medial *e* is represented by either the *pṛṣṭhamātrā* or the slanting stroke placed above the letter.
6. Medial *ai* is expressed more frequently by *pṛṣṭhamātrā*s at either end of the top and less regularly by two superscribed strokes. In the later sections of the manuscript, the sign is expressed only by the superscribed strokes.
7. Medial *o* is formed as in the inscriptions in three ways: (i) by superscribed flourish; (ii) by small strokes, wedges or buttons attached to both ends of the top bar; and (iii) by the top stroke of *e* combined with the sign for medial *ā*.
8. Medial *au* is expressed by a superscribed flourish combined with the sign of medial *ā*.

LIGATURES

1. The letter *k* retains its archaic form when forming the first member of the ligature. As a final element it retains its complete form. Same is the case, as we noticed above, in the inscriptions.
2. *ñ* as the final element changes its form completely as in the inscriptions and assumes the same form we noticed above in the inscriptions.
3. *r* as the first element of a ligature usually loses its lower part and is denoted by a small vertical. In combination with *v*, it is inserted in the left limb of *v* as is the case in early Śāradā inscriptions.
4. As in the inscriptions, final *r* is rendered by a long stroke drawn from left to right.
5. *th* as the second member in ligature *sth* occurs only in the spiral form as in the early Śāradā inscriptions.

6. In *ṣṭ* and *ṣṭh*, the original forms of *ṭ* and *ṭh* are more or less preserved but a downward stroke is added to the right of *ṭ*. Sometimes the downward stroke is replaced by a hook.

Another Śāradā manuscript of the 12th century, containing a commentary on Sanskrit grammar and discovered by Bhikkhu Rahul in Tibet, is referred to by R.S. Pandit in his book *River of Kings*.[6] But unfortunately no details are given and the manuscript is not accessible.

Our next accessible manuscript in point of time is an old birch bark manuscript of *Muni-mata-maṇi-mālā*.[7] The manuscript bears no date but on certain palaeographic considerations recounted below it can be assigned to the 14th century CE. The manuscript is the earliest known and accessible manuscript discovered so far in Kashmir where Śāradā has been the alphabet *par excellence*. The exact nature of the contents of the manuscript is not known. Even the title of the manuscript is not traceable now. According to Shri Dinanath Shastri, Ex-Head Pandit of the Manuscript Library of the Jammu & Kashmir State Research Department, the manuscript contains a *tāntrik* work. The manuscript is in an extremely worn out condition and the proper study of its contents is not possible in view of the extremely fragile and brittle condition of its birch leaves. However, notwithstanding its contents, the manuscript is of great importance from palaeographic point of view. It is the only accessible manuscript which enables us to study the developments and changes that the Śāradā characters undergo in the manuscripts from 12th century CE to the 14th century CE.

We shall now discuss below the forms of Śāradā characters used in the manuscript and see what developments do they display when compared to those of the Bakshali Manuscript noted above.

**Details of the Forms** (see Table 5, col. II)

VOWELS

1. The initial vowels *a* and *ā* occur regularly with closed tops. The earlier forms with open tops found fairly common in the Bakshali Manuscript are conspicuous by their absence. As noted above, the practice of closing the tops of *a* and *ā* by means of horizontal top bars becomes fairly regular and common in the inscriptions only after the 13th century CE.
2. In initial *i*, the top upper dots are converted into curve with small upward strokes attached to its both ends. The similar form has been noticed above in the Khonamuh stone slab inscription of 1428 (see Table 4, col. II).

---

6. Appendix J, p. 627, fn. 14.
7. The manuscript is now preserved in the Manuscripts Library of the Department of Libraries and Archives, Jammu & Kashmir Government. I owe the information about the title of the manuscript to ex-Head Pandit of the Department.

3. The initial *ī*, *u* and *ū* do not manifest any spectacular change.
4. In initial *e* and *o*, the wedges at the left top ends have been replaced by the vertical downward strokes and their forms agree closely with those of the Koṭiher stone slab inscription dated CE 1369 (Table 4, col. I).
5. The initial *au* is formed like *o* with the addition of a wedge at the right top end.

CONSONANTS

1. *k* occurs regularly in a double looped form, the form which became common in the inscriptions only after the 13th century CE. A peculiarity worth noticing in the *k* of our manuscript is that it occurs regularly without the top bar and the curve forming the loop on the left side of the vertical shows a slight twist towards the left at the upper end.
2. The other gutturals *kh*, *g*, *gh* and *ṅ* do not present anything remarkable.
3. *c* occurs often in quadrangular form though the ancient circular form also occurs occasionally.
4. The conservative characters, *ch* and *j*, display no change.
5. No instance of *jh* could be traced in a few folios of the manuscript that were examined by the writer for palaeographic study.
6. In *ñ*, the earlier wedge at the left top end is changed into a vertical stroke. The same development was noticed above in the form of the letter in the Khonamuh inscription (Table 4, col. II).
7. *ṭ* shows a fork at the right top end in place of the usual wedge or serif.
8. The letter *ṭh* and *ḍ* remain constant.
9. In *ḍh*, the curve at the right end usually forms a circular loop with the base stroke.
10. *ṇ* occurs both with and without the left-hand tail. When without the tail, it does not present anything remarkable. But in the tailed form, a significant peculiarity is noticed in the treatment of the tail which is represented by the vertical stroke instead of the usual long drawn slanting stroke.
11. Nothing noteworthy is presented by the dental group.
12. *p* also remains unchanged.
13. *ph* is without the inverted curve or a loop and resembles the letter *h*.
14. A distinction appears to be made in the formation of *b* and *v*. The former is made more cursive and the latter angular. Moreover, the right-hand vertical is

lengthened downwards in case of *v* while in case of *b* it retains the same level as the left-hand loop.

15. In *bh,* the curve at the lower end is sometimes drawn upwards to touch the loop in the middle. This circular form of *bh* is commonly met with in the later Śāradā manuscripts of the 17th and the subsequent centuries.
16. *y* occurs in both forms with the open or closed top. It, besides, shows an inverted stroke like that found in the forms of the Koṭiher and Khonamuh inscriptions noted above (see Table 4, cols. I, II).
17. The consonants *r, l, v, ś, ṣ, s,* and *h* do not materially differ from those of the Bakshali Manuscript except that the curve forming the loop on the left side of the vertical in *v* shows a twist to the left at the upper end as in the case of *k* noted above.
18. Nothing is particularly remarkable about the *jihvāmūlīya* and the *upadhmānīya* which occur in the same form as in the Bakshali Manuscript except that *upadhmānīya* shows an additional small upward stroke at the right end.
19. The long drawn slanting stroke is replaced by a small vertical in *virāma.*

MEDIAL VOWELS

1. The medial vowel *ā* is expressed as in the Bakshali Manuscript by a wedge, serif or a cursive hook. The hook sometimes develops into a loop in case of *ṇā*. Peculiarity is noticed in *jā* where the vowel is expressed by a small triangle suspended from the right end of the top horizontal bar. This method of expressing medial *ā* in *jā* is noticed only in one case in the Baijnāth Śiva Temple inscription (Table 3, col. XIV), but becomes fairly common both in the inscriptions and the manuscripts after the 13th century.
2. The medial *i* and *ī* are formed by long curves drawn to the left and the right of the consonant, respectively. The old smaller curves found occasionally in the Bakshali Manuscript are rare.
3. The medial *u* and *ū* continue to be rendered in the old fashion, the former by a wedge, a curve or a downward stroke (in case of *rū)* and the latter by the flag like line or by the sign of subscribed initial *ū.*
4. The medial *ṛ* does not materially differ in shape from that of the Bakshali Manuscript. It occurs both in the angular and the cursive forms. A peculiar form of the sign is noticed in *kṛ.*
5. The medial *e* is expressed either by the *pṛṣṭhamātrā* or by the superscribed stroke above the consonant. The former is important as it constitutes an important proof of the age of the manuscript. The practice of forming the medial *e* by the

*pr̥ṣṭhamātrā* had become obsolete in Kashmir in the 15th century as is attested to by the evidence of Jonarāja who while recounting an anecdote regarding a forgery in a deed of sale (*vikrayapattraka*) remarks, "in order to express the *e* following a consonant the clerks formerly used to write a stroke behind the consonants. But as in course of time the script (*lipi*) became changed, writers of today write the stroke expressing *e* over the consonant."[8] This would show that our manuscripts, where the earlier method is frequently employed, must belong to a period earlier than the 15th century. The above evidence of Jonarāja is corroborated by the rare use of *pr̥ṣṭhamātrā* in forming medial *e* in later Śāradā manuscripts where the *pr̥ṣṭhamātrā,* as will be subsequently shown, is resorted to only occasionally to denote the medial *ai.*

6. The medial *ai* is likewise expressed either by the two superscribed horizontal strokes placed over the top of the consonant or by a *pr̥ṣṭhamātrā* combined with the superscribed *e* stroke.
7. The medial *o* is expressed as in the Bakshali Manuscript and in early Śāradā inscriptions in three different ways. They are (i) by a *pr̥ṣṭhamātrā* combined with the sign for medial *ā;* (ii) by the superscribed *e* stroke combined with the symbol for medial *ā;* and (iii) by the superscribed flourish. The first two methods were rarely employed in the inscriptions after the 13th century. In the manuscripts of the 16th and the subsequent centuries also, the two methods become obsolete and it is only the third method that is frequently employed.
8. The medial *au* is expressed as usual by a superscribed flourish combined with the sign for medial *ā.*

LIGATURES

Among the ligatures, the following deserve attention:

1. *kṣ* where the superscribed *k* consists of a small curve to the left and a long drawn cursive stroke to the right reaching the level of the bottom of the subscribed *ṣ.*
2. *jñ* where the subscribed *ñ* has an unusual looped form.
3. *ry* where the right half of the subscribed *y* is suppressed.
4. *rth* which closely agrees with the form of the Bakshali Manuscript noted above.
5. *r̥ṇ* where the small vertical representing the superscribed *r* is missing and the *ṇ* sign is attached direct to the top bar. The shape of subscribed *ṇ* with a long drawn curve on the left and a loop on the right is noteworthy.

---

8. Jonarāja, *Dvitīya Rājataraṅgiṇī* 1025-37 (Jonarāja was a contemporary of Zain-ul-Ābidin, CE 1428-70).

6. *rgh* where the small vertical for superscribed *r* suspended from the horizontal top bar is blended with the central stroke of the superscribed *gh*.

7. The superscribed *th* in ligature *sth* is always S-like in shape as is usually the case in the Śāradā records of the 12th and the subsequent centuries. The spiral form found in the earlier inscriptions of 10th and the 11th centuries and quite frequently found in the Bakshali Manuscript is rare.

8. Nothing special is noteworthy in ligatures *ṣṭ* and *ṣṭh*.

We have studied above in detail the forms of the Śāradā characters employed in the manuscript. Some characters show developed forms not noticed in the Śāradā records earlier than the 13th century. The manuscript employs methods of expressing medial *e* and *o* which became obsolete in Kashmir after the 15th century. This would show that the manuscript belongs to a period which is later than the 13th century and earlier than the 15th century. We may not be wrong if we assign the manuscript to the 14th century.

There is no literary specimen available to study the development of the Śāradā alphabet in the manuscripts of 15th century. In the 16th century, the Śāradā alphabet reached the final stage of its development as is illustrated by the following Śāradā manuscripts discovered from Kashmir, which though, are bearing no date, appear to belong to the 16th century on palaeographic considerations.

1. The birch bark manuscript of *Śakuntalā*.[9]
2. The birch bark manuscript of the Ādi and the Sabhā Parva of the *Mahābhārata*.[10]
3. The birch bark manuscript of *Kathā-sarit-sāgara*.[11]

The Śāradā characters used in these manuscripts agree closely in the majority of cases with those of the birch bark manuscript of *Muni-mata-maṇi-mālā* noted above. A few characters, however, display some significant changes. We shall study below these changes in detail.

---

9. The manuscript represents the Kashmirian recension of Kālidāsa'a *Abhijñāna-Śakuntalā*. It was purchased by George Bühler in CE 1875 in Kashmir and is mentioned in the Deccan College Collection under No. 192. It has been described by Bühler in his *Kashmir Report*, p. 62. The forms of the letters in the table have been taken from Bühler's *Indian Palaeography*, plate VI, col. VIII and *Anecdota oxonancia*, Ariana Series, l. 3, plate 6.

10. This manuscript was also purchased by Bühler in Kashmir and has been described by him in his *Kashmir Report*, p. 64. It is mentioned in the Deccan College Collection of 1875-76 under No. 159 and has been utilized for the critical edition of the *Mahābhārata* (ed. Dr. V.S. Sukhthankar) and its siglum is SI in the critical apparatus of the said edition.

11. It is now preserved in the MSS Library of the aforementioned department of Jammu & Kashmir Government.

VOWELS (See Table 5, Cols. III-V)

1. The initial *i* occurs in its earlier form with two dots above and a curve below in the manuscript of *Śakuntalā* (col. III). In two other manuscripts (cols. IV, V), the vowel is found in its later form as in the manuscript of *Muni-mata-maṇi-mālā* (col. II) noted above. In the manuscript of *Mahābhārata,* the lower curve is very small as in the Bower Manuscript noted above.
2. The initial *i* resembles the forms of the Baijnāth Śiva Temple inscription (Table 3, col. XIV) and the Khonamuh stone inscription of 1428 (Table 4, col. II).
3. The initial *u* shows an unusual form in the manuscript of *Śakuntalā* in as much as the curve marking the length of the vowel is attached to the bottom of *u* instead of to its back.
4. The initial *ṛ* occurs in exactly the same form as in the Bakshali Manuscript (col. I).
5. The initial *e* with a vertical to the left agrees closely with the form of the *Muni-mata-maṇi-mālā* (col. II). The left-hand vertical is straight in the manuscript of *Śakuntalā* (col. III) but shows a slight twist to the right at the lower end in the manuscripts of the *Mahābhārata,* (col. IV) and the *Kathā-sarit-sāgara* (col. V).
6. The initial *o* resembles the form of the *Muni-mata-maṇi-mālā* (col. II). In the manuscript of *Śakuntalā* (col. III), the vertical is drawn close in front of *u* with the result that the letter looks like the Roman capital letter B.
7. In the initial *au,* the earlier wedge at the right top end is replaced by a small triangle.

CONSONANTS

Among the consonants the developments are noticed only in the following letters:

1. In *ṅ,* where the earlier wedge at the right top end is sometimes replaced by a semi-circle, e.g. in the manuscript of *Śakuntalā* (col. III) and sometimes by a small circle, e.g. in the manuscript of the *Mahābhārata* (col. IV).
2. *j,* which retained its conservative character from the ancient Brāhmī to the 15th century CE, now undergoes significant change and can be fairly regarded as a reliable criterion for age. The letter drops the central stroke and the top stroke is replaced by two small connecting curves with a small upward stroke attached to them at the right end.
3. In *jh,* the left half consisting of a vertical with a wedge attached to its lower end remains unchanged. The right half, however, is replaced by the sign which resembles the letter *dh* in shape.

4. Clear distinction is made between *b* and *v* in making the loop which is triangular in case of *b* and the usually cursive in case of *v*. Besides, the right-hand vertical in *v* is protruded downwards.
5. *bh* shows a well pronounced wedge or a solid loop in the middle. The circular form of the letter noticed above in the manuscript of the *Muni-mata-maṇi-mālā* (col. II) occurs occasionally in the manuscript of the *Mahābhārata* (col. IV). In our other two manuscripts the earlier form with a semi-circular curve prevails.
6. *y* occurs exclusively with its top closed by means of a horizontal stroke. The form with an open top found occasionally in the manuscript of the *Muni-mata-maṇi-mālā* (col. II) is rare.

MEDIAL VOWELS

As regards the medial vowels, the following peculiarities and developments deserve notice:

1. The medial *ā* in *jā* is expressed by a small circular loop attached to the right end of the top horizontal bar, in the manuscripts of the *Mahābhārata* (col. IV) and the *Kathā-sarit-sāgara* (col. V). In the manuscripts of *Śakuntalā* (col. III), it is denoted by a curve issuing from the right end of the top horizontal bar that touches the left-hand vertical in the middle. The similar method of expressing the medial *ā* in *jā* is followed in the later Śāradā manuscripts with the only difference that the curve touches the left-hand vertical at its upper end instead of in the middle. It needs to be pointed out here that in the letter *j*, when accompanied by medial *ā*, the two newly developed curves at the top are regularly replaced by the older horizontal bar.
2. The medial *u* is expressed, besides the usual flag-like line attached to the lower end of the consonant, by the combination of two curves of initial *u*. These curves are attached to the bottom of the consonant, sometimes one below the other, sometimes back to back and occasionally they form very peculiar combinations, e.g. in *bhū* and *Śru* in the manuscript of *Śakuntalā* (col. III).
3. The medial *ṛ* is expressed generally by a semi-circular curve facing upwards. The peculiar forms are noticed in *kṛ* in the manuscript of the *Mahābhārata* (col. IV) and *śru* in the manuscript of the *Kathā-sarit-sāgara* (col. V).
4. The medial *e* is expressed exclusively by a horizontal stroke placed above the consonant.
5. The medial *ai* is formed throughout by the superscribed strokes except in the manuscript of the *Kathā-sarit-sāgara* (col. V) where the older method consisting

of a *pṛṣṭhamātrā* combined with the superscribed stroke is also employed occasionally.

6. The medial *o* is also expressed generally by a superscribed flourish except in a very few cases in the manuscript of the *Kathā-sarit-sāgara* (col. V) where it has been expressed in the older fashion, viz. by a *pṛṣṭhamātrā* combined with the sign of medial *ā*.

VIRĀMA

The long drawn streamer which represents the *virāma* in the earlier records becomes a long vertical in the manuscript of *Śakuntalā* (col. III) and occurs in the same form in the later Śāradā manuscripts.

LIGATURES

Nothing is specially remarkable about the ligatures except what has already been stated above while discussing the ligatures of the manuscript of the *Muni-mata-maṇi-mālā*. Mention may, however, be made of the ligatures where *k* forms the first member. The shape of *k* in such cases continues to be the same as in that of the manuscript of *Muni-mata-maṇi-mālā* (col. II) but the long-drawn curve to the right is now made comparatively thinner than the smaller one to the left. Also worthy of note are the ligatures where *r* forms the second member. In such a case, *r* is represented by a cursive downward stroke attached to the upper consonant on the right side.

As has been pointed out above, none of our manuscripts bears any date. But the detailed study of the forms used in them would show that they belong to a period which is later than the 15th century and earlier than the 17th century CE. They show developed forms of *j, jh* and *jā* which are not traced in the manuscript of the *Muni-mata-maṇi-mālā* or in the Khonamuh stone inscription of 1428 CE or the Peshawar Museum inscription of 1461 CE. Besides, the form of *bh* which is often semi-circular in shape, the top bars which are comparatively shorter in length and the use of *pṛṣṭhamātrā* for the formation of medial *ai* and *o* point to a period earlier than the 17th century CE.

## Modern Śāradā

With 17th century we enter into a period of what may be called the modern Śāradā. Though the alphabet remained in use for another three centuries, it remained almost static and did not show essential differences from earlier forms except in the case of a few letters. This latest stage of the alphabet is exemplified by a birch bark manuscript of *Bālabodhinī*[12] which contains a Sanskrit grammatical text for beginners and the paper manuscript of the same work dated *Saṁvat* (*Laukika*) (48) 21 *Hijrī* 1158 or CE 1745. These manuscripts contain a complete list of all Śāradā characters in use at the time. The latter

12. Same as above f.n.

have not displayed any significant change since then as Śāradā alphabet gradually went into limited use with the introduction and popularization of the Devanāgarī script, the vehicle of the Indian national language, Hindi.

We now discuss below the forms of the modern Śāradā alphabet illustrated in Table 5 (cols. VI-X). Col. VI contains the letters from the aforementioned manuscript of the *Bālabodhinī*. Characters in col. VII have been taken from an undated manuscript of a *Brāhmaṇa* text.[13] Col. VIII illustrates the letters based on a manuscript dated CE 1905 of a text on *śrāddha* ritual,[14] while the col. IX represents those found in a manuscript dated CE 1933 of *Śivamahimnastotra*.[15] Col. X represents the letters taken from a horoscope prepared in CE 1963.[16] It may be pointed out here that till a couple of decades ago the horoscopes in Kashmir were exclusively written in the Śāradā.

**Details of Forms** (see Table 5, cols. VI-X)

VOWELS AND CONSONANTS

1. Initial *a* and *ā* in horoscopes (col. X) assume typical forms with left limb looking like *dh* with a slight projection towards the left at the upper end.
2. The old form of *i* with two dots above and a curve below is found in the manuscript of a *Brāhmaṇa* text (col. VII) but gradually becomes rare.
3. The rarely occurring characters *ṝ, ḷ, ḹ* occur only in the list of the letters of the Śāradā alphabet given in the manuscripts of the *Bālabodhinī* (col. VI). The initial *ṝ* is formed like *ṛ* with the addition of a small triangle at the right top end. *ḷ* is similar to *n* in shape but has in addition the curve of medial *r* attached to the right limb at the lower end. *ḹ* is formed like *e* with the addition of a small triangle at the right upper end as in the case of *ṝ*.
4. In the manuscript of the *Brāhmaṇa* text (col. VII), *j* shows a form where instead of two curves connected with small loops at the top, we find two downward strokes suspended from the top horizontal bar.
5. In *ṇ*, the tailed form observed earlier becomes rare.
6. Clear distinction is made between *b* and *v*. While the letter looks like the modern Devanāgarī *v*, the former is more triangular than cursive in shape with the right-hand vertical rarely protruding downwards.
7. The use of *jihvāmūlīya* and *upadhmānīya* gradually becomes rare.

---

13. Personal collection.
14. Personal collection.
15. Personal collection.
16. Personal collection.

MEDIAL VOWELS

1. Medial *ā* is expressed more often by a knob at the right top end of the consonant and also sometimes by a small downward stroke. In case of *jā,* the medial sign is either triangular or circular, while in *ṇā* it displays significant development inasmuch as the curve denoting medial *ā* is lengthened and drawn further towards the left to cover the entire bottom surface of the letter.
2. In *ka, ku* and *kṛ* (and in ligatures), *k* presents typical form with its right limb showing long ornamental curve (cols. IX and X).
3. In *ṛ*, the right upper end of the curve is lengthened upwards sometimes to reach the level of the top upper letter (col. X).
4. The medial *e* and *ai* are only expressed by strokes which are more horizontal than slanting. The use of *pṛṣṭhamātrā* is invariably absent.
5. The medial *o* is also rendered exclusively by a flourish over the top of the letter which sometimes assumes ornamental form (col. IX).

LIGATURES

1. The ligature *rv,* having passed through successive stages of development from the old form with excrescence on the left, now assumes the form which closely resembles the modern letter *c* of the Devanāgarī. In *ry,* we have sometimes addition of another curve below the shortened curve of the subscript *y* (col. IX). The forms of *rdh, rth* and *rja* are typically noteworthy.
2. Subscript *r* is rendered by an ornamental flag-like line with a slight loop at the upper end.
3. Subscript *th* in *rth* and *sth* shows significant development from the earlier spiral or *S*-like forms. It may be described as subscript *t* with ornamental flag-like curve or downward stroke placed at its back.
4. Another marked development is found in ligatures with subscript *dh* where the latter is hardly distinguishable from subscribed *ṭ* or *ṭh* in ligatures *sṭ* or *sṭh.* Quite unusually sometimes the subscript *ṭ* is rendered in its initial form (col. IX).

**Conclusion**

This brings our study of the development of the Śāradā alphabet to a close so far as its use in inscriptions, manuscripts and documents of general use is concerned. It would not be out of place here to recount the opinions of some earlier eminent epigraphists about the nature of the Śāradā alphabet and see how far they hold good in the light of our present knowledge of the script.

The earlier epigraphists like Kielhorn and Hoernle described Śāradā as the most conservative alphabet which remained constant all through and showed but little change during the course of several centuries. Thus, Kielhorn while editing the copper-plate inscription of Somavarman and Āsaṭa observed, "It would have been impossible to determine the age of that inscription even approximately from the characters in which it is written."[17] Dr Hoernle similarly opined that "the Śāradā characters are no guide as to age" and that "any undated manuscript or inscription written in the Śāradā alphabet must be placed any time after CE 500."[18]

However, the observations of the learned epigraphists seem to be evidently based on the insufficient evidence of the limited number of Śāradā records accessible to them. The present study of the origin and the development of the Śāradā alphabet based on a very wide range of inscriptions and manuscripts dating from the 9th to the 20th century and covering the entire region of north-western Himalayas, makes it sufficiently clear that the Śāradā alphabet undergoes sure and distinct changes right from its first appearance in the 9th century till its final development in the 20th century and that there is no justification to label it as a conservative alphabet. Secondly, Dr Hoernle's suggestion that "the Śāradā characters are no guide to age" does not seem to be wholly true. For, keeping in view the forms that Śāradā characters display in the course of different centuries, it should not be impossible to determine the approximate date of any undated Śāradā record.

17. *Indian Antiquary*, vol. XVII, p. 7, n. 2.

18. Ibid., vol. XII, p. 89.

# 6

## Numerals of the Śāradā Alphabet*

In the Śāradā inscriptions, numerals are generally used for recording the dates. They are also sometimes used for denoting verse numbers in longer inscriptions written in verse. In the copper-plate grants of Chamba, numerals have also been used for denoting the quantity of the donated pieces of land. In the manuscripts, numerals are used for recording verse numbers, and also the number of leaves or folios, chapters or cantos. In the Bakshali Manuscript, numerals have been used for arithmetical notation.

In general, our records employ the system of decimal numeration. In an image inscription from Chamba, now preserved in the National Museum, New Delhi, and in the Peshawar inscription of Vaṇhaḍaka of (*Laukika*) 538, the numerical signs have also been expressed in words. The signs of numerical figures are fairly uniform on the whole though variations in certain cases are also observed. Below is given a brief description of each figure. The figures are illustrated in the accompanying Table 6.

1. The figure 1 is represented mostly by a semi-circle and occasionally by a complete circle. In modern Śāradā, the figure is exclusively represented by the latter sign. In the Bakshali Manuscript, besides the semi-circle, the figure is also denoted especially in fractions by a (i) dot; (ii) by a dot with tail; or (iii) by a short horizontal.
2. The sign for the figure 2 generally consists of two curves placed one below the other and open to the left. In the Bakshali Manuscript, the figure is also denoted by a sign resembling the figure 2 of modern Devanāgarī. An advanced form is, however, noticed in the Koṭiher inscription (col. XVI) and in the Śāradā birch bark manuscript of the *Mahābhārata* (col. XXII) where the sign has been formed like the circular figure for 1 with the addition of a tail. The same sign is used in modern Śāradā (col. XXIII).
3. The figure 3 is formed like the figure 2 with the addition of a small tail or a curve below the second curve.
4. The figure 4 occurs in our records in three distinct forms. The one that is found in the Sungal copper-plate inscription of Vidagdha (col. V), resembles the Śāradā ligature *tk*. The second, which is most common among the three, looks like the

* *The references of the inscriptions and the manuscripts cited in this section have already been given in the previous sections.*

ligature *ṅk*. The third, which is found in the Koṭiher inscription (col. XVIII) and in the manuscript of the *Mahābhārata* (col. XXII), and which is more commonly used in modern Śāradā, is developed from the second with the omission of the subscribed *k*. The sign used in the Bakshali Manuscript agrees closely with that used in the Sungal grant.

5. The symbol for the figure 5 resembles the Śāradā letter *p* with the right-hand vertically lengthened downwards and turned towards the right. Its shape is generally consistent throughout.

6. The figure 6 shows distinct variations in shape. In the Hund inscription (col. VI) and the S.P.S. Museum Srinagar bronze image inscription (col. III), its form agrees with Nāgarī figure 6. In the Devī-rī-koṭhī inscription of Nāgapāla (col. XIV), it is represented by an *S*-like form. In the Salhi inscription (col. XV), it shows a peculiar looped form. In the Bakshali Manuscript it resembles the final *m* (with *virāma*). In the Hariparbat inscription (col. XX) it is semi-circular in shape with the lower end of the curve lengthened upwards towards the left. The form of the manuscript of the *Mahābhārata* (col. XXII) agrees closely but is narrower in shape. The sign used in the modern Śāradā (col. XXIII) is the development of this form with the upper end of the lengthened curve turned sharply round towards the right. The sign in this respect closely resembles that of the figure 7 of the Devanāgarī.

7. The sign for the figure 7 closely agrees with that used in the Nāgarī to denote the figure 1. Its form remains generally consistent throughout.

8. The symbol for the figure 8 may be described as the Śāradā *ṅ* without the wedge at the right top end and with the base stroke slanting downwards. In the modern Śāradā (col. XXIII), the base stroke is converted into a curve turning sharply towards the left. A peculiar cursive form occurs in the Peshawar Museum inscription (col. XIX) where the figure shows a big circular loop at the lower end.

9. The sign for figure 9 in the Hund inscription of Kāmeśvarī Devī (col. VI), does not materially differ from that of the figure 7 noted above. In the Bakshali Manuscript (col. XXI) and the manuscript of the *Mahābhārata* (col. XXII), the sign is denoted by a small circle with a curve attached to it on the right. The sign of the figure is the same in modern Śāradā (col. XXIII) with the curve turned round and lengthened towards the left.

10. The zero is rendered throughout by a dot.

As pointed out above, the numerical signs in the National Museum, New Delhi image inscription and the Peshawar Museum inscription have also been expressed in words. Thus in the former, the years 53 in the date has been expressed by word *shara* (standing for 5) and *guṇa* (standing for 3). In the latter inscription, the figures of the date 538 have been expressed by *shara* (5) and hundred augmented by *gaja* (8) and thirty.

# 7

# Ṭākarī Alphabet Origin and Development (14th-16th Centuries)

ṬĀKARĪ the popular alphabet of Himachal Pradesh is the direct descendant of the Śāradā alphabet which, as seen above, remained the predominant script of the region from 9th to 13th century. The Ṭākarī makes its appearance in the 14th century under its earlier denomination of Devāśeṣa. The most significant peculiarity of this script, distinguishing it from its mother script Śāradā, is the use of loops and triangles in place of the knobs and wedges which is the distinguishing trait of the Śāradā.

## Name

As regards the origin of the term Ṭākarī, J. Ph. Vogel[1] suggests two etymologies. "It may be connected with *ṭaṅka* which would point to its having been in the first instance a commercial alphabet. A parallel is furnished by the word *mahājanī* (from *mahājan* "a banker"). Another possibility is to connect it with *ṭhākur* (Sanskrit *ṭhakkura*) in which case it may have been the original character used by Rājpūt land-holders." Ṭākarī also denotes, as pointed out by Vogel,[2] the commercial shorthand used by the *baniyā*s, the trading community of certain districts of Punjab. However, the relation of the latter script with the Ṭākarī of the hills and with the Śāradā is not explicitly clear as the two appear to be two distinct systems of writing. It appears that while the script that was popular with the elite class of the society and used for official purpose was known as Devāśeṣa, the popular version of the same used by the common man and the business community for maintaining records of accounts came to be called Ṭākarī. B. Ch. Chabra[3] suggests that Ṭākarī is the later development of Devāśeṣa. The nomenclature Devāśeṣa once popular with the local paṇḍits is no longer used now and the people today are familiar with only one appellation Ṭākarī.

In course of time Ṭākarī developed a great number of varieties, each neighbouring hill state or tract having its own peculiar Ṭākarī. As pointed out by Vogel,[4] the popular

1. Chabra, B. Ch., *Antiquities of Chamba State,* Part I, p. 47 f.
2. Ibid.
3. Ibid., Part II, p. 3 fn.
4. loc. cit.

Ṭākarī is in general very difficult to read and most of the documents, in which it is used, are very difficult to decipher as they are generally written in a very quick hand. Vogel[5] was not wrong when he made the prediction that the Ṭākarī alphabet would be the despair of future epigraphists.

Even with the popularization of the Indian National language Hindi and its script Devanāgarī, Ṭākarī continued to be used side by side with Devanāgarī till the 19th century. But later it lost the race and was finally replaced by Devanāgarī which was adopted as the official script.

**Details of Forms** (see Table 7)

We may now discuss the details of the characters of Ṭākarī-Devāśeṣa as found in the epigraphic records, mostly copper-plate inscriptions, which are available in uninterrupted succession and in large numbers from 14th to 18th centuries. Since it is impossible to discuss the forms used in all the inscriptions, the following inscriptions have been selected to represent the study:

1. Guroli copper-plate inscription of Vairasivarman, *Vikram Saṁvat* 1387 (1330 CE),[6]
2. Mhesa copper-plate of Bhoṭavarman, Śaka 1318 (CE 1396),[7]
3. Jungrar plate of Bhoṭavarman (undated),[8]
4. Saṅgrāmavarman's grant to Badu Legha (*Śāstra*) 22 (CE 1446),[9]
5. Mindha copper-plate of Saṅgrāmavarman (undated),[10]
6. Chamba plate of Ānandavarman (son of Saṅgrāmavarman),[11]
7. Chamba plate of Gaṇeśavarman, *Śāstra* 97 (CE 1521-22),[12]
8. Ganguya grant of Gaṇeśavarman,[13]
9. Chamba plate of Balabhadra VS 1652 (CE 1595),[14] and
10. Kulu copper-plate grant of Bahādur Singh.[15]

5. loc. cit.
6. Chabra, B.Ch., *Antiquities of Chamba State*, Part II, plate I A.
7. Ibid., plate I B.
8. Ibid., plate III.
9. Ibid., plate IV B.
10. Ibid., plate V A.
11. Ibid., plate VI A.
12. Ibid., plate VII A.
13. Ibid., plate IX A.
14. Ibid., plate XIX B.
15. *Annual Report of the Archaeological Survey of India*, 1903-04, plate LXXI.

VOWELS

1. The initial *a* and *ā* occur in two forms. One, with the two curves open to the left connected with the right-hand vertical by means of a small horizontal bar, is the direct descendant of the Śāradā. The other, with two slanting strokes one connected to the top bar and the other to the right-hand vertical, appears to be close to the form found in the old Nāgarī inscriptions. Both the letters occur mostly with their top closed by means of a horizontal bar though in some records the letters occur with open tops (cols. III, V, X). While a small triangle at the foot of the vertical on the left reminiscent of the earlier wedge of the Śāradā letter is the distinguishing feature of *a*, the length of the vowel in *ā* is marked by a curve open to the left and attached to the foot of the vertical as is the case in the Śāradā.
2. The initial *i* with two dots and a curve below, occurs in the same form as in early Śāradā. A peculiar form with a horizontal stroke at the base occurs in the Jungrar plate of Bhoṭavarman (col. III).[16] Another peculiar form with the curve inordinately lengthened upwards on the left and the two dots placed on the right occurs in the Guroli plate of Vairaśivarman (col. I).
3. In initial *ī*, which occurs very rarely, the wedge at the foot of the vertical of the Śāradā letter has been replaced by a triangle. The two dots are placed at the top as in the Śāradā.
4. The initial *u* occurs in the same form as in the Śāradā. Sometimes the curve is inordinately lengthened to cover the top of the letter (cols. I, II).
5. *ū* does not occur independently but is found as a subscript representing the medial sign of the vowel. It is the same as initial *u* with a curve attached to it at the back. The letter occurs in the same form in the Śāradā.
6. *r̥* which in its initial form is met with only in a couple of inscriptions, does not differ much from the cerebral *ṭ* described below.
7. Initial *e* with a triangle on the right and a vertical stroke on the left does not differ much from the sign of the later Śāradā. Only occasionally we find the position of the triangle and the vertical reversed.
8. *ai* is formed like *e* with a horizontal stroke representing the length of the vowel placed at the top of the letter. In the text of the inscription itself the sign represents the initial *e*.
9. The initial *o* does not occur independently but is found in the benedictory syllable *oṁ*. It is formed like *u* with a small slanting stroke suspended from the top bar on

16. Ref. p. 70, f.n. 8.

the left. The small stroke gradually becomes a full-fledged vertical in the later Ṭākarī as is the case in the Śāradā.

10. Only one instance of initial *au* formed like *o* with the flourish of medial *o* over the top is found in the Guroli plate of Vairaśivarman (col. I).

11. *anunāsika* crescent below and the circle in place of the usual dot above is found in the Jungrar plate (col. III). In all other inscriptions under reference, the crescent and the dot occur in reverse order. Same is the case in the later Śāradā.

CONSONANTS

12. *k* occurs in double looped form, though the single looped form of the sign with a loop on the left and the downward curve on the right is not uncommon.

13. *kh* usually denoted by *s* in the Ṭākarī inscriptions, has the same form as in the Śāradā.

14. In *g,* the distinguishing feature is a triangle in place of the wedge of the Śāradā letter.

15. *gh,* with the right-hand vertical protruding downwards does not differ materially from the Śāradā form of the letter.

16. The guttural nasal *ṅ* is found only in ligatures where it is usually the first member. Instead of the wedge of the Śāradā, the letter occurs usually with a serif or small upward stroke at the right top end.

17. The distinguishing feature of *c* making it look distinct from the Śāradā form of the letter, is the circular loop on the left. The letter occurs both in cursive and quadrangular forms. In some instances it is difficult to distinguish it from *ś* (cols. III, V).

18. *ch* retains its conservative character with two loops but in certain cases it assumes the form of the double looped *k* and the two letters become hard to distinguish.

19. The letter *jh* does not occur rarely. It consists of two parts. The left part resembles the letter *r* and the right comprises two connecting curves, one short and the other lengthening downwards.

20. The palatal nasal of which only a couple of examples are seen in the inscriptions does not occur independently and is usually seen in the ligature *jñ*. However, it also occurs as a first member in the ligature *ñc* in the Ganguya plate of Gaṇeśavarman (col. VIII). It differs from the Śāradā *ñ* in two respects. The left-hand vertical is cursive and the right-hand curve moves towards the right instead of slanting downwards as is the case in the Śāradā.

21. *ṭ* shows well developed top bar and occurs both with or without a serif at the right end of the top bar.

22. *ṭh,* represented by a circle, retains its archaic form.
23. *ḍ* shows a material change from the corresponding letter in the Śāradā. It shows a loop in the middle and a triangle at the lower end representing the wedge of the Śāradā.
24. The letter *ḍh* shows a prominent loop on the left and a kink or another loop on the right.
25. The cerebral nasal has the same form as in the Śāradā. It mostly occurs without left-hand tail though the tailed forms are not uncommon.
26. *t,* the most conservative character in Śāradā, does not show any significant change in Devāśeṣa-Ṭākarī as well.
27. *th,* with well developed top bar, is lozenge in shape and the right-hand vertical usually protrudes downwards.
28. *d* occurs with a prominent loop on the left.
29. The only distinguishing feature in *dh* is that it has well developed top bar.
30. *n* does not present anything remarkable except that it sometimes shows a loop in the middle (col. VII).
31. *p,* which occurs throughout without top bar, is akin to the Śāradā form of the letter.
32. *ph* retains the old form with the curve on the right turning inwards but not forming contact with the base.
33. *b* is represented by *v* as is usually the case in the Śāradā and will be described subsequently.
34. *bh* shows a prominent circular or triangular loop in the middle on the left.
35. In *m,* the distinguishing feature is a loop on the left in place of the knob of the Śāradā.
36. *y* occurs mostly with its top closed though the examples with open top are not rare.
37. In keeping with the predominant trait of Devāśeṣa-Ṭākarī *r* shows triangular loop in place of the Śāradā wedge on the left.
38. *l* with a well developed top bar, does not materially differ from its Śāradā counterpart. The position of the two curves and their connection with the right-hand vertical and the top bar present, however, interesting varieties.
39. *v,* with a horizontal top bar and the right-hand vertical protruding downwards, does not differ from the Śāradā and Nāgarī forms of the letter.

40. *ś* is akin to *m* but with its top closed by means of a horizontal bar.

41. *ṣ*, another conservative letter, retains its old form. The only distinguishing feature is the downward lengthening of the right-hand vertical. In the Devāśeṣa-Ṭākarī the letter also represents the letter *kh* owing to the fact that the *ṣ* in the local vernacular is pronounced as *kh*.

42. *s* is akin to *m* but the loop is generally triangular and not circular as is the case with *m*.

43. *h* shows two forms. In one where the letter occurs independently, the right-hand curve usually turns sharply round and moves towards the left. In combination with other letters it usually retains its older form.

44. *Virāma* is represented by a long-drawn slanting stroke, occasionally vertical, at the right end of the letter. The letters with which the *virāma* occurs retain their full form which is not always the case in the Śāradā.

MEDIAL VOWELS

1. Medial *ā* is expressed by a serif, by a serif with inverted loop or a looped upward stroke or by a short vertical attached to the right end of the top stroke. In case of *nā, tā,* and sometimes *jā,* it is expressed by a curve facing down attached to the right top end. In case of *nā,* the curve turns round and moves towards the left. In case of *jā,* sometimes the upward vertical is attached to the right end of the middle stroke making at times contact with the top horizontal.

2. Medial *i* and *ī* are expressed in the old fashion by long curves drawn to the left and the right of the letter, respectively. The curves are at times very short (col. V) as in the old inscriptions.

3. Medial *u* is expressed as in the Śāradā in two ways, either by a curve open to the left attached to the base of the consonant or by a small triangle representing the older wedge attached to the foot of the vertical on the left. In case of *ru,* it is expressed by a cursive downward stroke attached to the middle of the letter on the right.

4. Medial *ū* is also expressed in different ways, either by a sign for initial *u* or two curves placed one below the other or side by side, or by a small horizontal stroke with a loop at the right end attached to the foot of the vertical on the left.

5. Medial *ṛ* is expressed by an upward curve attached to the foot of the vertical or the base of the letter where vertical is absent on the right.

6. Medial *e* and *ai* are expressed by horizontal strokes (one in case of *e* and two in case of *ai*) placed above the top of the letter. No instance of the earlier *pṛṣṭhamātrā* is found.

7. Medial *o* is fashioned as in the Śāradā by a flourish (two connected small curves) placed above the top of the letter.

8. The same flourish accompanied by the sign of medial *ā* represents medial *au.*

LIGATURES

1. *k* as the first member of a ligature or accompanied by medial vowels *r, u* or *ū* assumes a peculiar shape distinct from the sign. Its loops are usually missing. It consists of a short horizontal bar in the middle on the left and a long-drawn downward slanting stroke on the right. In rare cases we find a small loop instead of the bar on the left (cols. I, II). As second member of the ligature it retains its complete form (cf. cols. II, III).

2. The palatal nasal *ñ* occurs in the ligatures *jña, jñā.* It assumes the shape of cerebral *ṇ* without the right-hand upward stroke.

3. *r,* as the first member of the ligatures in *rca* and *rna, rva, rya* looses its left-hand loop as is the case in the Śāradā. With other consonants, it retains its usual shape. In case of *rva,* the sign is inserted into the loop of the letter which at times assumes the shape of Devanāgarī *c.*

4. As a second or the third member of the ligature, *r* is represented by horizontal bar attached to the foot of the vertical on the left as is the case in the Śāradā. Sometimes the stroke has a loop at the upper end and the direction also changes from left to the right. This is a peculiar feature of the Devāśeṣa-Ṭākarī.

5. As in the Śāradā we have peculiar ligature *rtha* in which *r* occurs without the loop and *th* is represented by an *S*-like form accompanied by a slanting stroke on the right.

6. Subscribed *ṭ* and *ṭh,* which usually have the same shape, are accompanied by a slanting stroke on the right. This stroke sometimes has a loop at the upper end.

7. The subscript *y* is represented by a curve open to the right.

8. The subscript *dh* in the ligature *ddha* has the same form as the subscript looped *r.*

# 8

## Ṭākarī Alphabet
### (17th and 18th Centuries)

In the epigraphic Devāśeṣa-Ṭākarī alphabet of the 17th and 18th centuries, found in the copper-plate inscriptions of the rulers of Chamba and a couple of stone inscriptions, we do not come across any major variations or changes to justify a different nomenclature. The characters mostly retain their earlier forms and do not display any significant change. Some minor variations are noticed in the case of some characters. The same have been illustrated in the accompanying table wherein the forms of characters have been taken from the well-written and well-preserved copper-plate inscriptions of king Balabhadra,[1] Pṛthvīsiṁha (Pṛthvīsingha)[2] and Śatrusiṁha (Chhaddasinha),[3] Lakṣmī Nārāyaṇa Temple Niche Inscription of the *Śāstra Saṁvat* 55[4] and the Cabūtrā stone inscription of *Vikram Saṁvat* 1717.[5]

**Vowels** (see Table 8)

1. The initial *a* occurs regularly with closed top. No instance of *a* with open top as noticed earlier in some inscriptions is found in Devāśeṣa-Ṭākarī after the 16th century.
2. The occurrence of *ā* becomes rarer.
3. A few instances of initial *i* are noticed (cols. IV, V, VII) where two dots have been replaced by a curve like that of medial *o* as in the case of later Śāradā. In one instance (col. VII), in place of curve, we find the sign of initial *u*.
4. *o* occurs only in the benedictory syllable *oṁ* as earlier and we find minor variations in col. IV where the curve is comparatively shorter and in col. VI where the two parts of the letter are vertical and *u* have been written separately.

---

1. Chabra, B. Ch., *Antiquities of Chamba State*, Part II, p. 127 ff., plates XXI, XXV, XXVI.
2. Ibid., p. 150 ff., plates XXVIII, XXIX.
3. Ibid., p. 159 f., plate XXX.
4. Ibid., p. 169 f., plate XXXIIA.
5. Ibid., p. 170 ff., plate XXXIIB.

### Consonants

5. *k* occurs mostly in double looped form. In many cases it is difficult to distinguish it from *ch*.
6. In the Niche inscription (col. VII), we find in the letter *ḍ* a small downward stroke in place of the usual triangle.
7. As in the earlier period, *ṇ* usually occurs without the left-hand tail but we do have a couple of instances where the letter has been provided with a tail (cols. V, VII) as is the case in some inscriptions of the earlier period.
8. *n* sometimes occurs with a loop (col. VI).
9. *y* occurs regularly with a closed top.

### Medial Vowels & Ligatures

Medial vowels continued to be expressed in the same way as in the earlier period. Some peculiarities may be noted below:

1. The sign for medial *ā* occurs mostly without loop. The medial *a* in *ṇā* has been expressed in one case (col. VI) by a straight downward stroke instead of the usual curve moving to the left.
2. In the sign for medial *u*, the loop is sometimes omitted.
3. The superscribed *k* occurs sometimes in a single looped form.
4. Superscript *r* continues to be written in the earlier fashion and is inserted in left limb of *y* and *v*.
5. The ligatures *gra* and *stra* in the Cabūtrā inscription (col. VIII), deserve notice.

## Numerals of the Ṭākarī Alphabet

Numerical figures found in the Devāśeṣa-Ṭākarī inscriptions follow the decimal system of notation as in the Śāradā. The forms of the figures maintain fair uniformity throughout though variations are noticed here and there.

We give below a brief description of each figure (see Table No. 9).

The figure 1 (one) is written more frequently by a semi-circular curve facing down. It is also represented in some cases by a circle. In modern Ṭākarī, the curve shows a loop on the left.

The figure 2 (two) is represented by two connected curves written one below the other. In modern Ṭākarī it resembles the initial *u*.

The figure 3 (three) is also formed like two with the addition of a small stroke at the foot on the right. In the modern Ṭākarī, the stroke is looped at the upper end.

The form of figure 4 (four) resembles the Devanāgarī figure of 4. In the Chamba plate of Ānandavardhana, it retains its earlier form.

The figure 5 (five) which closely resembles the sign of *p*, is almost the same as in the Śāradā. In the Treaty document (col. VIII), the right-hand vertical is replaced by a cursive stroke with a bend towards the right at the bottom.

The figure 6 (six) in Ṭākarī is a complex figure though written in a single stroke of pen. It has a loop at the upper end and cursive strokes on the left and the right.

The figure 7 (seven) looks like the Nāgarī figure 1.

The numerical figure 8 (eight) has an *S*-like form with a curve (col. I) or a slanting stroke (cols. VI, VII) or a short horizontal (col. VIII) at the top.

A long-drawn curve on the right moving towards the left attached to a circular loop at the top makes the figure 9 (nine). It is not materially different from the Śāradā figure.

Small dot or a circle (in modern Ṭākarī) represents the figure of zero.

# Tables

## TABLE 1A
## BRĀHMĪ ALPHABET OF NORTH-WESTERN INDIA
## (c. 300 BCE TO c. CE 300)
## CHIEF PECULIARITIES

| I | II | III | IV | V | VI | VII | VIII | IX | | |
|---|---|---|---|---|---|---|---|---|---|---|
| Kalsi Edicts | Delhi-Topra ED. VI ED. VII | Pathyar Rock Inscription | Mathurā Inscription | Inscriptions of Śoḍāsa | Kanihara Rock Inscription | Mora (Mathurā) Inscription | Coins of Agathocles & Pantaleon | Mathurā Kuṣāṇa Inscriptions | | |
| a | a | | | a ā | ā | | | a | y | sy |
| k | | | | k | | | | ā | sh | rta |
| kh | kh | | khi | | | | | i | ṣ | tra pra |
| ch | | | | | | | | u | ch | |
| j | j | | | | | | | e | | |
| t | ḷ | | n | d | | | | k | mā | |
| y | ḍh | y | m | m | m | | | kh | si | |
| sh | | | | sh | sh | sh | | ṇ | ku | |
| ṣ | | | s | ṣ | ṣ | ṣ | | d | gṛ | |
| shā | | | si | r | | r | | n | ge | |
| ke she | | u | u | chi si ni go | kṛ | vo vṛ | | | ṣo | |

## TABLE 1B (a)
## BRĀHMĪ ALPHABET OF NORTH-WESTERN INDIA
## (4th - 5th Centuries CE)

| | I | II | III | IV | V | VI | VII |
|---|---|---|---|---|---|---|---|
| Transcript Characters in Roman | Abottabad Inscription | Mathurā Inscription G.E. 61 | Mathurā Inscription | Tusam Inscription | Shorkoṭ Inscriptions | Bower Manuscript | Chilas Inscription |
| a | | | | | | | |
| ā | | | | | | | |
| i | | | | | | | |
| ī | | | | | | | |
| u | | | | | | | |
| ū | | | | | | | |
| ṛ | | | | | | | |
| e | | | | | | | |
| ai | | | | | | | |
| o | | | | | | | |
| au | | | | | | | |
| k | | | | | | | |
| kh | | | | | | | |
| g | | | | | | | |

## TABLE 1B (b)
## BRĀHMĪ ALPHABET OF NORTH-WESTERN INDIA
## (4[th] - 5[th] Centuries CE)

| | I | II | III | IV | V | VI | VII |
|---|---|---|---|---|---|---|---|
| Transcript Characters in Roman | Abottabad Inscription | Mathurā Inscription G.E. 61 | Mathurā Inscription | Tusam Inscription | Shorkoṭ Inscriptions | Bower Manuscript | Chilas Inscription |
| gh | | | | 𑀖 | | 𑀖 | |
| ṅ | | 𑀗 | | 𑀗 | | 𑀗 | |
| c | | 𑀘 | 𑀘 | 𑀘 | 𑀘 | 𑀘 | |
| ch | | | 𑀙 | | | 𑀙 | |
| j | 𑀚 | 𑀚 | 𑀚 | 𑀚 | | 𑀚 | 𑀚 |
| jh | | | | | | 𑀛 | |
| ñ | | 𑀜 | | | | 𑀜 | |
| ṭ | | 𑀝 | 𑀝 | | | 𑀝 𑀝 | 𑀝 |
| ṭh | | 𑀞 | | | | 𑀞 | |
| ḍ | | 𑀟 | | 𑀟 | | 𑀟 | 𑀟 |
| ḍh | | | | | | 𑀠 | 𑀠 |
| n | 𑀡 | 𑀡 | 𑀡 | 𑀡 | | 𑀡 | 𑀡 |
| t | 𑀢 | 𑀢 | 𑀢 | 𑀢 | 𑀢 | 𑀢 𑀢 | 𑀢 |
| th | 𑀣 | 𑀣 | | 𑀣 | 𑀣 | 𑀣 | |
| d | 𑀤 | 𑀤 | 𑀤 | 𑀤 | 𑀤 | 𑀤 𑀤 | 𑀤 |

### TABLE 1B (c)
### BRĀHMĪ ALPHABET OF NORTH-WESTERN INDIA
### (4th - 5th Centuries CE)

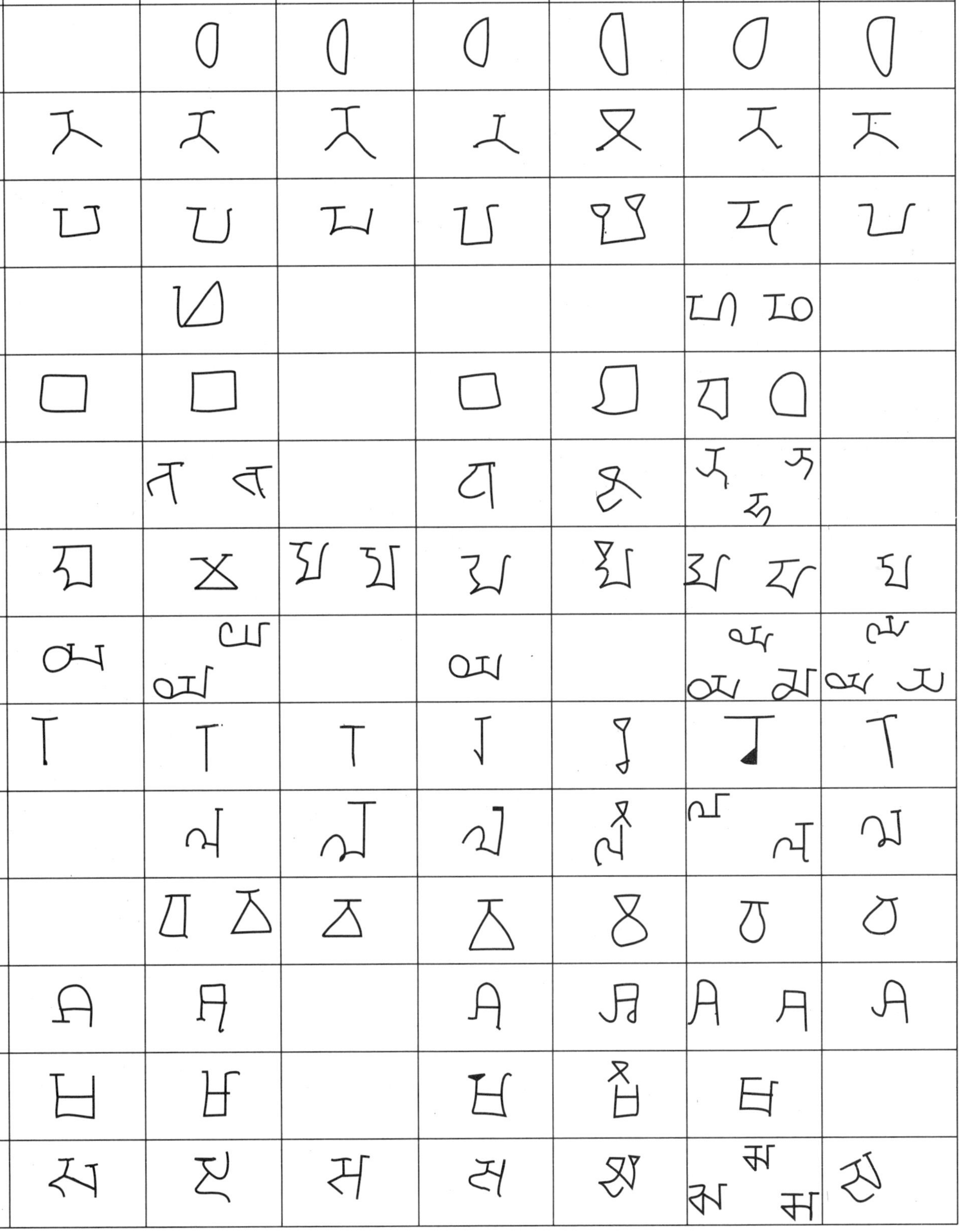

| | I | II | III | IV | V | VI | VII |
|---|---|---|---|---|---|---|---|
| Transcript Characters in Roman | Abottabad Inscription | Mathurā Inscription G.E. 61 | Mathurā Inscription | Tusam Inscription | Shorkoṭ Inscriptions | Bower Manuscript | Chilas Inscription |
| dh | | | | | | | |
| n | | | | | | | |
| p | | | | | | | |
| ph | | | | | | | |
| b | | | | | | | |
| bh | | | | | | | |
| m | | | | | | | |
| y | | | | | | | |
| r | | | | | | | |
| l | | | | | | | |
| v | | | | | | | |
| ś | | | | | | | |
| ṣ | | | | | | | |
| s | | | | | | | |

## TABLE 1B (d)
## BRĀHMĪ ALPHABET OF NORTH-WESTERN INDIA
### (4th - 5th Centuries CE)

| | I | II | III | IV | V | VI | VII |
|---|---|---|---|---|---|---|---|
| Transcript Characters in Roman | Abottabad Inscription | Mathurā Inscription G.E. 61 | Mathurā Inscription | Tusam Inscription | Shorkoṭ Inscriptions | Bower Manuscript | Chilas Inscription |
| h | | | | | | | |
| x<br>ḥ | | | | | | : | |
| | | | | | | | |
| **MEDIAL VOWELS** | | | | | | | |
| ā | | | jā | | | kā ṅgā ṭhā | |
| i | | | | | | | |
| ī | | | | | | | |
| u | | | | | | | |
| ū | | | | | | | |
| ṛ | | | | | ghṛ | | |
| e | | | | | | | |
| ai | | | | | | | |
| o | | | | | | | |
| au | | | | | | | |

## TABLE 1B (e)
## BRĀHMĪ ALPHABET OF NORTH-WESTERN INDIA
## (4th - 5th Centuries CE)
## LIGATURES

| | I | II | III | IV | V | VI | VII |
|---|---|---|---|---|---|---|---|
| Transcript Characters in Roman | Abottabad Inscription | Mathurā Inscription G.E. 61 | Mathurā Inscription | Tusam Inscription | Shorkoṭ Inscriptions | Bower Manuscript | Chilas Inscription |
| kṣa | | | | | | | |
| ccha | | | | | | | |
| jña | | | | | | | |
| sup. r | rg | | ryy | ryy | rvv | rṇṇ | rm |
| sub. r | pr | tre | pr | kr | | Sri tpr | pr |
| ṣta ṣṭh | | | ṣṭha | | | ṣṭ | |
| sub. y | | vya | ṣya jya | sya | tya | khya sya | |
| s th | | | | | | | |
| sup. r | tr | tr | | str | | tr | |
| sup. s, v, t, p | sv | tp pt | pt | tp | | sc | |
| sup. t, d, n | | | tt | ddhy | ddh | nut ddhy | |
| | | | tthy | kṣm | | ñch | śmī |
| | | | ssy | sya | | tmya | mbu |
| | | | myā | | | nstri | ryā |

## TABLE 1C (a)
## BRĀHMĪ ALPHABET OF NORTH-WESTERN INDIA
## ($6^{th}$ - $8^{th}$ Centuries CE)

| | I | II | III | IV | V | VI | VII |
|---|---|---|---|---|---|---|---|
| Transcript Characters in Roman | Kura Inscription | Nirmand Copper-Plate Inscription | Gilgit Inscriptions | Brahmor and Chattrahi Inscriptions | Gum Inscription of Āṣāḍhadeva | Hatun Manuscript | Suaim Inscription |
| a |  | |  | |  |  | |
| ā |  |  |  |  | | | |
| i |  | |  | | | | |
| ī | | | |  | | | |
| u |  |  |  | | | | |
| ū |  | |  |  | | | |
| e | | |  |  | | | |
| o | | |  | | | | |
| k |  |  |  |  |  |  |  |
| kh |  |  | 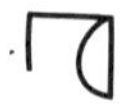 | | | | |
| g | 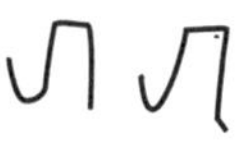 |  |  |  |  |  |  |

## TABLE 1C (b)
## BRĀHMĪ ALPHABET OF NORTH-WESTERN INDIA
### ($6^{th}$ - $8^{th}$ Centuries CE)

| | I | II | III | IV | V | VI | VII |
|---|---|---|---|---|---|---|---|
| Transcript Characters in Roman | Kura Inscription | Nirmand Copper-Plate Inscription | Gilgit Inscriptions | Brahmor and Chattrahi Inscriptions | Gum Inscription of Āṣāḍhodeva | Hatun Inscription | Suaim Inscription |
| gh |  | | 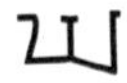 | | |  | |
| ṅ | |  |  | |  |  | |
| c |  |  |  |  | | | |
| ch | |  |  | | | | |
| j |  |  |  |  |  |  | |
| jh | | | | | | | |
| ñ |  |  | 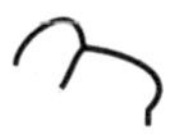 | | | | |
| ṭ |  | |  | | |  |  |
| ṭh |  |  | | | | | |
| ḍ | |  | | | | | |
| ḍh | |  |  | |  | | |

## TABLE 1C (c)
## BRĀHMĪ ALPHABET OF NORTH-WESTERN INDIA
### (6th - 8th Centuries CE)

| | I | II | III | IV | V | VI | VII |
|---|---|---|---|---|---|---|---|
| Transcript Characters in Roman | Kura Inscription | Nirmand Copper-Plate Inscription | Gilgit Inscriptions | Brahmor and Chattrahi Inscriptions | Gum Inscription of Āṣāḍhadeva | Hatun Inscription | Suaim Inscription |
| ṇ | | | | | | | |
| t | | | | | | | |
| th | | | | | | | |
| d | | | | | | | |
| dh | | | | | | | |
| n | | | | | | | |
| p | | | | | | | |
| ph | | | | | | | |
| b | | | | | | | |
| bh | | | | | | | |
| m | | | | | | | |

## TABLE 1C (d)
## BRĀHMĪ ALPHABET OF NORTH-WESTERN INDIA
### ($6^{th}$ - $8^{th}$ Centuries CE)

| | I | II | III | IV | V | VI | VII |
|---|---|---|---|---|---|---|---|
| Transcript Characters in Roman | Kura Inscription | Nirmand Copper-Plate Inscription | Gilgit Inscriptions | Brahmor and Chattrahi Inscriptions | Gum Inscription of Āṣāḍhadeva | Hatun Inscription | Suaim Inscription |
| y | | | | | | | |
| r | | | | | | | |
| l | | | | | | | |
| v | | | | | | | |
| ś | | | | | | | |
| ṣ | | | | | | | |
| s | | | | | | | |
| h | | | | | | | |
| jih. | | | | | | | |
| up. | | | | | | | |

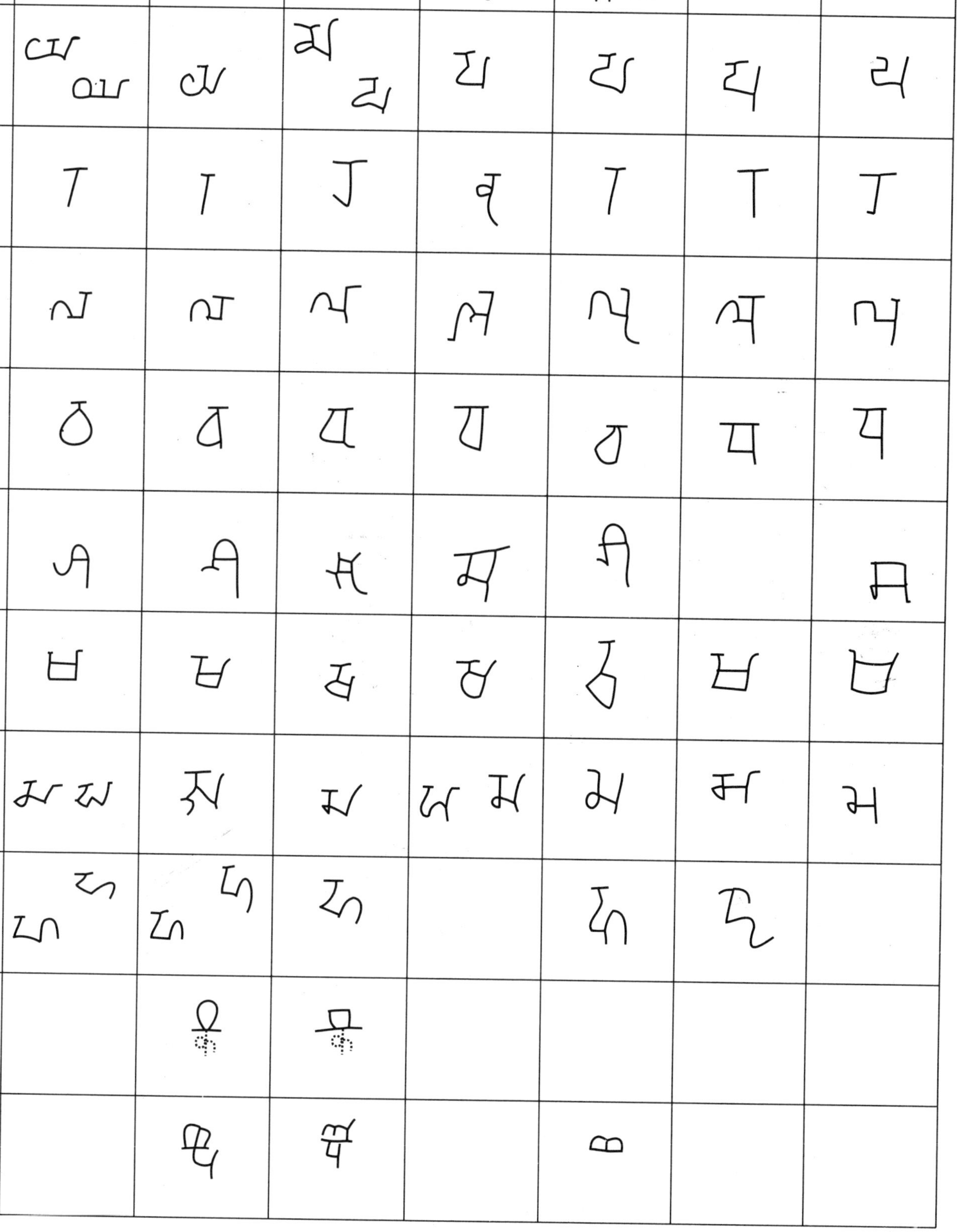

## TABLE 1C (e)
## BRĀHMĪ ALPHABET OF NORTH-WESTERN INDIA
### (6th - 8th Centuries CE)

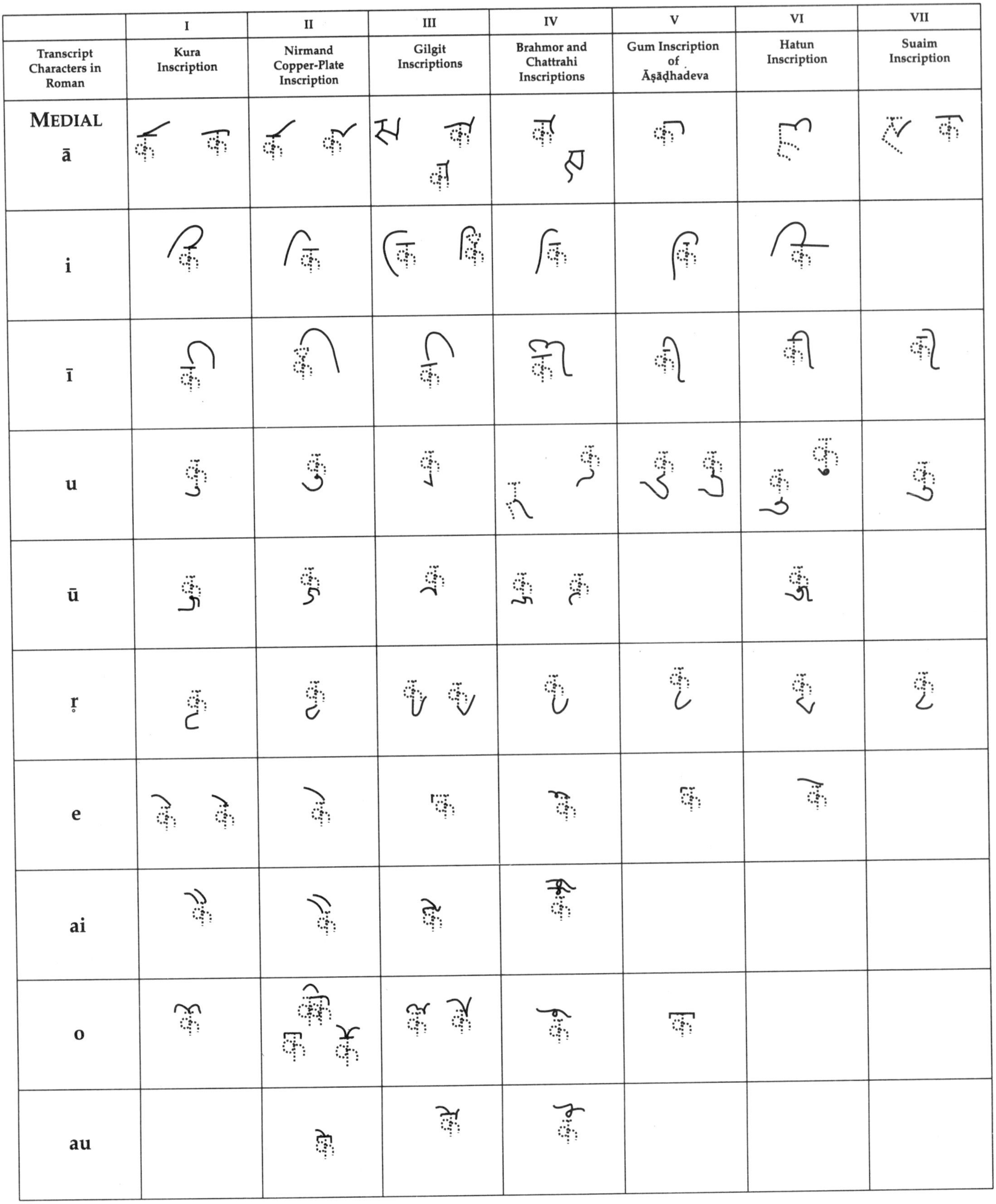

## TABLE 1C (f)
## BRĀHMĪ ALPHABET OF NORTH-WESTERN INDIA
## (6th - 8th Centuries CE)
## LIGATURES

| | I | II | III | IV | V | VI | VII |
|---|---|---|---|---|---|---|---|
| Transcript Characters in Roman | Kura Inscription | Nirmand Copper-Plate Inscription | Gilgit Inscriptions | Brahmor and Chattrahi Inscriptions | Gum Inscription of Āṣāḍhadeva | Hatun Inscription | Suaim Inscription |
| **kṣa** |  |  | 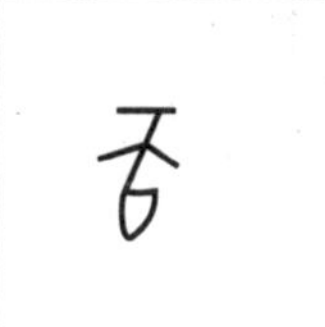 |  |  | | |
| **jña** |  | |  | | | | |
| **cch** | |  | | | | | |
| **sup. r** |  | 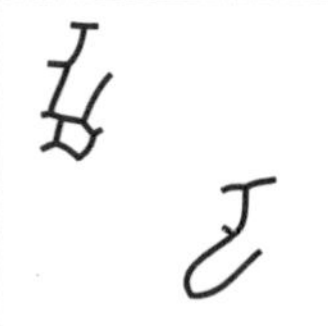 |  | 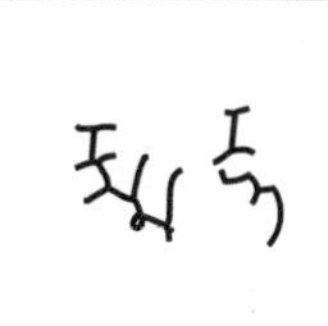 | 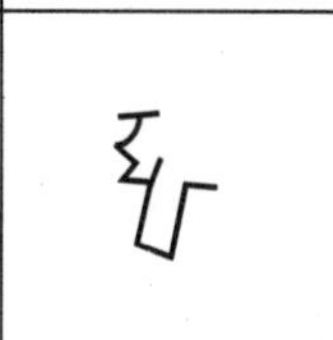 | 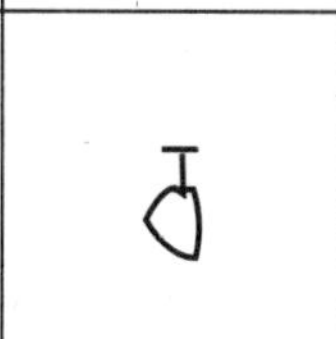 | |
| **s.r** |  |  |  |  | 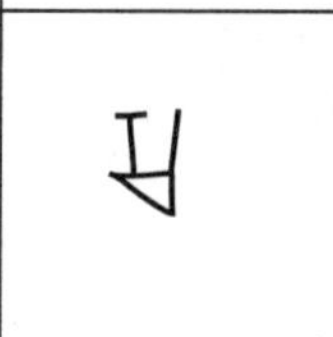 | 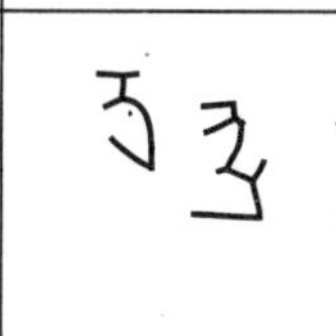 | |
| **ṣṭ, ṣṭh** | 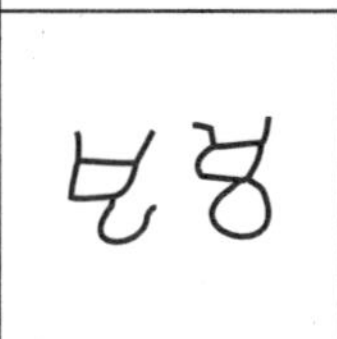 | 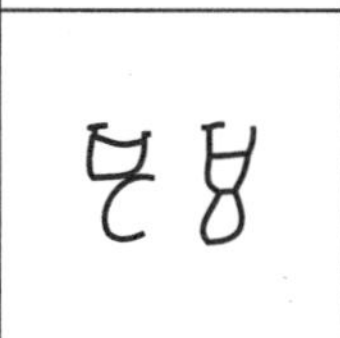 |  |  | 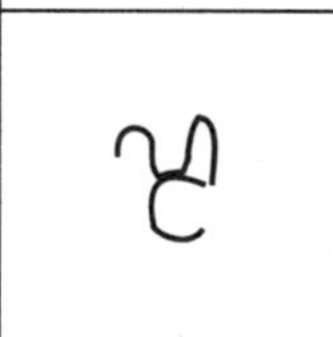 | | |
| **ṣ/ś/s.ya** | 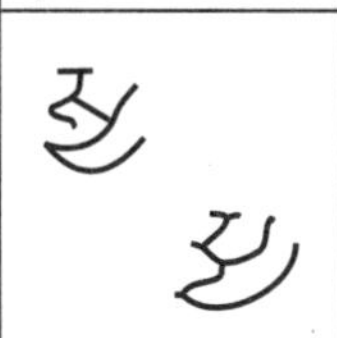 |  |  | | 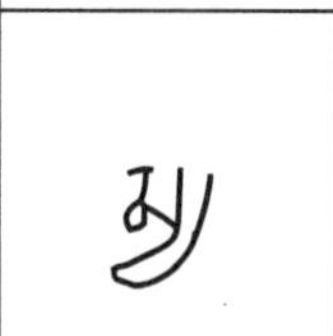 |  | 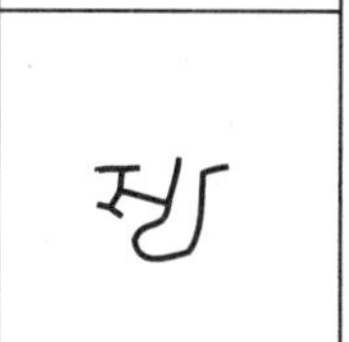 |
| **śca** |  |  | 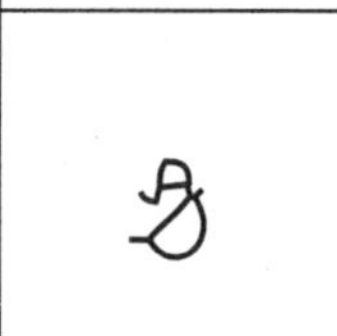 | | | | |
| **sup. - t/th** | 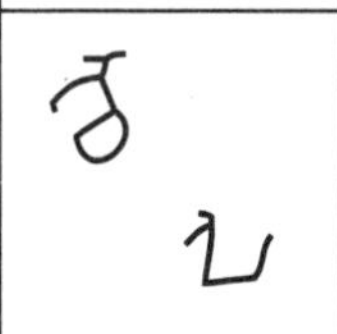 | 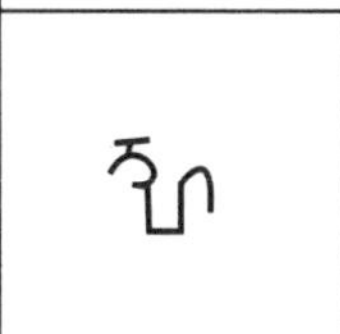 | 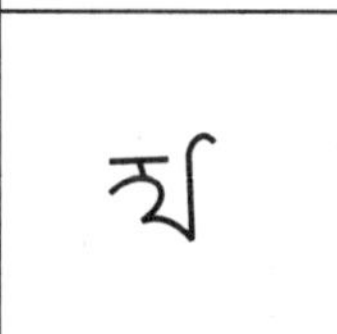 | 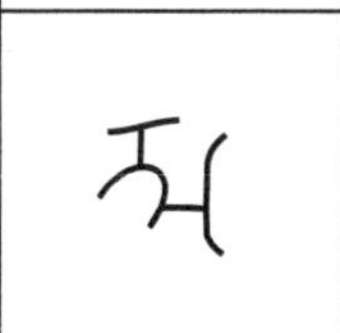 | 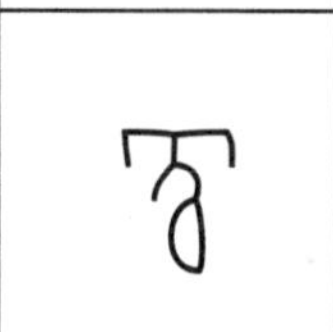 | 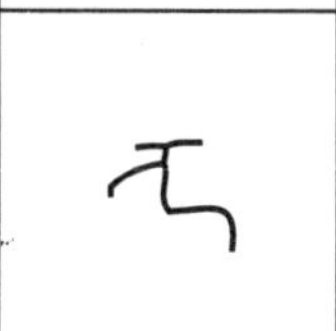 | |

## TABLE 1C (g)
## BRĀHMĪ ALPHABET OF NORTH-WESTERN INDIA
## (6[th] - 8[th] Centuries CE)
## LIGATURES

| | I | II | III | IV | V | VI | VII |
|---|---|---|---|---|---|---|---|
| Transcript Characters in Roman | Kura Inscription | Nirmand Copper-Plate Inscription | Gilgit Inscriptions | Brahmor and Chattrahi Inscriptions | Gum Inscription of Āṣāḍhadeva | Hatun Inscription | Suaim Inscription |
| | pta  | sta  | stha  | ṭv  | ṭv  | | |
| | ddh  | | rtha  | śrī 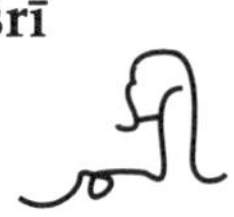 | śrī  | | śrī  |
| | | rkk  | ñj  | śl  | rmmy  | | |
| | | myi  | tth  | śr  | | nnṛ  | ṣk  |
| | | rṇṇ  | | gg  | | sca  | |
| | | | | ṇḍa  | | | |

## TABLE 1D (a)
## BRĀHMĪ ALPHABET OF NORTH-WESTERN INDIA
## (c. 300 BCE TO c. CE 800)

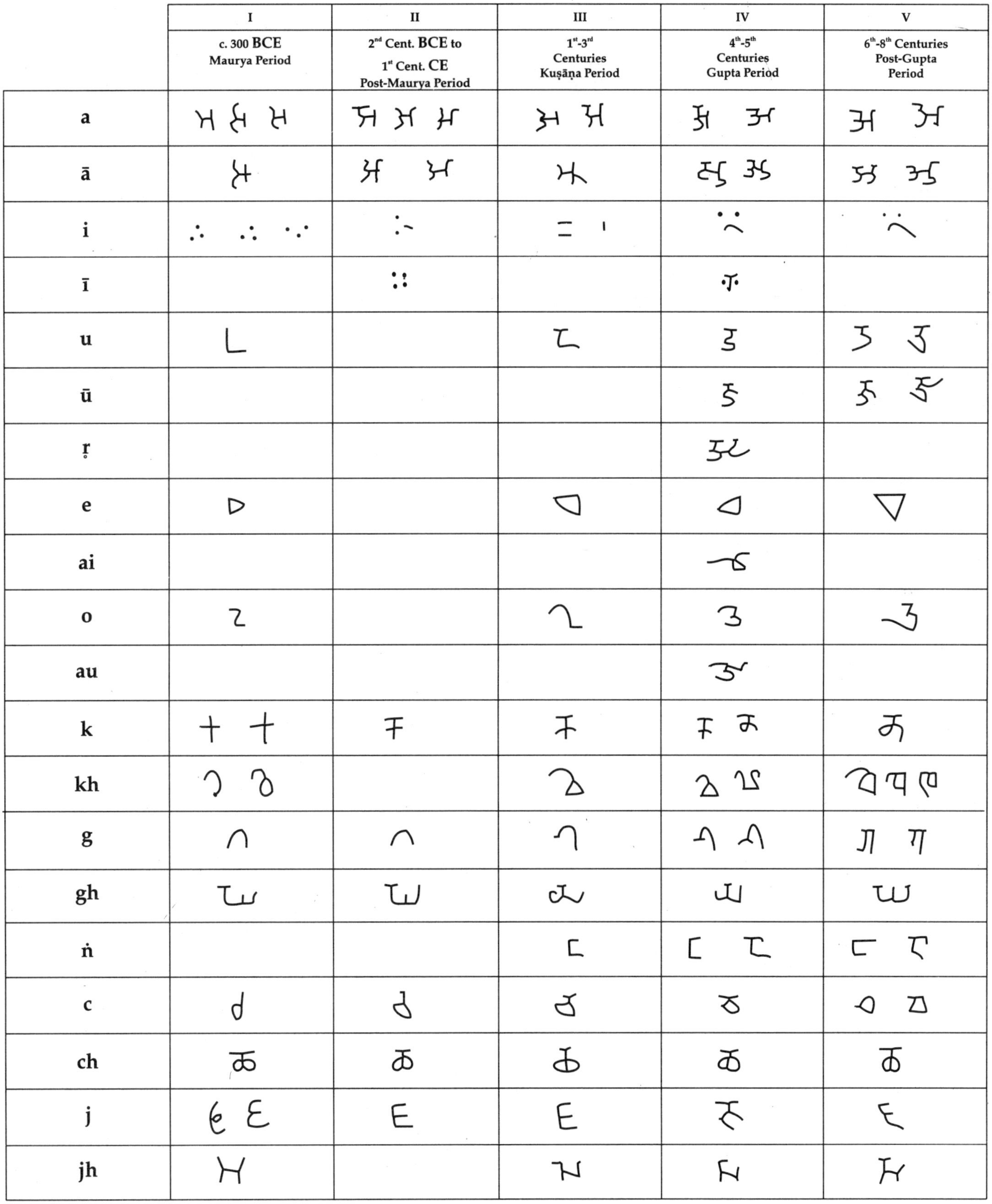

| | I | II | III | IV | V |
|---|---|---|---|---|---|
| | c. 300 BCE Maurya Period | 2nd Cent. BCE to 1st Cent. CE Post-Maurya Period | 1st-3rd Centuries Kuṣāṇa Period | 4th-5th Centuries Gupta Period | 6th-8th Centuries Post-Gupta Period |
| a | | | | | |
| ā | | | | | |
| i | | | | | |
| ī | | | | | |
| u | | | | | |
| ū | | | | | |
| ṛ | | | | | |
| e | | | | | |
| ai | | | | | |
| o | | | | | |
| au | | | | | |
| k | | | | | |
| kh | | | | | |
| g | | | | | |
| gh | | | | | |
| ṅ | | | | | |
| c | | | | | |
| ch | | | | | |
| j | | | | | |
| jh | | | | | |

## TABLE 1D (b)
## BRĀHMĪ ALPHABET OF NORTH-WESTERN INDIA
## (c. 300 BCE TO c. CE 800)

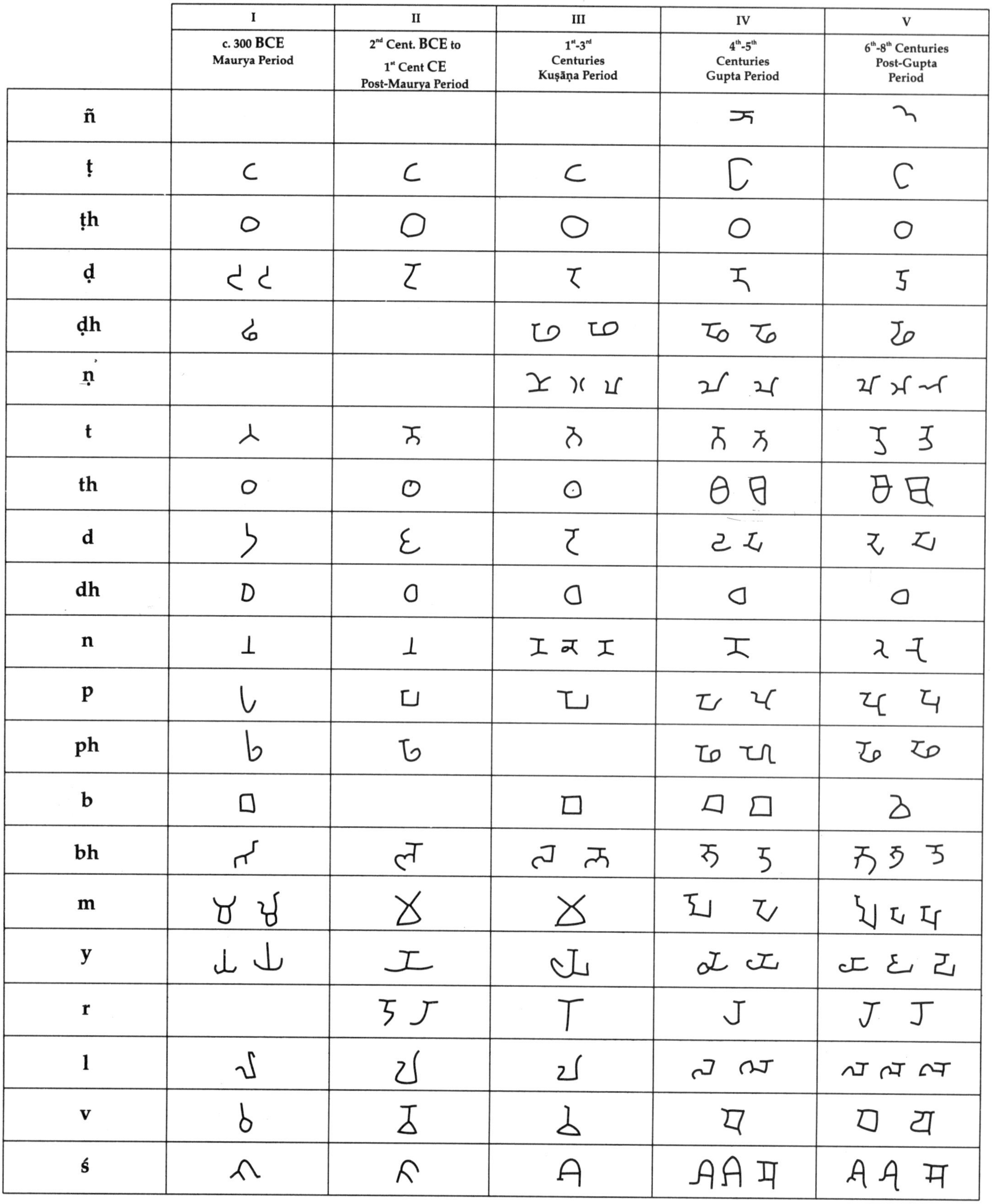

## TABLE 1D (c)
## BRĀHMĪ ALPHABET OF NORTH-WESTERN INDIA
## (c. 300 BCE TO c. CE 800)

| | I | II | III | IV | V | |
|---|---|---|---|---|---|---|
| | c. 300 BCE Maurya Period | 2[nd] Cent. BCE to 1[st] Cent CE Post-Maurya Period | 1[st]-3[rd] Centuries Kuṣāṇa Period | 4[th]-5[th] Centuries Gupta Period | 6[th]-8[th] Centuries Post-Gupta Period | |
| ṣ | | | | | | |
| s | | | | | | |
| h | | | | | | |
| jihvā-mūlīya | | | | | | |
| upadh-mānīya | | | | | | |
| | | MEDIAL VOWELS | | | | |
| ā | | | | | | |
| i | | | | | | |
| ī | | | | | | |
| u | | | | | | |
| ū | | | | | | |
| ṛ | | | | | | |
| e | | | | | | |
| ai | | | | | | |
| o | | | | | | |
| au | | | | | | |
| | | LIGATURES | | | | |
| | | | | | | |
| | | | | | | |
| | | | | | | |

# TABLE 2 (a)
# ŚĀRADĀ ALPHABET
# EARLY PHASE (9th-10th Centuries)

| | I | II | III | IV | V | VI | VII | VIII | IX | X | XI | XII |
|---|---|---|---|---|---|---|---|---|---|---|---|---|
| Characters in Roman | Ghaṭa Inscrip. of A(va)ntivarman | Chilas Inscription Nos. 63-65 | Sarahan Praśasti | Dewai Inscrip. of Bhīmadeva Shāhī | Hund Inscription of Jayapāladeva | Hund Inscription of Vijayapāla | Barikoṭ Inscription of Jayapāladeva | S.P.S. Museum Inscription | Srinagar Inscription | Brahmor Copper-Plate Inscription | Sungal Copper-Plate Inscription | Tur Image Inscription |
| a |  |  |  | |  |  | | |  |  |  |  |
| ā | | |  | |  |  | | | |  |  | |
| i | | |  | |  |  | | | | |  | |
| ī | | |  | | | | | | | | | |
| u | | | | | | |  |  |  |  |  | |
| ū | | |  | |  | | | | | |  | |
| e | | |  | | | |  | | |  |  | |
| o | | | | | | | | | |  |  | |

## TABLE 2 (b)
## ŚĀRADĀ ALPHABET
## EARLY PHASE (9th-10th Centuries)

## TABLE 2 (c)
## ŚĀRADĀ ALPHABET
## EARLY PHASE (9th-10th Centuries)

| | I | II | III | IV | V | VI | VII | VIII | IX | X | XI | XII |
|---|---|---|---|---|---|---|---|---|---|---|---|---|
| Characters in Roman | Ghaṭa Inscrip. of A(va)ntivarman | Chilas Inscription Nos. 63-65 | Sarahan Praśasti | Dewai Inscrip. of Bhīmadeva Shāhī | Hund Inscription of Jayapāladeva | Hund Inscription of Vijayapāla | Barikoṭ Inscription of Jayapāladeva | S.P.S. Museum Inscription | Srinagar Inscription | Brahmor Copper-Plate Inscription | Sungal Copper-Plate Inscription | Tur Image Inscription |
| ṭh | | | | | | | | | | | | |
| ḍ | | | | | | | | | | | | |
| ḍh | | | | | | | | | | | | |
| ṇ | | | | | | | | | | | | |
| t | | | | | | | | | | | | |
| th | | | | | | | | | | | | |
| d | | | | | | | | | | | | |
| dh | | | | | | | | | | | | |
| n | | | | | | | | | | | | |
| p | | | | | | | | | | | | |
| ph | | | | | | | | | | | | |
| b | | | | | | | | | | | | |
| bh | | | | | | | | | | | | |

# TABLE 2 (d)
# ŚĀRADĀ ALPHABET
# EARLY PHASE (9th-10th Centuries)

| | I | II | III | IV | V | VI | VII | VIII | IX | X | XI | XII |
|---|---|---|---|---|---|---|---|---|---|---|---|---|
| Characters in Roman | Ghaṭa Inscrip. of A(va)ntivarman | Chilas Inscription Nos. 63-65 | Sarahan Praśasti | Dewai Inscrip. of Bhīmadeva Shāhī | Hund Inscription of Jayapāladeva | Hund Inscription of Vijayapāla | Barikoṭ Inscription of Jayapāladeva | S.P.S. Museum Inscription | Srinagar Inscription | Brahmor Copper-Plate Inscription | Sungal Copper-Plate Inscription | Tur Image Inscription |
| m | | | | | | | | | | | | |
| y | | | | | | | | | | | | |
| r | | | | | | | | | | | | |
| l | | | | | | | | | | | | |
| v | | | | | | | | | | | | |
| ś | | | | | | | | | | | | |
| ṣ | | | | | | | | | | | | |
| s | | | | | | | | | | | | |
| h | | | | | | | | | | | | |
| jih. | | | | | | | | | | | | |
| up. | | | | | | | | | | | | |
| halanta | | | | | | | | | | | | |
| | | | | | | | | | | | | |
| | | | | | | | | | | | | |
| | | | | | | | | | | | | |

## TABLE 2 (e)
## ŚĀRADĀ ALPHABET
## EARLY PHASE (9th-10th Centuries)

| | I | II | III | IV | V | VI | VII | VIII | IX | X | XI | XII |
|---|---|---|---|---|---|---|---|---|---|---|---|---|
| Characters in Roman | Ghaṭa Inscrip. of A(va)ntivarman | Chilas Inscription Nos. 63-65 | Sarahan Praśasti | Dewai Inscrip. of Bhīmadeva Shāhī | Hund Inscription of Jayapāladeva | Hund Inscription of Vijayapāla | Barikoṭ Inscription of Jayapāladeva | S.P.S. Museum Inscription | Srinagar Inscription | Brahmor Copper-Plate Inscription | Sungal Copper-Plate Inscription | Tur Image Inscription |
| **Medial ā** | | | | | | | | | | | | |
| **ā** | | | **mā** | | **sā** | | **pā** | | | | | |
| **jā** | | | | | | | | | | | | |
| **ā** | | | **ṅā** | **ṅā** | **ṇā** | | **ṅā** | | **ṇā** | **ṅā** | **ṅā** | **ṅā** |
| **i** | | | | | | | | | | | | |
| **ī** | | | | | | | | | | | | |
| **u** | | **hu** | **ku śu** | | | | | | | | | |
| **u** | | **hu** | **hu** | | **hu** | **nu** | | **pu** | **pu** | **pu** | **pu** | **pu** |
| **ru** | | | | | | | | | | | | |
| **ū** | | | **bhū** | | **mū** | **mū** | | | | **rū** | **rū** | |
| **ū** | | | | | | | | | | | | |
| **ū** | | | **rū** | | | | | | | | | |
| **ṛ** | | | **dhṛ hṛ** | | **kṛ** | **tṛ** | | **kṛ** | | | | |
| **e** | | | | | | | | | | | | |
| **ai** | | | | | | | | | | | | |

## TABLE 2 (f)
## ŚĀRADĀ ALPHABET
## EARLY PHASE (9th-10th Centuries)

| | I | II | III | IV | V | VI | VII | VIII | IX | X | XI | XII |
|---|---|---|---|---|---|---|---|---|---|---|---|---|
| Characters in Roman | Ghaṭa Inscrip. of A(va)ntivarman | Chilas Inscription Nos. 63-65 | Sarahan Praśasti | Dewai Inscrip. of Bhīmadeva Shāhī | Hund Inscription of Jayapāladeva | Hund Inscription of Vijayapāla | Barikoṭ Inscription of Jayapāladeva | S.P.S. Museum Inscription | Srinagar Inscription | Brahmor Copper-Plate Inscription | Sungal Copper-Plate Inscription | Tur Image Inscription |
| Med o | | | no | | to | | | | | | to | |
| o | | to so | ko | | no | go | | do | no ro | yo | go ṭo | ṇo |
| au | | | gau rau | | vau | pau | | | gau | ḍau | dau śau | |
| LIG. sup. k | | kṣa | kta kṣa | | kya | kta | | | kta | kta kya | kta kya kṣa | |
| sub. k | | | ṣka | | rka | | | | ṅka | ḍka | ṣka | kka |
| sup. ñ | | | ñja | | | | | | | | | |
| sub. ñ | | | | | | | | | jña | jña | jñā | |
| ṣṭa ṣva | | | | | | | | | | | ṣva | ṣva |
| sub.y | | | dya | | mya | jya | syā | sya | sya | dya | dya hya | śya |
| sup.r | rma | | rta | | rya | rya | ryā | rda | rma | rma | rṇa | |
| rya | | | | | | | | | | | | |
| rva | | | | | | | | | | | | |
| sub.r | śra | ṣra | pra nmra | gra | pra | | | | śra | śra | śra pra | pra |
| | | pra | rkṣya | | | | | | | | tpra | |
| sub.th | | | rtha ktha | | | | stha | | | stha rtha | | |

## TABLE 3 (a)
## ŚĀRADĀ ALPHABET
## (11th - 13th Centuries)

| | I | II | III | IV | V | VI | VII | VIII | IX | X | XI | XII | XIII | XIV | XV |
|---|---|---|---|---|---|---|---|---|---|---|---|---|---|---|---|
| Transcribed letter in Roman | Coins of Rulers of Kashmir & Mahmud of Ghazni | Hund Inscrip. of Kāmeśvarī Devī (Shāhī) 168-69. CE 1018-19 | Bhahund Fountain Inscrip. Śāstra (410)4 (CE 1028-29) | Daechan Stone Inscription (Laukika) (41)12 CE 1036 | Kulait Copper-Plate Inscrip. of Somavarman & Āṣatavarman 11th Cent. | Chamba Copper-Plate Inscrip. of Somavarman 11th Cent. | Thunda Copper-Plate Inscrip. of Āṣatavarman 11th Cent. | Luj Fountain Inscrip. Śāstra (41) 81 CE 1105-06 | S.P.S. Museum Inscrip. of Jayasiṁha (Laukika) (42)25 CE 1149 | Tapar Inscrip. Paramandadeva (Laukika) (42) 33 CE 1157 | Devī-rī-koṭhī Inscrip. of Rājānaka Nāga-pāla & Ramapāla CE 1159-61 | Sathi Fountain Inscrip. of Ludrapala Śāstra (42)46 CE 1170 | Arigom Stone Inscrip. (Laukika) (42)73 CE 1197 | Baijināth Śiva Temple Inscrip. Śaka 1126. CE 1204 | Vejibror Stone Inscrip. of Rājadeva (Śaka) 58 CE 1236 |
| a | | | | | | | | | | | | | | | |
| ā | | | | | | | | | | | | | | | |
| i | | | | | | | | | | | | | | | |
| ī | | | | | | | | | | | | | | | |
| u | | | | | | | | | | | | | | | |
| ū | | | | | | | | | | | | | | | |
| e | | | | | | | | | | | | | | | |

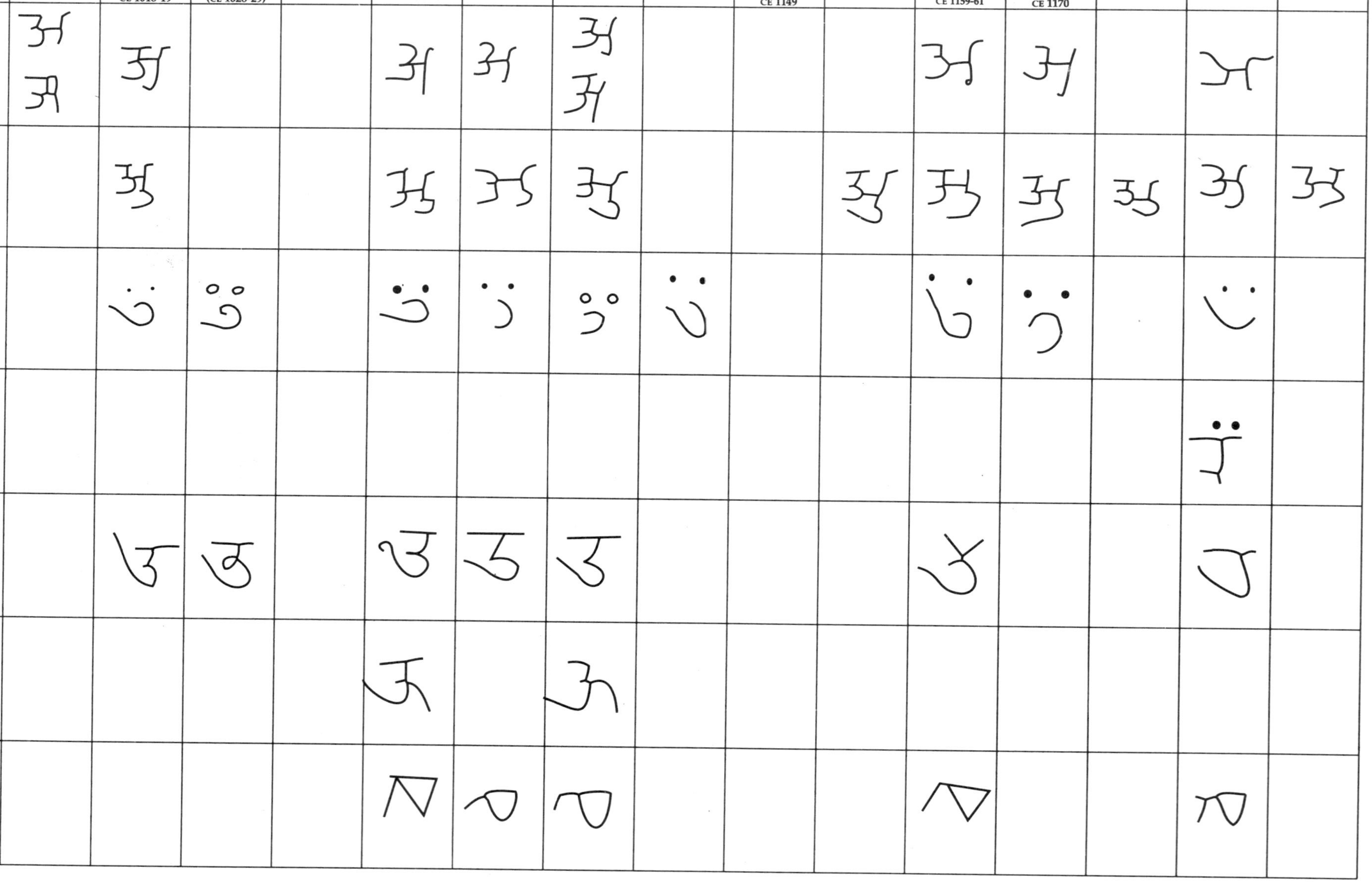

## TABLE 3 (b)
## ŚĀRADĀ ALPHABET
## (11th - 13th Centuries)

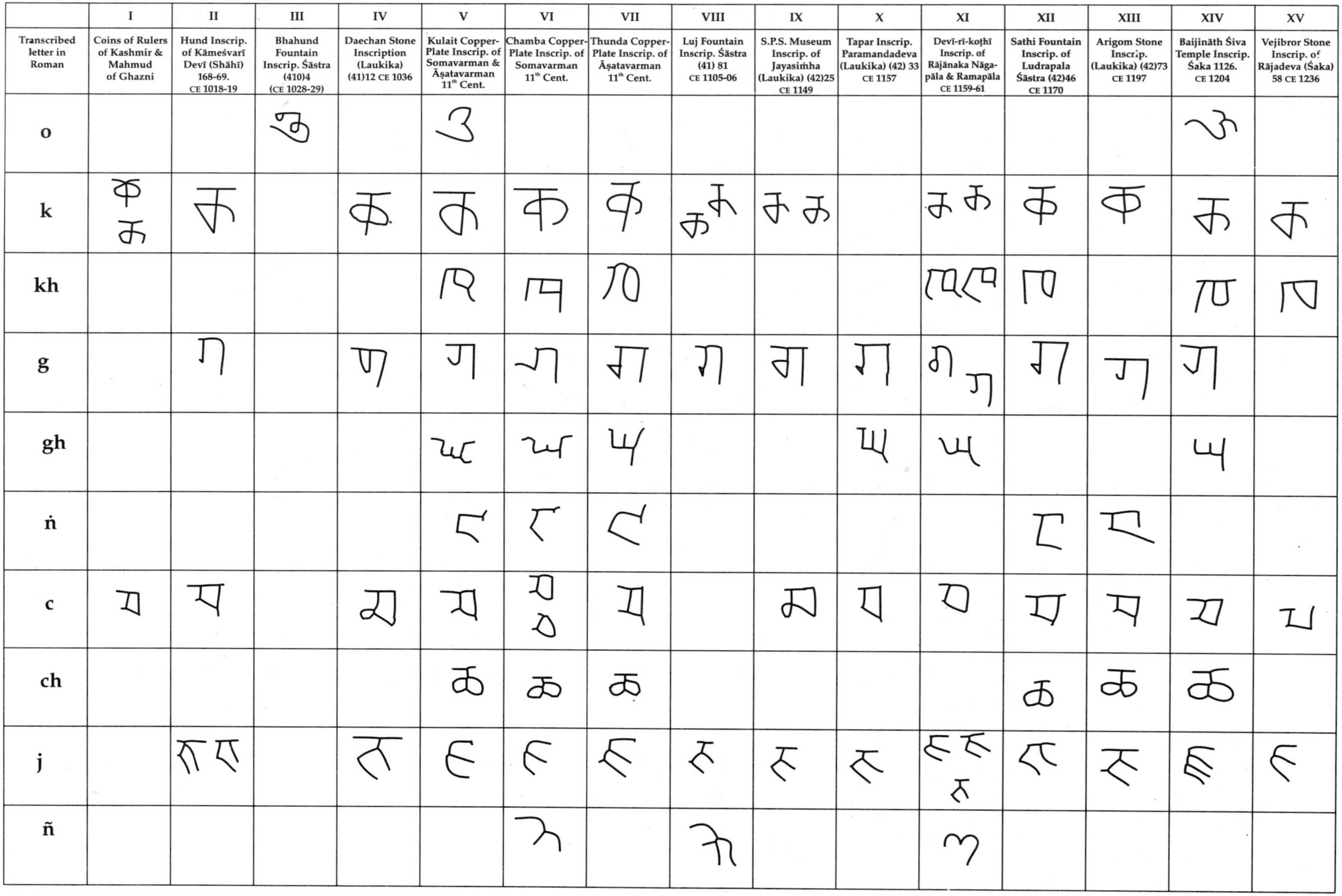

## TABLE 3 (c)
## ŚĀRADĀ ALPHABET
## (11th - 13th Centuries)

| | I | II | III | IV | V | VI | VII | VIII | IX | X | XI | XII | XIII | XIV | XV |
|---|---|---|---|---|---|---|---|---|---|---|---|---|---|---|---|
| Transcribed letter in Roman | Coins of Rulers of Kashmir & Mahmud of Ghazni | Hund Inscrip. of Kāmeśvarī Devī (Shāhī) 168-69. CE 1018-19 | Bhahund Fountain Inscrip. Śāstra (410)4 (CE 1028-29) | Daechan Stone Inscription (Laukika) (41)12 CE 1036 | Kulait Copper-Plate Inscrip. of Somavarman & Āṣatavarman 11th Cent. | Chamba Copper-Plate Inscrip. of Somavarman 11th Cent. | Thunda Copper-Plate Inscrip. of Āṣatavarman 11th Cent. | Luj Fountain Inscrip. Śāstra (41) 81 CE 1105-06 | S.P.S. Museum Inscrip. of Jayasiṁha (Laukika) (42)25 CE 1149 | Tapar Inscrip. Paramandadeva (Laukika) (42) 33 CE 1157 | Devī-rī-koṭhī Inscrip. of Rājānaka Nāga-pāla & Ramapāla CE 1159-61 | Sathi Fountain Inscrip. of Ludrapala Śāstra (42)46 CE 1170 | Arigom Stone Inscrip. (Laukika) (42)73 CE 1197 | Baijināth Śiva Temple Inscrip. Śaka 1126. CE 1204 | Vejibror Stone Inscrip. of Rājadeva (Śaka) 58 CE 1236 |
| ṭ | | | | | | | | | | | | | | | |
| ṭh | | | | | | | | | | | | | | | |
| ḍ | | | | | | | | | | | | | | | |
| ḍh | | | | | | | | | | | | | | | |
| ṇ | | | | | | | | | | | | | | | |
| t | | | | | | | | | | | | | | | |
| th | | | | | | | | | | | | | | | |
| d | | | | | | | | | | | | | | | |

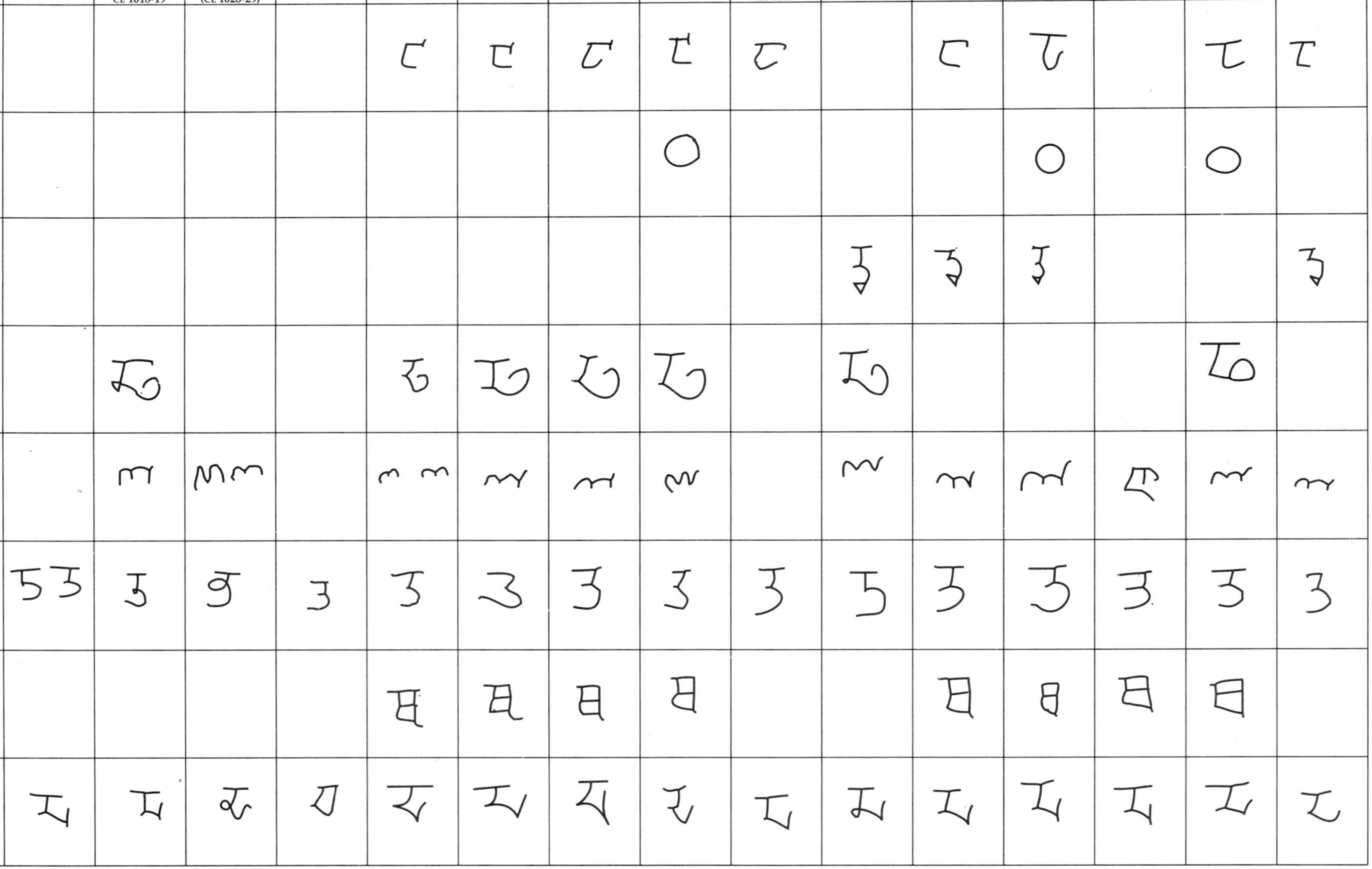

**TABLE 3 (d)**
**ŚĀRADĀ ALPHABET**
**($11^{th}$ - $13^{th}$ Centuries)**

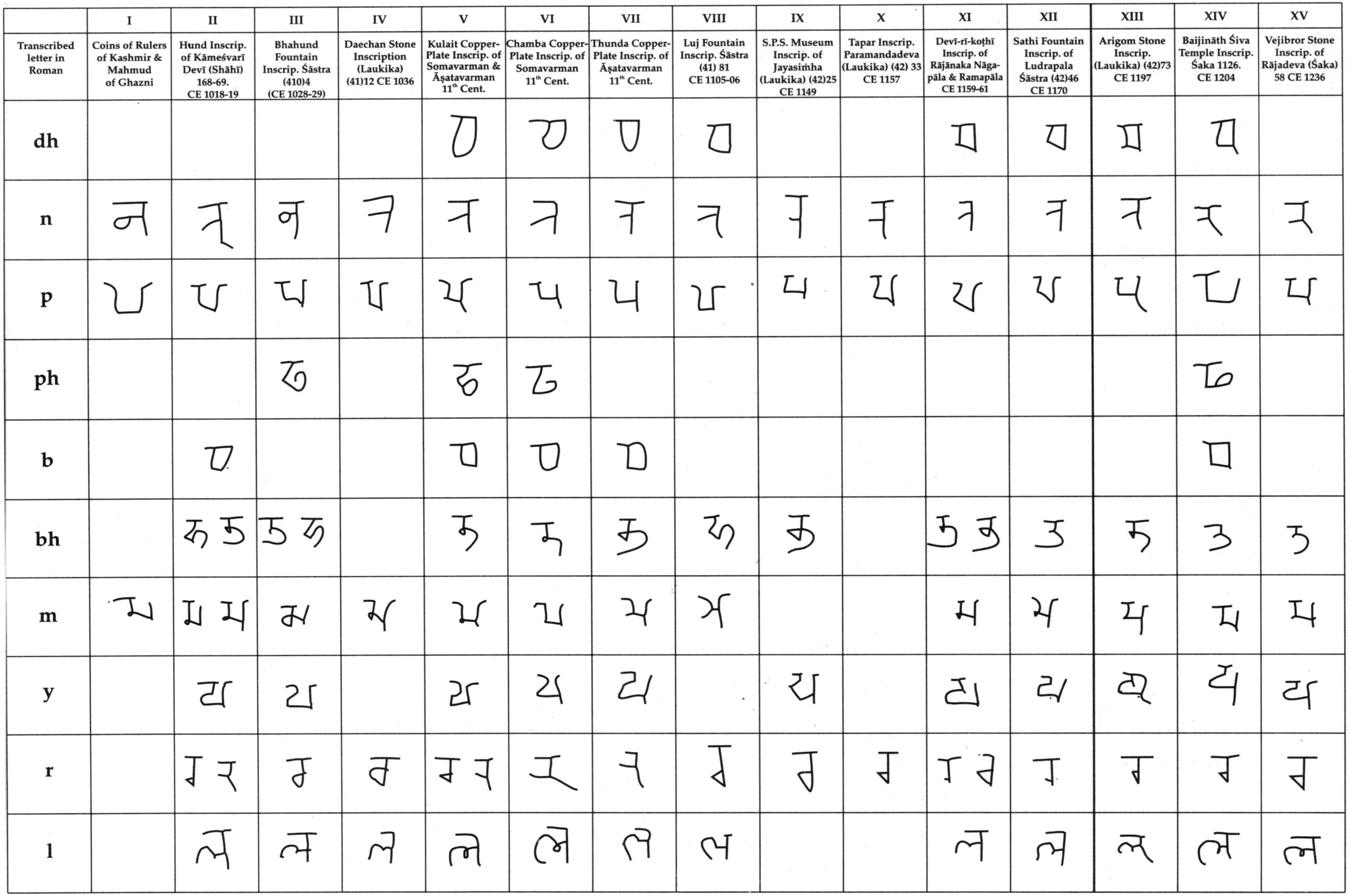

**TABLE 3 (e)**
**ŚĀRADĀ ALPHABET**
**(11th - 13th Centuries)**

| | I | II | III | IV | V | VI | VII | VIII | IX | X | XI | XII | XIII | XIV | XV |
|---|---|---|---|---|---|---|---|---|---|---|---|---|---|---|---|
| Transcribed letter in Roman | Coins of Rulers of Kashmir & Mahmud of Ghazni | Hund Inscrip. of Kāmeśvarī Devī (Shāhī) 168-69. CE 1018-19 | Bhahund Fountain Inscrip. Śāstra (410)4 (CE 1028-29) | Daechan Stone Inscription (Laukika) (41)12 CE 1036 | Kulait Copper-Plate Inscrip. of Somavarman & Āṣatavarman 11th Cent. | Chamba Copper-Plate Inscrip. of Somavarman 11th Cent. | Thunda Copper-Plate Inscrip. of Āṣatavarman 11th Cent. | Luj Fountain Inscrip. Śāstra (41) 81 CE 1105-06 | S.P.S. Museum Inscrip. of Jayasiṁha (Laukika) (42)25 CE 1149 | Tapar Inscrip. Paramandadeva (Laukika) (42) 33 CE 1157 | Devī-rī-koṭhī Inscrip. of Rājāraka Nāga-pāla & Ramapāla CE 1159-61 | Sathi Fountain Inscrip. of Ludrapala Śāstra (42)46 CE 1170 | Arigom Stone Inscrip. (Laukika) (42)73 CE 1197 | Baijināth Śiva Temple Inscrip. Śaka 1126. CE 1204 | Vejibror Stone Inscrip. of Rājadeva (Śaka) 58 CE 1236 |
| v | | | | | | | | | | | | | | | |
| ś | | | | | | | | | | | | | | | |
| ṣ | | | | | | | | | | | | | | | |
| s | | | | | | | | | | | | | | | |
| h | | | | | | | | | | | | | | | |
| jih. up. | | | | | | | | | | | | | | | |
| halanta | | | | | | | | | | | | | | | |

## TABLE 3 (f)
## ŚĀRADĀ ALPHABET
## (11th - 13th Centuries)

| | I | II | III | IV | V | VI | VII | VIII | IX | X | XI | XII | XIII | XIV | XV |
|---|---|---|---|---|---|---|---|---|---|---|---|---|---|---|---|
| Transcribed letter in Roman | Coins of Rulers of Kashmir & Mahmud of Ghazni | Hund Inscrip. of Kāmeśvarī Devī (Shāhī) 168-69. CE 1018-19 | Bhahund Fountain Inscrip. Śāstra (410)4 (CE 1028-29) | Daechan Stone Inscription (Laukika) (41)12 CE 1036 | Kulait Copper-Plate Inscrip. of Somavarman & Āṣatavarman 11th Cent. | Chamba Copper-Plate Inscrip. of Somavarman 11th Cent. | Thunda Copper-Plate Inscrip. of Āṣatavarman 11th Cent. | Luj Fountain Inscrip. Śāstra (41) 81 CE 1105-06 | S.P.S. Museum Inscrip. of Jayasiṁha (Laukika) (42)25 CE 1149 | Tapar Inscrip. Paramandadeva (Laukika) (42) 33 CE 1157 | Devī-rī-koṭhī Inscrip. of Rājānaka Nāga-pāla & Ramapāla CE 1159-61 | Sathi Fountain Inscrip. of Ludrapala Śāstra (42)46 CE 1170 | Arigom Stone Inscrip. (Laukika) (42)73 CE 1197 | Baijināth Śiva Temple Inscrip. Śaka 1126. CE. 1204 | Vejibror Stone Inscrip. of Rājadeva (Śaka) 58 CE 1236 |
| **MEDIAL VOWELS** | | | | | | | | | | | | | | | |
| **ā** | | rā | śā | rā | kā jā ṇā ṭā | tā | dā | thā yā ṇā | rā | bhā | yā | ṭā ṅā | nā ṣā | rā jā | pā ṭā |
| **i** | pi | ti | bhi | hi | khi li ki | ti ni | ni | pi | bhi | bhi | ti | li | bhi | pi chi | ti |
| **ī** | thī | śrī | ṇī | śrī | śī | nī dī | śrī nī | rī | | śrī | śrī | śī | śrī | dhī | śrī |
| **u** | | ku pu | pu śu ru | śu | pu ru śu | pu ru ku | gu hu ru | su śu | śu | pu śu | śu gu | du ku ru | pu ru | pu ru dhu | śu |
| **ū** | | sū | pū | | hū śū rū kū | dū kū | pū rū | sū | | | śū rū | | tū | pū | |
| **ṛ** | | kṛ dhṛ | | kṛ | kṛ | kṛ gṛ | kṛ | | | | kṛ | | kṛ | gṛ | |
| **e** | | pe le | de | te | se de śe | de | de le | de | de | je | de le | se | te | the | ye |
| **ai** | | | tai | dai | kai | kai | | | | | bhai | trai | nai | dhai | dhai |
| **o** | | ho ko | lo | | no | yo go | go no ko | ho | go | | ro | yo | lo | mo | lo |
| **au** | | nau | | | kau | chau | kau | | | | sau | | dhau | jau | |

## TABLE 3 (g)
## ŚĀRADĀ ALPHABET
## (11[th] - 13[th] Centuries)

| | I | II | III | IV | V | VI | VII | VIII | IX | X | XI | XII | XIII | XIV | XV |
|---|---|---|---|---|---|---|---|---|---|---|---|---|---|---|---|
| Transcribed letter in Roman | Coins of Rulers of Kashmir & Mahmud of Ghazni | Hund Inscrip. of Kāmeśvarī Devī (Shāhī) 168-69. CE 1018-19 | Bhahund Fountain Inscrip. Śāstra (410)4 (CE 1028-29) | Daechan Stone Inscription (Laukika) (41)12 CE 1036 | Kulait Copper-Plate Inscrip. of Somavarman & Āṣatavarman 11[th] Cent. | Chamba Copper-Plate Inscrip. of Somavarman 11[th] Cent. | Thunda Copper-Plate Inscrip. of Āṣtavarman 11[th] Cent. | Luj Fountain Inscrip. Śāstra (41) 81 CE 1105-06 | S.P.S. Museum Inscrip. of Jayasiṁha (Laukika) (42)25 CE 1149 | Tapar Inscrip. Paramandadeva (Laukika) (42) 33 CE 1157 | Devī-rī-koṭhī Inscrip. of Rājānaka Nāga-pāla & Ramapāla CE 1159-61 | Sathi Fountain Inscrip. of Ludrapala Śāstra (42)46 CE 1170 | Arigom Stone Inscrip. (Laukika) (42)73 CE 1197 | Baijināth Śiva Temple Inscrip. Śaka 1126. CE 1204 | Vejibror Stone Inscrip. of Rājadeva (Śaka) 58 CE 1236 |
| **sup.k** | | | kṣ | kv | kk | | kṣ | | | | | kt | ky | | |
| **sub.k** | | tk | | | sk .rk | ṅk | ṅk | | | | ṅk | ṅk rk | | | |
| **sup. ṅ** | | | | | ṅk ṅgh ṅg | ṅkṛ | ṅg | | | | | ṅg | ṅg | ṅg | |
| **sup. ñ** | | | | | | | ñj | | | | ñc | | | | |
| **sub. ñ** | | jñ | | | jñ | jñ | jñ | | | | jñ | jñ | | jñ | |
| **sub. t** | | nt | st | nt | kt st | kt | kt | | | | rt st kt | kt rt | | | |
| **sub. th rth** | | | | | | | | | | | | | | | |

# TABLE 3 (h)
# ŚĀRADĀ ALPHABET
## (11th - 13th Centuries)

| | I | II | III | IV | V | VI | VII | VIII | IX | X | XI | XII | XIII | XIV | XV |
|---|---|---|---|---|---|---|---|---|---|---|---|---|---|---|---|
| Transcribed letter in Roman | Coins of Rulers of Kashmir & Mahmud of Ghazni | Hund Inscrip. of Kāmeśvarī Devī (Shāhī) 168-69. CE 1018-19 | Bhahund Fountain Inscrip. Śāstra (410)4 (CE 1028-29) | Daechan Stone Inscription (Laukika) (41)12 CE 1036 | Kulait Copper-Plate Inscrip. of Somavarman & Āṣatavarman 11th Cent. | Chamba Copper-Plate Inscrip. of Somavarman 11th Cent. | Thunda Copper-Plate Inscrip. of Āṣatavarman 11th Cent. | Luj Fountain Inscrip. Śāstra (41) 81 CE 1105-06 | S.P.S. Museum Inscrip. of Jayasiṁha (Laukika) (42)25 CE 1149 | Tapar Inscrip. Paramandadeva (Laukika) (42) 33 CE 1157 | Devī-rī-koṭhī Inscrip. of Rājānaka Nāga-pāla & Ramapāla CE. 1159-61 | Sathi Fountain Inscrip. of Ludrapala Śāstra (42)46 CE 1170 | Arigom Stone Inscrip. (Laukika) (42)73 CE 1197 | Baijināth Śiva Temple Inscrip. Śaka 1126. CE 1204 | Vejibror Stone Inscrip. of Rājadeva (Śaka) 58 CE 1236 |
| (2) sth | | | | | | | | | | | | | | | |
| sub. y | | bhy | ny | jy | gny jy | | nchy | gy | jy | jy | jy sny | śy | ky | | jy |
| sup. r | | rm | rm | ry | rś rp | rg | rph rṇ rṭh | rl | | | rm | rd rt | | | |
| ry | | | | | | | | | | | | | | | |
| rv | | | | | | | | | | | | | | | |
| sub. r | | nmr | śtr | tr | pr cchr | | tr | pr | tr | tr | dr kr | sr dr tr | rdr | pr | |
| ṣṭ | | | | | | | | | | | | | | | |
| ṣṭh | | | | | | | | | | | | | | | |

## TABLE 4 (a)
## ŚĀRADĀ ALPHABET
## (14th - 16th Centuries)

| | I | II | III | IV | V | VI |
|---|---|---|---|---|---|---|
| Transcribed Letter in Roman | Koṭiher Stone Slab Inscription (Laukika) Saṁ (44)45 (CE 1369) | Khonamuh Inscription Kali 4530 (CE 1428) | Peshawar Museum Inscriptions (Laukika) Saṁ (4)538 (CE 1462) | Hariparbat Grave Stone Inscrip. (Laukika) Saṁ (45)60 (CE 1484) | Wularhama Bathroom Gate Inscriptions | Zajinai Stone Inscription |
| **a** | 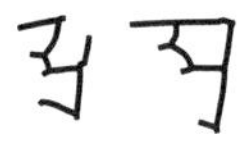 |  |  | | |  |
| **ā** | | | |  |  |  |
| **i** | |  | | | | |
| **ī** | | |  | | | |
| **u** | | |  | | | |
| **e** | | | |  | | |
| **o** |  | |  | | | |
| **k** |  |  |  |  |  |  |
| **kh** |  |  |  |  |  | |
| **g** |  |  |  |  |  |  |
| **gh** |  | |  | | |  |

# TABLE 4 (b)
# ŚĀRADĀ ALPHABET
## ($14^{th}$ - $16^{th}$ Centuries)

| | I | II | III | IV | V | VI |
|---|---|---|---|---|---|---|
| Transcribed Letter in Roman | Koṭiher Stone Slab Inscription (Laukika) Saṁ (44)45 (CE 1369) | Khonamuh Inscription Kali 4530 (CE 1428) | Peshawar Museum Inscriptions (Laukika) Saṁ (4)538 (CE 1462) | Hariparbat Grave Stone Inscrip. (Laukika) Saṁ (45)60 (CE 1484) | Wularhama Bathroom Gate Inscriptions | Zajinai Stone Inscription |
| ṅ |  |  |  | | |  |
| c |  |  |  | |  | |
| ch | |  |  | | | |
| j |  |  |  |  |  | |
| ñ | |  | | | | |
| ṭ |  |  | | | |  |
| ṭh |  |  | | | | |
| ḍ |  |  |  | | | |
| ḍh | |  | | | | |
| ṇ |  |  |  | | | |
| t |  |  |  |  |  |  |

## TABLE 4 (c)
## ŚĀRADĀ ALPHABET
## ($14^{th}$ - $16^{th}$ Centuries)

| | I | II | III | IV | V | VI |
|---|---|---|---|---|---|---|
| Transcribed Letter in Roman | Koṭiher Stone Slab Inscription (Laukika) Saṁ (44)45 (CE 1369) | Khonamuh Inscription Kali 4530 (CE 1428) | Peshawar Museum Inscriptions (Laukika) Saṁ (4)538 (CE 1462) | Hariparbat Grave Stone Inscrip. (Laukika) Saṁ (45)60 (CE 1484) | Wularhama Bathroom Gate Inscriptions | Zajinai Stone Inscription |
| th | 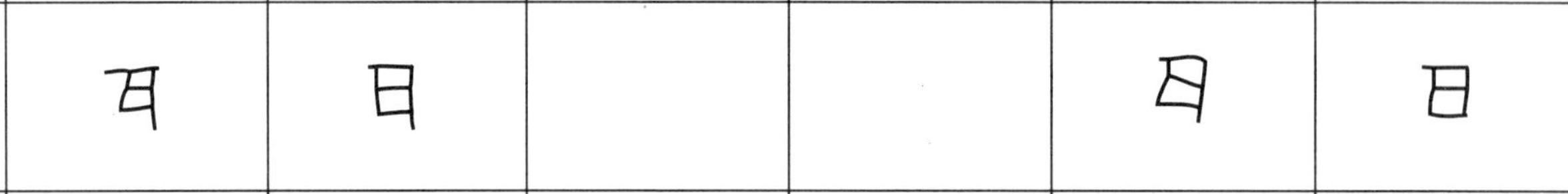 | | | | | |
| d | 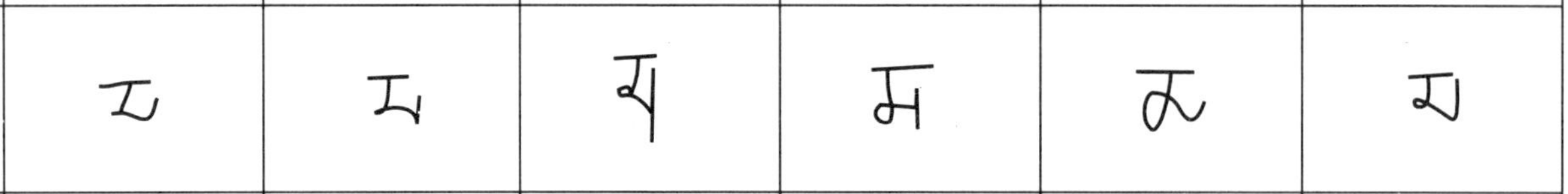 | | | | | |
| dh | 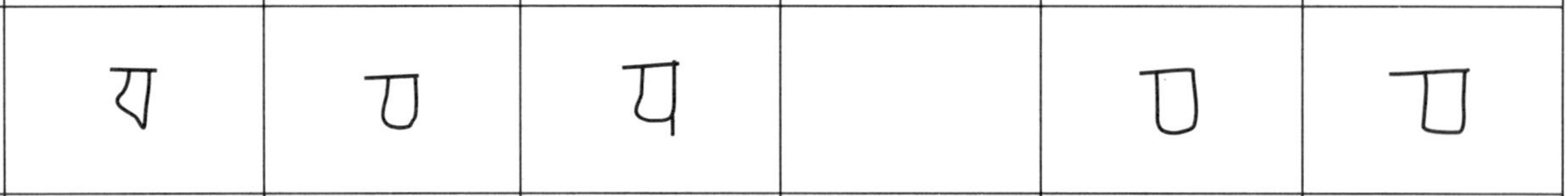 | | | | | |
| n | 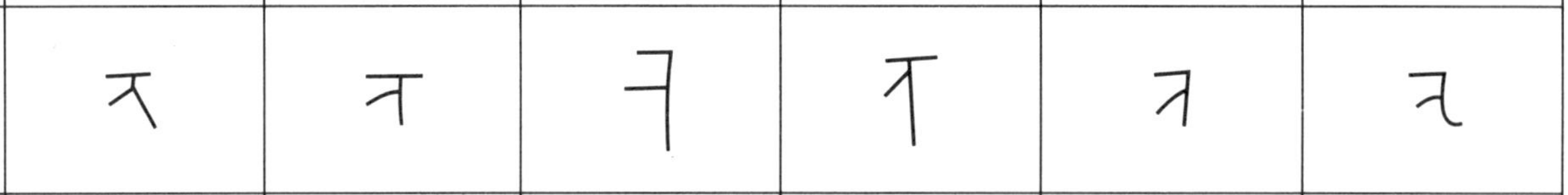 | | | | | |
| p | 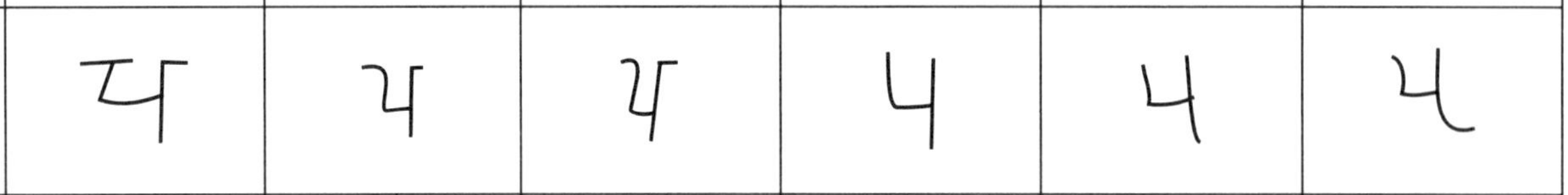 | | | | | |
| ph | 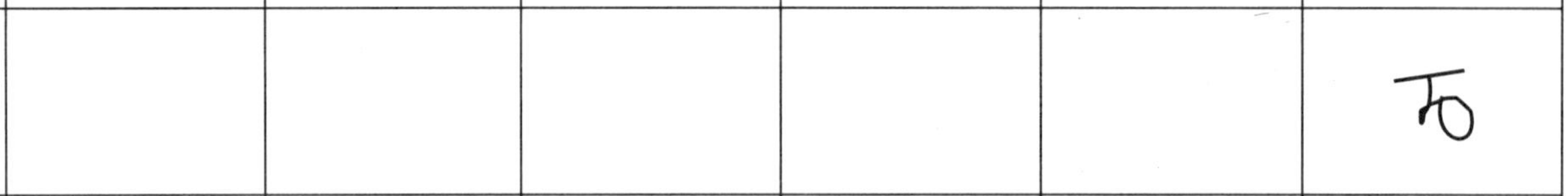 | | | | | |
| b | 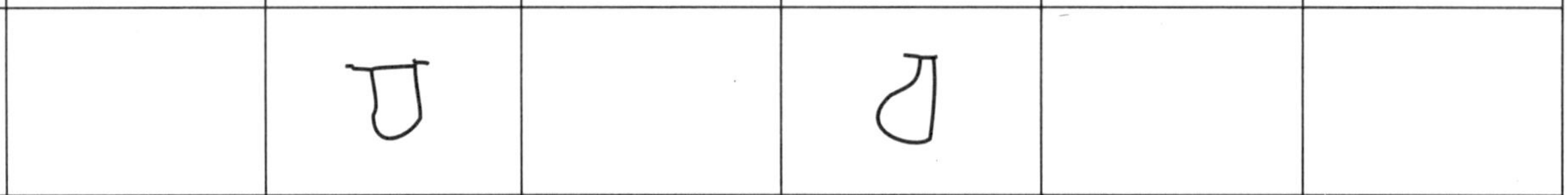 | | | | | |
| bh | 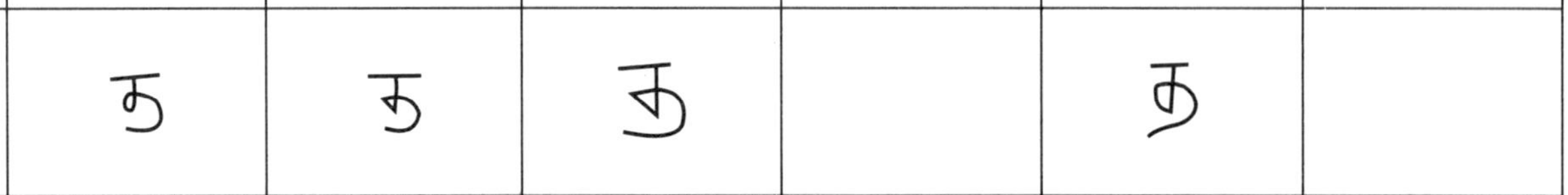 | | | | | |
| m | 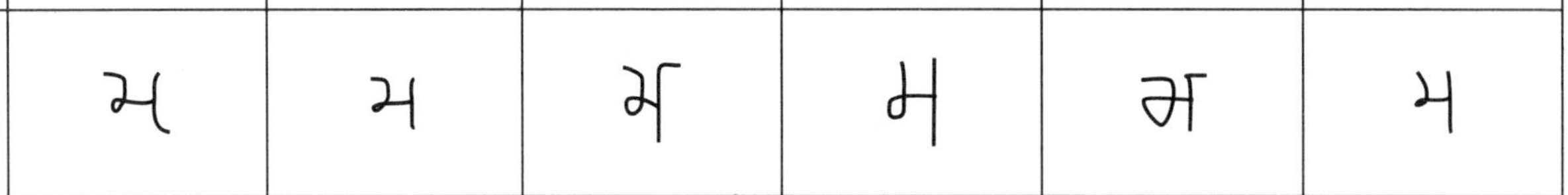 | | | | | |
| y | 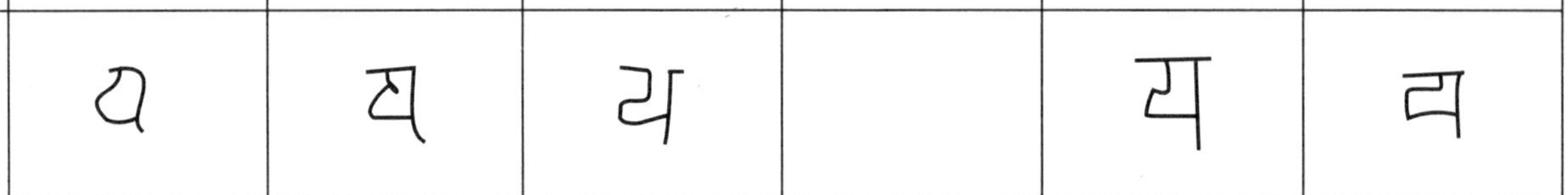 | | | | | |
| r | 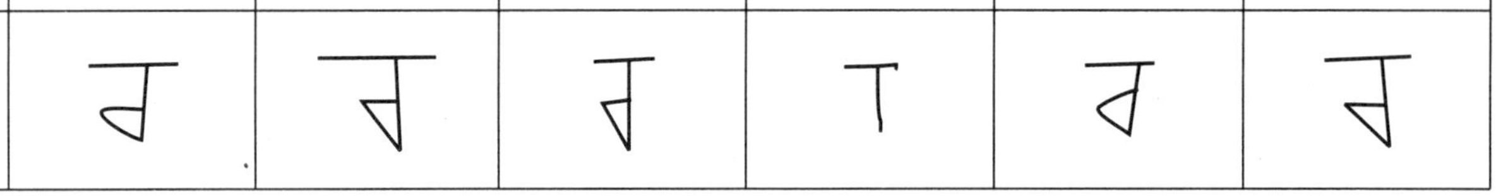 | | | | | |

## TABLE 4 (d)
## ŚĀRADĀ ALPHABET
## (14th - 16th Centuries)

| . | I | II | III | IV | V | VI |
|---|---|---|---|---|---|---|
| **Transcribed Letter in Roman** | **Koṭiher Stone Slab Inscription (Laukika) Saṁ (44)45 (CE 1369)** | **Khonamuh Inscription Kali 4530 (CE 1428)** | **Peshawar Museum Inscriptions (Laukika) Saṁ (4)538 (CE 1462)** | **Hariparbat Grave Stone Inscrip. (Laukika) Saṁ (45)60 (CE 1484)** | **Wularhama Bathroom Gate Inscriptions** | **Zajinai Stone Inscription** |
| l |  |  |  |  | |  |
| v |  |  |  |  | |  |
| ś |  |  |  |  |  |  |
| ṣ |  |  |  |  | | |
| s |  |  |  |  |  |  |
| h |  |  |  |  | | |
| up. |  | 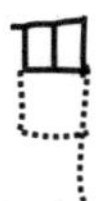 | | | | |
| halanta |  |  |  | | | |

## TABLE 4 (e)
## ŚĀRADĀ ALPHABET
## ($14^{th}$ - $16^{th}$ Centuries)

| | I | II | III | IV | V | VI |
|---|---|---|---|---|---|---|
| Transcribed Letter in Roman | Koṭiher Stone Slab Inscription (Laukika) Saṁ (44)45 (CE 1369) | Khonamuh Inscription Kali 4530 (CE 1428) | Peshawar Museum Inscriptions (Laukika) Saṁ (4)538 (CE 1462) | Hariparbat Grave Stone Inscrip. (Laukika) Saṁ (45)60 (CE 1484) | Wularhama Bathroom Gate Inscriptions | Zajinai Stone Inscription |
| **MEDIAL** ā | ḍā ṅā jā | dā | kā | hā | vā jā | vā |
| i with **k** | | | | | | |
| ī with **k** | | | | | | |
| u with **k** | | | | | | |
| ū | pū ndū | bhrū | yū śū | | | |
| ṛ | tṛ dṛ | dhṛ | ghṛ | | | kṛ |
| e | he | | te ke | le | te | |
| ai | rai | nai | | | | kai |
| o | so gho | to mo | lo | | | |
| au | | trau | nau | | | pau |

TABLE 4 (f)
ŚĀRADĀ ALPHABET
(14[th] - 16[th] Centuries)

| | I | II | III | IV | V | VI |
|---|---|---|---|---|---|---|
| Transcribed Letter in Roman | Koṭiher Stone Slab Inscription (Laukika) Saṁ (44)45 (CE 1369) | Khonamuh Inscription Kali 4530 (CE 1428) | Peshawar Museum Inscriptions (Laukika) Saṁ (4)538 (CE 1462) | Hariparbat Grave Stone Inscrip. (Laukika) Saṁ (45)60 (CE 1484) | Wularhama Bathroom Gate Inscriptions | Zajinai Stone Inscription |
| k in Ligatures | kṣ  | kt  | ky ṣk 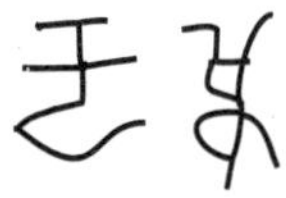 | kra  | jk 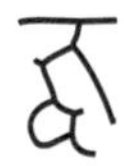 | |
| ṅ in Ligatures | ṅg  | ṅgā 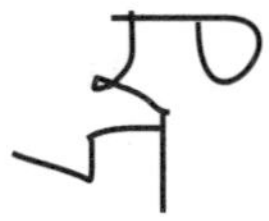 | ṅgā ṅg 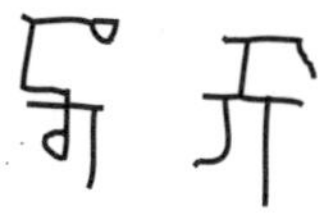 | | | |
| ñ in Ligatures | ñj  | ñc jñ 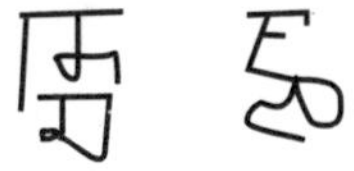 jñā  | | | | |
| rth and sth | | rth sth  |  | | | |
| r in Ligatures | rṇā gra 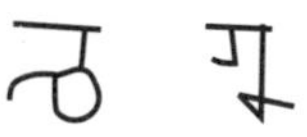 tra  | rṇ tr  rv  | rtr rg 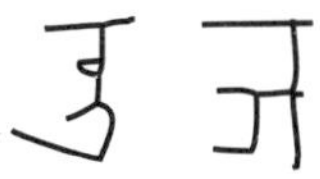 | dr vr  | rd tr 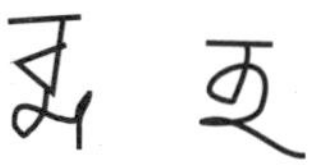 | |
| ṣṭ and ṣṭh | |  |  | 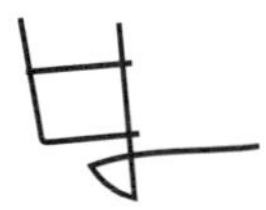 | ṇṭh  |  |

# TABLE 5 (a)
# ŚĀRADĀ ALPHABET IN MANUSCRIPTS
## (12th - 20th Centuries)

MODERN ŚĀRADĀ

| | I | II | III | IV | V | VI | VII | VIII | IX | X |
|---|---|---|---|---|---|---|---|---|---|---|
| Roman letters in transcription | Bhakshali Manuscript c. 12th Century | Manuscript of Muni-mata-maṇi-mālā c.14th Century | Manuscript of Śakuntalā c. 17th Century | Manuscript of Ādi & Sabhāparvan of Mahābhārata c. 16th century | Manuscript of Kathā-Sarit-Sāgara c. 16th Century | Manuscript of Bālabodhinī H.1158, (CE 1745) | Manuscript of C. Brāhmaṇa c. 18th Century | Manuscript of A Ritual Text 1905 CE | Manuscript of Śiva-Mahimnastota 1933 CE | Śāradā Horoscope 1963 CE |
| a | | | | | | | | | | |
| ā | | | | | | | | | | |
| i | | | | | | | | | | |
| ī | | | | | | | | | | |
| u | | | | | | | | | | |
| ū | | | | | | | | | | |
| ṛ ḷ | | | | | | | | | | |
| e | | | | | | | | | | |
| ai | | | | | | | | | | |
| o | | | | | | | | | | |
| au | | | | | | | | | | |
| k | | | | | | | | | | |
| kh | | | | | | | | | | |
| g | | | | | | | | | | |
| gh | | | | | | | | | | |

## TABLE 5 (b)
## ŚĀRADĀ ALPHABET IN MANUSCRIPTS
## (12th - 20th Centuries)

MODERN ŚĀRADĀ

| | I | II | III | IV | V | VI | VII | VIII | IX | X |
|---|---|---|---|---|---|---|---|---|---|---|
| Roman letters in transcription | Bhakshali Manuscript c. 12th Century | Manuscript of Muni-mata-maṇi-mālā c.14th Century | Manuscript of Śakuntalā c. 17th Century | Manuscript of Ādi & Sabhāparvan of Mahābhārata c. 16th Century | Manuscript of Kathā-Sarit-Sāgara c. 16th Century | Manuscript of Bālabodhinī H.1158, (CE 1745) | Manuscript of C. Brāhmaṇa c. 18th Century | Manuscript of A Ritual Text 1905 CE | Manuscript of Śiva-Mahimnastota 1933 CE | Śāradā Horoscope 1963 CE |

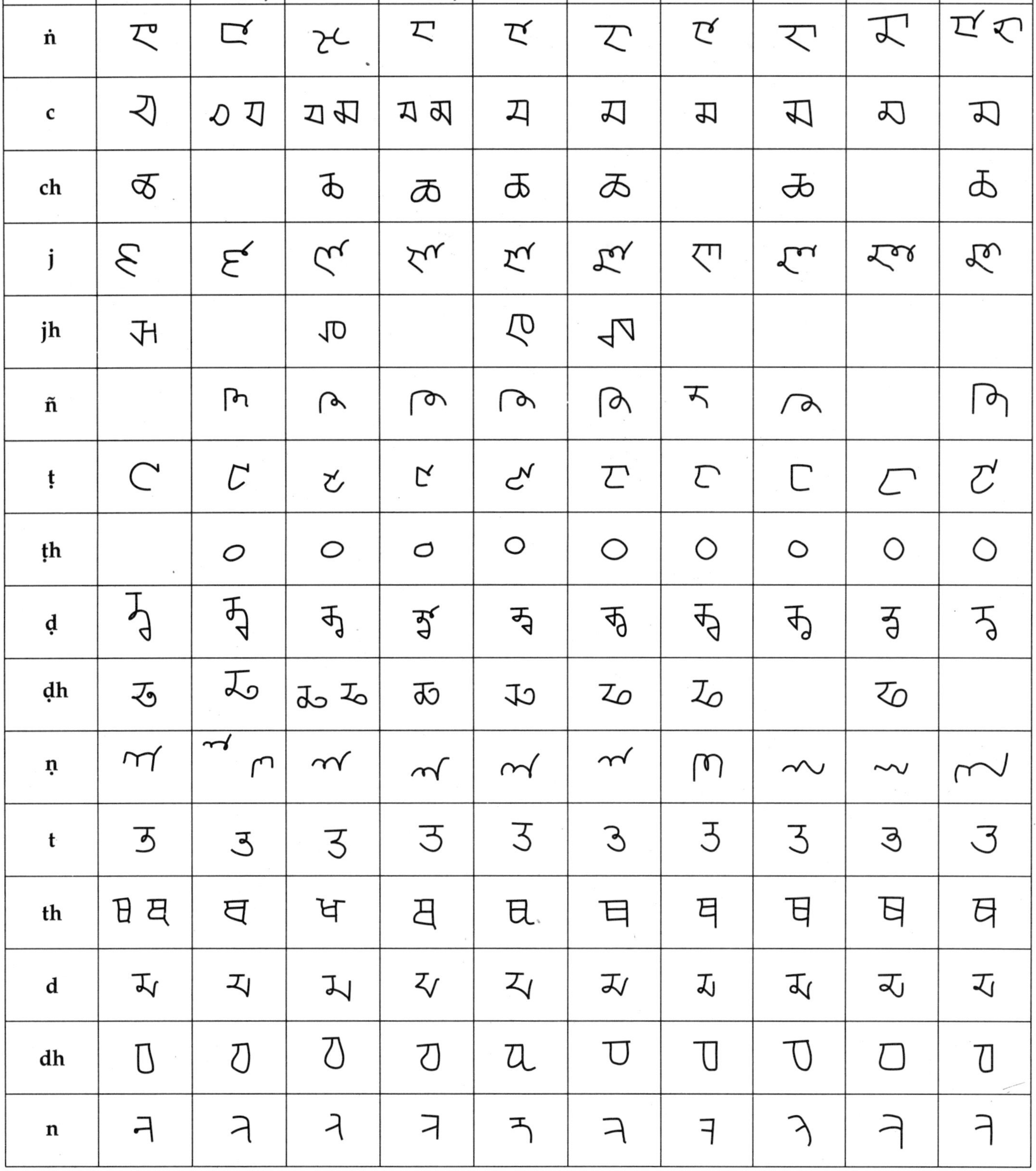

## TABLE 5 (c)
## ŚĀRADĀ ALPHABET IN MANUSCRIPTS
## (12th - 20th Centuries)

| | I | II | III | IV | V | VI | VII | VIII | IX | X |
|---|---|---|---|---|---|---|---|---|---|---|
| | | | | | | | MODERN ŚĀRADĀ | | | |
| Roman letters in transcription | Bhakshali Manuscript c. 12th Century | Manuscript of Muni-mata-maṇi-mālā c.14th Century | Manuscript of Śakuntalā c. 17th Century | Manuscript of Ādi & Sabhāparvan of Mahābhārata c. 16th Century | Manuscript of Kathā-Sarit-Sāgara c. 16th Century | Manuscript of Bālabodhinī H.1158, (CE 1745) | Manuscript of C. Brāhmaṇa c. 18th Century | Manuscript of A Ritual Text 1905 CE | Manuscript of Śiva-Mahimnastota 1933 CE | Śāradā Horoscope 1963 CE |
| p | | | | | | | | | | |
| ph | | | | | | | | | | |
| b | | | | | | | | | | |
| bh | | | | | | | | | | |
| m | | | | | | | | | | |
| y | | | | | | | | | | |
| r | | | | | | | | | | |
| l | | | | | | | | | | |
| v | | | | | | | | | | |
| ś | | | | | | | | | | |
| ṣ | | | | | | | | | | |
| s | | | | | | | | | | |
| h | | | | | | | | | | |
| jih. | | | | | | | | | | |
| up. | | | | | | | | | | |
| halant | | | | | | | | | | |

# TABLE 5 (d)
# ŚĀRADĀ ALPHABET IN MANUSCRIPTS
## (12th - 20th Centuries)

MODERN ŚĀRADĀ

| | I | II | III | IV | V | VI | VII | VIII | IX | X |
|---|---|---|---|---|---|---|---|---|---|---|
| Roman letters in transcription | Bhakshali Manuscript c. 12th Century | Manuscript of Muni-mata-maṇi-mālā c.14th Century | Manuscript of Śakuntalā c. 17th Century | Manuscript of Ādi & Sabhāparvan of Mahābhārata c. 16th Century | Manuscript of Kathā-Sarit-Sāgara c. 16th Century | Manuscript of Bālabodhinī H.1158, (CE 1745) | Manuscript of C. Brāhmaṇa c. 18th Century | Manuscript of A Ritual Text 1905 CE | Manuscript of Śiva-Mahimnastota 1933 CE | Śāradā Horoscope 1963 CE |
| MEDIAL VOWELS ā | bhā ṇā | ṇā nā | nā | tā | vā gā | nā kā | dhā tā | mā kā | nā śā | sā vā |
| ā | jā ṇā | ṇā ṭā | jñā | ṅā ṇā | ṅā ṇā | ṅā ṇā | jā ṇā | jā ṇā | ṅā ṇā | jā ṇā ṭā |
| i with k | | | | | | | | | | |
| ī with k | | | | | | | | | | |
| u | ru gu | su ru gu | pu | su śu hu | pu tu | ṭu cu pu ru | thu ru gu | mu ku tu | su gu ru tu | ku śu |
| ū | mū rū vrū | pū hū rū | pū sū rū | pū bhū rū | bhū hū | mū bhū rū | sū rū bhū | yū tū | pū tū bhū | mū bhū |
| ṛ | hṛ kṛ | gṛ kṛ | nṛ | bhṛ | dṛ stṛ | mṛ | vṛ | | hṛ kṛ sṛ | tṛ nṛ |
| e with k | | | | | | | | | | |
| ai with k | | | | | | | | | | |
| o with k | | | | | | | | | | |
| au with k | | ṇau | | | | | | | | |
| LIGATURE kṣ | | | rkṣ | | | | | | | |
| jñ sub. ñ | | | jñā | jñā | | jñā | jñā | | | |
| sup. r | rg rg rg | rṭ rgh rṇ | rc ryā | rd rj rth ry | rp rṇ rgh | rv rṇ rth | rṇ rv rk rm | rd rc rth | rv rth | rk rṇ rjā rgh rdh |
| sub. r | dvr dr | sr | pr | | śru | tr pr kru | mr vr tr kr | pr śr | pr sr kr str | pr kr |
| sth | | | | | | | | | | |
| ṣṭ ṣṭh sub. dh | | | | | | | dh | | ṣṭ gdh ddh | ṣṭh nṭh ddh nṭh |

## TABLE 6
## NUMERALS OF THE ŚĀRADĀ ALPHABET

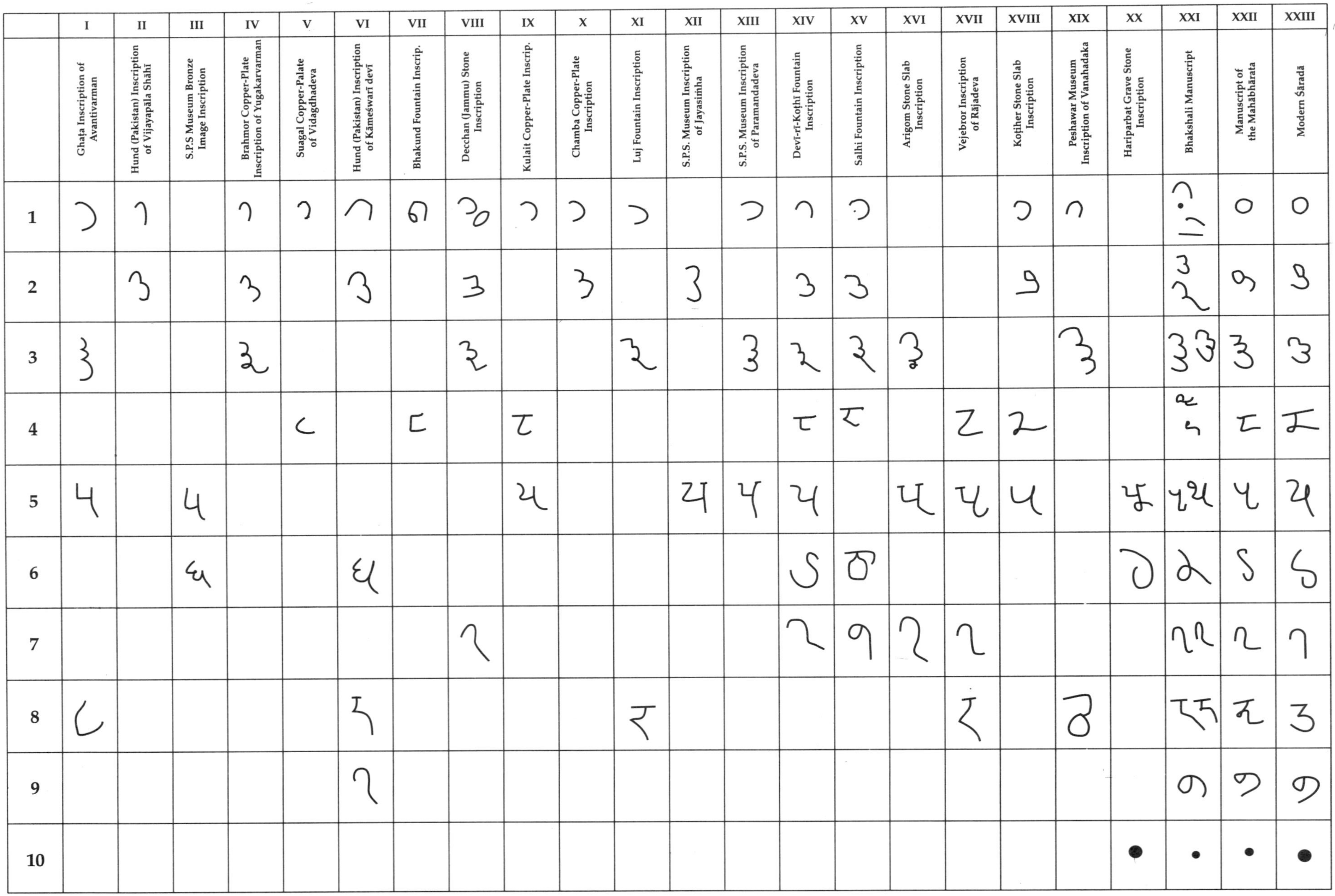

# RESUME

## ŚĀRADĀ ALPHABET

### EARLY PHASE (9th - 10th Centuries)

| a | ā | i | ī | u | ū | e | o | k | kh |
|---|---|---|---|---|---|---|---|---|---|
| g | gh | ṅ | c | c | chh | j | jh | ñ | ṭ ṭ |
| ṭh | ḍ | ḍh | ṇ | ṇ | ṇ | t | th | th | d |
| dh | dh | n | p | p | ph | b | bh | m | m |
| y | r | l | v | ś | ṣ | ṣ | s | h | |
| tā | jā | ṭā | ṇā | di | tī | ku | śu | pu | yu |
| bhū | sū | kṛ | hṛ | pṛ | gṛ | de | le | dai | pai |
| no | ro | gau | pau | kṣ | jñ | ṣṭ | ṣṭh | ṣṭh | sth |
| sy | rd | ry | ry | pr | ddhy | nt | ho | | |

### SECOND PHASE (11th - 13th Centuries)

| a | a | ā | i | ī | u | ū | e | o | k k |
|---|---|---|---|---|---|---|---|---|---|
| kh | g | gh | ṅ | c | ch | j | ñ | ṭ | ṭh |
| ḍ | ḍh | ṇ | ṇ | t | th | d | dh | n | p |
| ph | b | bh | m | m | y | r | l | v | ś |
| ṣ | s | h | | | | | | | |
| rā | jā | ṭā | ṇā | di | rī | śu | pu | bhū | sū |
| de | te | te | ge | khai | tai | chai | go | lo | bho sau |
| sth | sth | rth | ṣṭh | pr | | | | | |

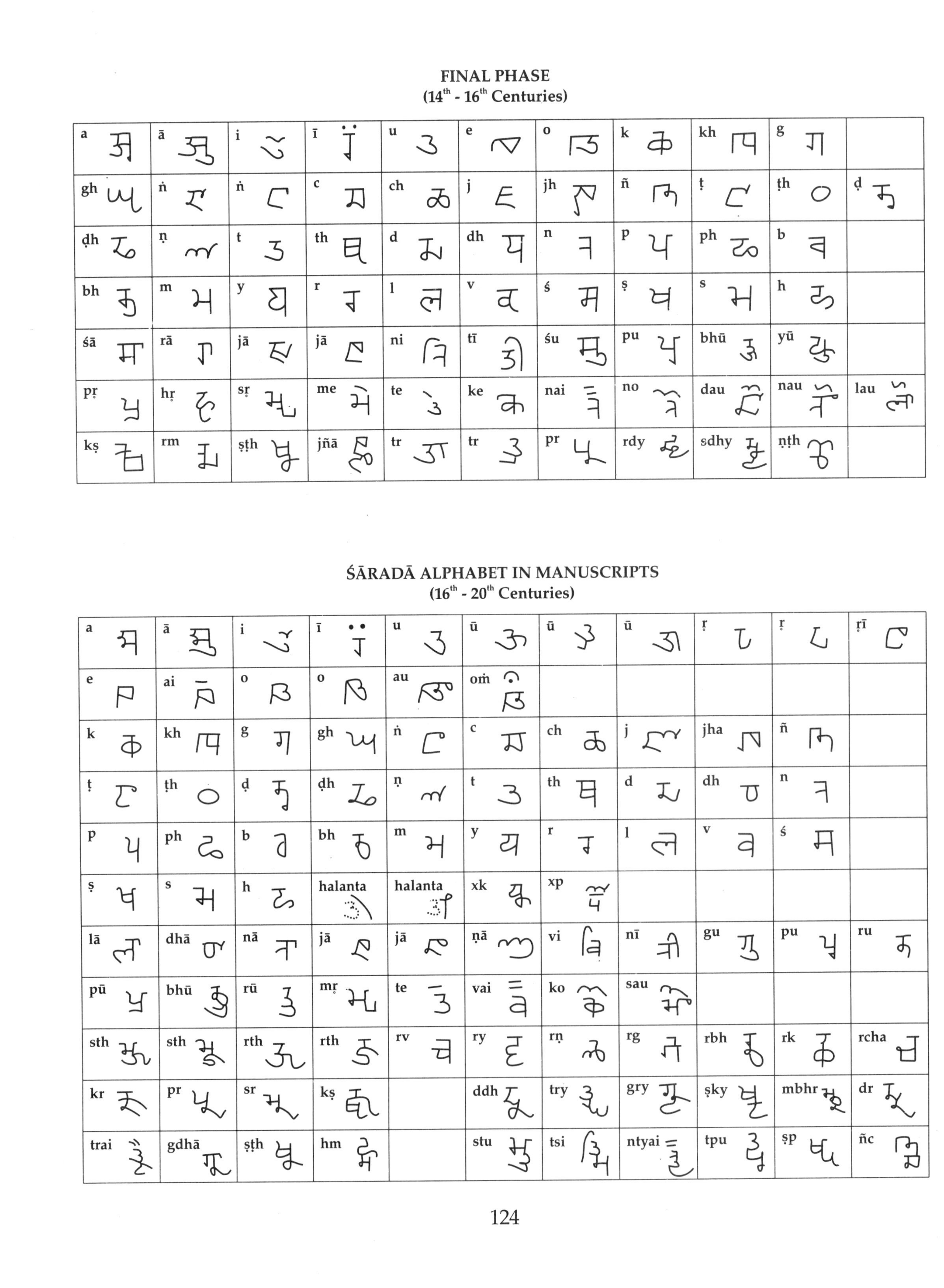

## FINAL PHASE
### (14th - 16th Centuries)

| a | ā | i | ī | u | e | o | k | kh | g | |
|---|---|---|---|---|---|---|---|---|---|---|
| gh | ṅ | ṅ | c | ch | j | jh | ñ | ṭ | ṭh | ḍ |
| ḍh | ṇ | t | th | d | dh | n | p | ph | b | |
| bh | m | y | r | l | v | ś | ṣ | s | h | |
| śā | rā | jā | jā | ni | tī | śu | pu | bhū | yū | |
| pṛ | hṛ | sṛ | me | te | ke | nai | no | dau | nau | lau |
| kṣ | rm | ṣṭh | jñā | tr | tr | pr | rdy | sdhy | ṇṭh | |

## ŚĀRADĀ ALPHABET IN MANUSCRIPTS
### (16th - 20th Centuries)

| a | ā | i | ī | u | ū | ū | ū | ṛ | ṛ | ṛī |
|---|---|---|---|---|---|---|---|---|---|---|
| e | ai | o | o | au | oṁ | | | | | |
| k | kh | g | gh | ṅ | c | ch | j | jha | ñ | |
| ṭ | ṭh | ḍ | ḍh | ṇ | t | th | d | dh | n | |
| p | ph | b | bh | m | y | r | l | v | ś | |
| ṣ | s | h | halanta | halanta | xk | xp | | | | |
| lā | dhā | nā | jā | jā | ṇā | vi | nī | gu | pu | ru |
| pū | bhū | rū | mṛ | te | vai | ko | sau | | | |
| sth | sth | rth | rth | rv | ry | rṇ | rg | rbh | rk | rcha |
| kr | pr | sr | kṣ | | ddh | try | gry | ṣky | mbhr | dr |
| trai | gdhā | ṣṭh | hm | | stu | tsi | ntyai | tpu | ṣp | ñc |

## TABLE 7 (a)
## DEVĀŚEṢA - ṬĀKARĪ ALPHABET
## ($14^{th}$-$16^{th}$ Centuries)

| | I | II | III | IV | V | VI | VII | VIII | IX | X |
|---|---|---|---|---|---|---|---|---|---|---|
| Characters in Roman | Guroli Copper-Plate Inscription of Vairasivarman | Mhesa Copper-Plate Inscription of Bhoṭavarman | Jungrar Copper-Plate Inscription of Bhoṭavarman | Saṅgrāmavarman's grant to Badhu Legha | Mindha Copper-Plate Inscription of Saṅgrāmavarman | Chamba Plate of Ānandavarman | Chamba Plate of Gaṇeśavarman | Ganguya grant of Gaṇeśavarman | Chamba Plate of Balabhadra | Kulu Copper-Plate Grant of Bahādur Singh |
| a | | | | | | | | | | |
| ā | | | | | | | | | | |
| i | | | | | | | | | | |
| ī [1] | | | | | | | | | | |
| u | | | | | | | | | | |
| ū | | | | | | | | | | |
| ṛ [2] | | | | | | | | | | |
| e | | | | | | | | | | |
| ai | | | | | | | | | | |
| o | | | | | | | | | | |
| au | | | | | | | | | | |
| anusvāra | | | anunāsika | | | | | | | |
| k | | | | | | | | | | |
| kh | | | | | | | | | | |
| g | | | | | | | | | | |
| gh | | | | | | | | | | |
| ṅ | | | | | | | | | | |

1. Chabra, op. cit, no. 38, lines 8-10; no. 39, line 11.
2. Ibid., no. 28, line 3; no. 37, line 3.

## TABLE 7 (b)
## DEVĀŚEṢA - ṬĀKARĪ ALPHABET
### (14th-16th Centuries)

| Characters in Roman | I Guroli Copper-Plate Inscription of Vairasivarman | II Mhesa Copper-Plate Inscription of Bhoṭavarman | III Jungrar Copper-Plate Inscription of Bhoṭavarman | IV Saṅgrāmavarman's grant to Badhu Legha | V Mindha Copper-Plate Inscription of Saṅgrāmavarman | VI Chamba Plate of Ānandavarman | VII Chamba Plate of Gaṇeshavarman | VIII Ganguya grant of Gaṇeshavarman | IX Chamba Plate of Balabhadra | X Kulu Copper-Plate Grant of Bahādur Singh |
|---|---|---|---|---|---|---|---|---|---|---|
| c | | | | | | | | | | |
| ch | | | | | | | | | | |
| j | | | | | | | | | | |
| jh | | | | | | | ñ | ñc | | |
| ṭ | | | | | | | | | | |
| ṭh | | | | | | | | | | |
| ḍ | | | | | | | | | ṇḍ | ṇḍ |
| ḍh | | | | | | | | | | |
| ṇ | | | | | | | | | ṣṇa | |
| t | | | | | | | | | | |
| th | | | | | | | | | | |
| d | | | | | | | | | | |
| dh | | | | | | | | | | |
| n | | | | | | | | | | |
| p | | | | | | | | | | |
| ph | | | | | | | | | | |

## TABLE 7 (c)
## DEVĀŚEṢA - ṬĀKARĪ ALPHABET
### ($14^{th}$-$16^{th}$ Centuries)

| | I | II | III | IV | V | VI | VII | VIII | IX | X |
|---|---|---|---|---|---|---|---|---|---|---|
| Characters in Roman | Guroli Copper-Plate Inscription of Vairasivarman | Mhesa Copper-Plate Inscription of Bhoṭavarman | Jungrar Copper-Plate Inscription of Bhoṭavarman | Saṅgrāmavarman's grant to Badhu Legha | Mindha Copper-Plate Inscription of Saṅgrāmavarman | Chamba Plate of Ānandavarman | Chamba Plate of Gaṇeshavarman | Ganguya grant of Gaṇeshavarman | Chamba Plate of Balabhadra | Kulu Copper-Plate Grant of Bahādur Singh |
| **bh** | | | | | | | | | | |
| **m** | | | | | | | | | | |
| **y** | | | | | | | | | | |
| **r** | | | | | | | | | | |
| **l** | | | | | | | | | | |
| **v** | | | | | | | | | | |
| **ś** | | | | | | | | | | |
| **ṣ** | | | | | | | | | | |
| **s** | | | | | | | | | | |
| **h** | | | | | | | | | | |
| **halanta** | | | | | | | | | | |
| | | | | | **MEDIAL VOWELS** | | | | | |
| **ā with k** | | | | | | | | | | |
| **ā** | jā ṇā | | jā ṭā | jā | jā ṭā ṇā | jā | | jā ṭā ṇā | ṇā jā | ṭā jā |
| **i** | | | | | | | | | | |
| **ī with k** | | | | | | | | | | |
| **u with k** | | | | | | | | | | |

## TABLE 7 (d)
## DEVĀŚEṢA - ṬĀKARĪ ALPHABET
### (14th-16th Centuries)

| | I | II | III | IV | V | VI | VII | VIII | IX | X |
|---|---|---|---|---|---|---|---|---|---|---|
| Characters in Roman | Guroli Copper-Plate Inscription of Vairasivarman | Mhesa Copper-Plate Inscription of Bhoṭavarman | Jungrar Copper-Plate Inscription of Bhoṭavarman | Saṅgrāmavarman's grant to Badhu Legha | Mindha Copper-Plate Inscription of Saṅgrāmavarman | Chamba Plate of Ānandavarman | Chamba Plate of Gaṇeshavarman | Ganguya grant of Gaṇeshavarman | Chamba Plate of Balabhadra | Kulu Copper-Plate Grant of Bahādur Singh |
| u with k | | | | pu | | | | | | |
| u with r | | | | | | | | | | |
| ū with k | | | | | | | | | | |
| ṛ | bhṛ | sṛ kṛ | kṛ vṛ | | kṛ tṛ tṛ | kṛ vṛ | pṛ | vṛ kṛ | kṛ stṛ | bhṛ |
| e with k | | | | | | | | | | |
| ai with k | | | | | | | | | | |
| o with k | | | | | | | | | | |
| au | | | | | | | | | | |
| sup. & sub. k | kṣ kt | kṣ rk | rk | | kṣ | kṣ | kṣ | kt kṣ | kṣ kt | kṣ kt |
| jñ. | | | | jñā | | | | jñā | | jñā |
| sup. r | rk ry rv | rv rgh rṇ ry | rjy ry | rm | rm rṇ rv | rm rṇ | rm rv rṇ | rm rṇ ry | rt rc rv | rt rd |
| sub. r | mr tr | pr śr | pr nmr | gr | kr tr | pr tr | tr | tr vr | kr gr dr | tr pr |
| rth sth | | | | | | | | | | |
| ṣṭ ṣṭh | | | | | | | | | | |
| sub. y | śy ly | py bhy | ṇy sy | dy py | sy gy | dy ry | ṇy jy | sy jy | sy śy hy | dhy sy |
| d dh | | | | | | | | | | |

## TABLE 8 (a)
## DEVĀŚEṢA - ṬĀKARĪ ALPHABET
## (17th - 18th Centuries)

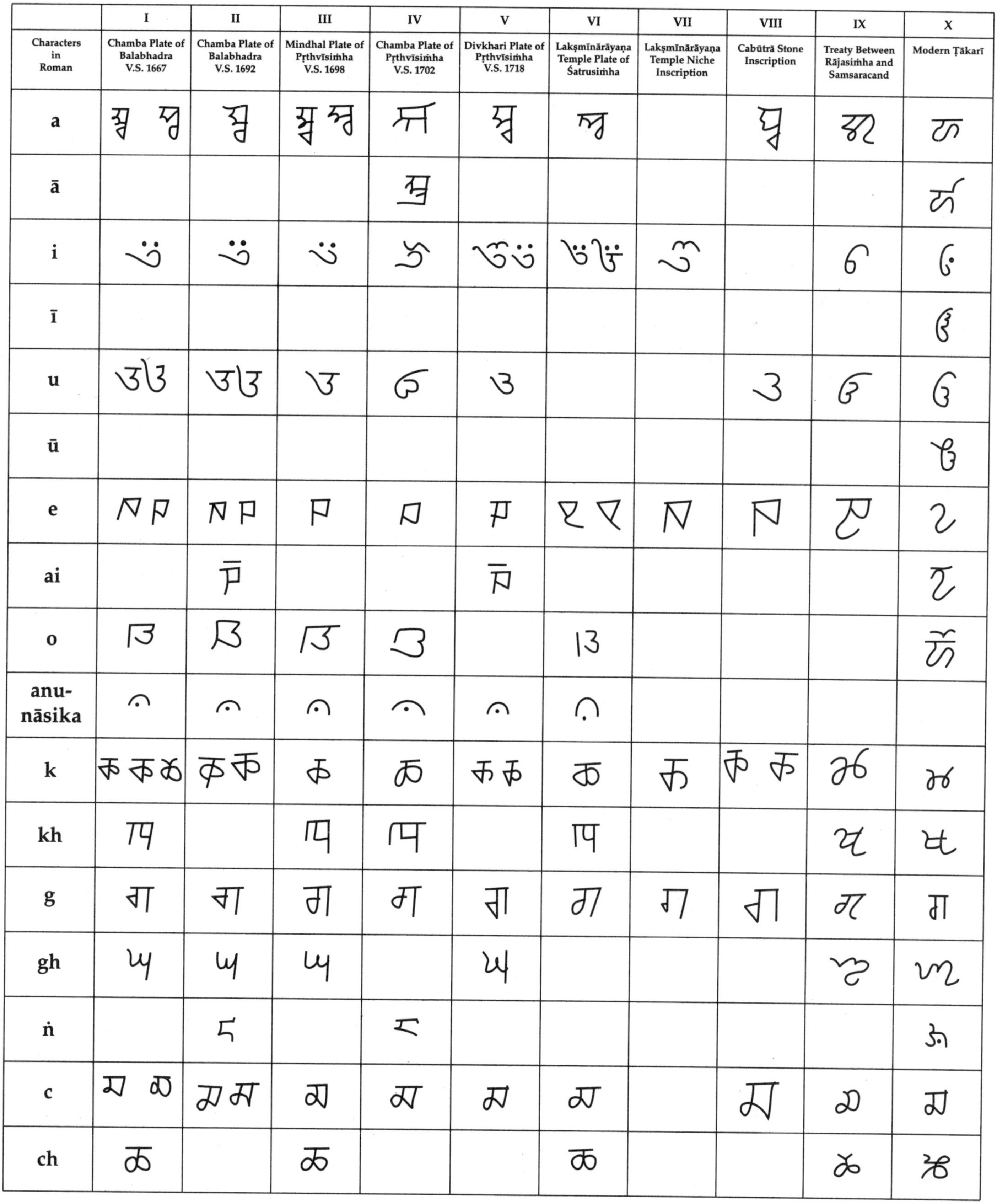

TABLE 8 (b)
DEVĀŚEṢA - ṬĀKARĪ ALPHABET
(17th - 18th Centuries)

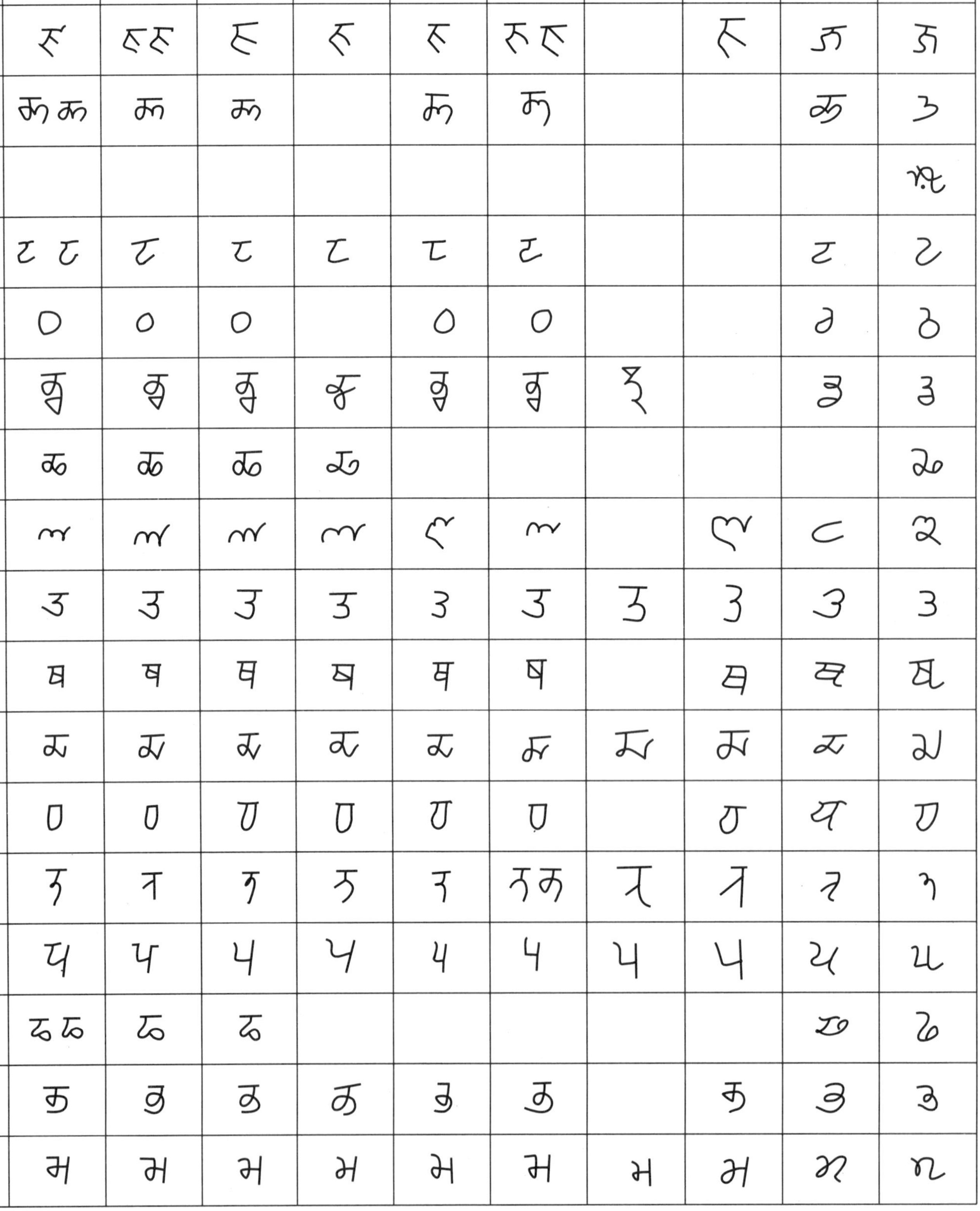

| | I | II | III | IV | V | VI | VII | VIII | IX | X |
|---|---|---|---|---|---|---|---|---|---|---|
| Characters in Roman | Chamba Plate of Balabhadra V.S. 1667 | Chamba Plate of Balabhadra V.S. 1692 | Mindhal Plate of Pṛthvīsiṁha V.S. 1698 | Chamba Plate of Pṛthvīsiṁha V.S. 1702 | Divkhari Plate of Pṛthvīsiṁha V.S. 1718 | Lakṣmīnārāyaṇa Temple Plate of Śatrusiṁha | Lakṣmīnārāyaṇa Temple Niche Inscription | Cabūtrā Stone Inscription | Treaty Between Rājasiṁha and Samsaracand | Modern Tākarī |
| j | | | | | | | | | | |
| jh | | | | | | | | | | |
| ñ | | | | | | | | | | |
| ṭ | | | | | | | | | | |
| ṭh | | | | | | | | | | |
| ḍ | | | | | | | | | | |
| ḍh | | | | | | | | | | |
| ṇ | | | | | | | | | | |
| t | | | | | | | | | | |
| th | | | | | | | | | | |
| d | | | | | | | | | | |
| dh | | | | | | | | | | |
| n | | | | | | | | | | |
| p | | | | | | | | | | |
| ph | | | | | | | | | | |
| bh | | | | | | | | | | |
| m | | | | | | | | | | |

## TABLE 8 (c)
## DEVĀŚEṢA - ṬĀKARĪ ALPHABET
### (17th - 18th Centuries)

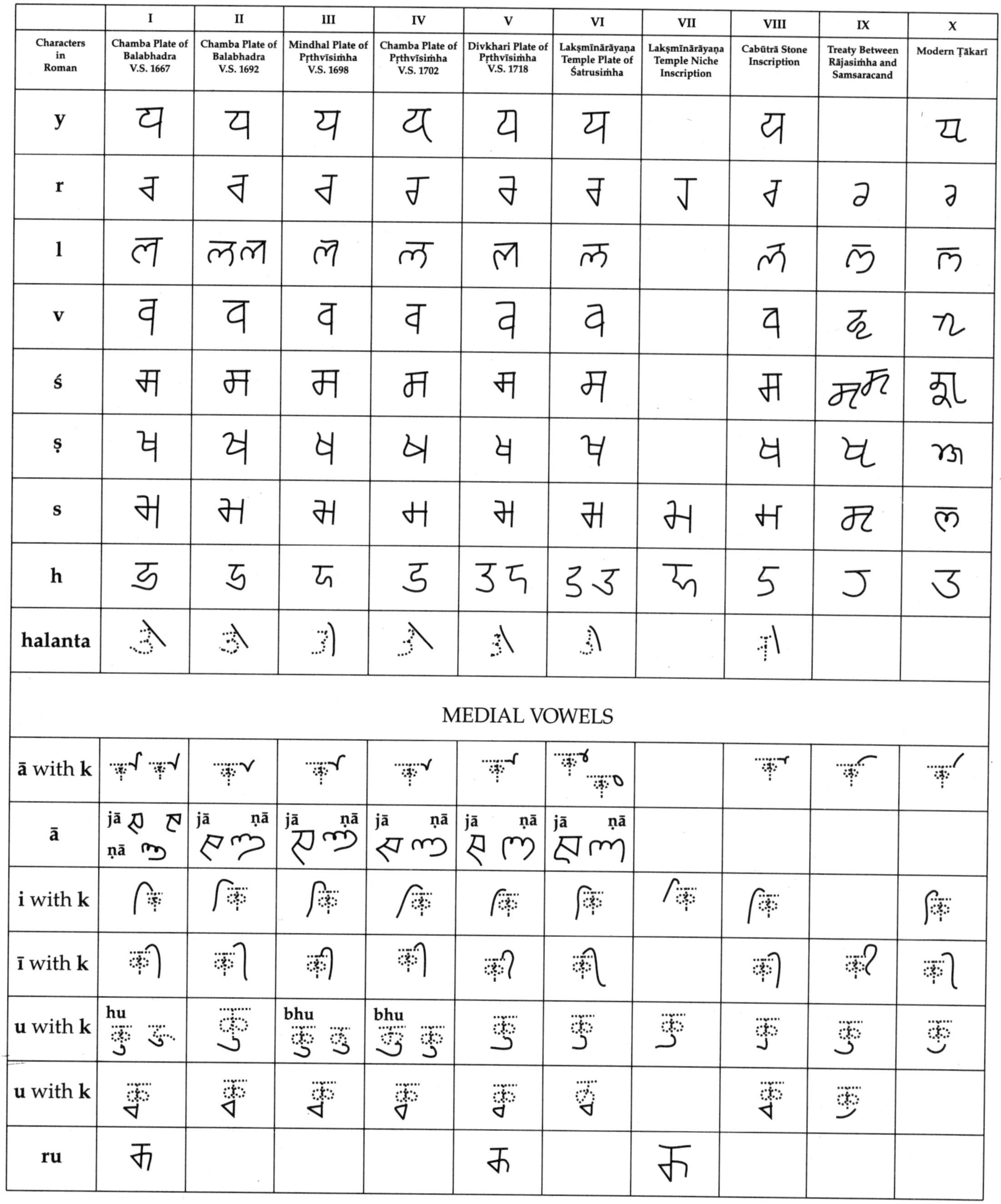

## TABLE 8 (d)
## DEVĀŚEṢA - ṬĀKARĪ ALPHABET
### (17th - 18th Centuries)

| | I | II | III | IV | V | VI | VII | VIII | IX | X |
|---|---|---|---|---|---|---|---|---|---|---|
| Characters in Roman | Chamba Plate of Balabhadra V.S. 1667 | Chamba Plate of Balabhadra V.S. 1692 | Mindhal Plate of Pṛthvīsiṁha V.S. 1698 | Chamba Plate of Pṛthvīsiṁha V.S. 1702 | Divkhari Plate of Pṛthvīsiṁha V.S. 1718 | Lakṣmīnārāyaṇa Temple Plate of Śatrusiṁha | Lakṣmīnārāyaṇa Temple Niche Inscription | Cabūtrā Stone Inscription | Treaty Between Rājasiṁha and Samsaracand | Modern Ṭākarī |
| **ū with k** | | | | | | | | | | |
| **ū with k** | | | | | | | | | | |
| **ṛ** | kṛ smṛ | kṛ | nṛ | nṛ | vṛ | bhṛ | | tṛ | | |
| **e with k** | | | | | | | | | | |
| **ai with k** | | | | | | | | | | |
| **o with k** | | | | | | | | | | |
| **au with k** | | | | | | | | | | |

### LIGATURES

| | I | II | III | IV | V | VI | VII | VIII | IX | X |
|---|---|---|---|---|---|---|---|---|---|---|
| **sup. k** | kl kṣ | kt kṣ kl | kṣ kv | kl kṣ | kv | kṣ | | | | |
| **sub. k** | | ṣk | ṣk | | | ṣk | | | | |
| **sup. r** | rt rm rṇ rc ry rv | rm rṇ rv ry rg | rm rṇ ry | rk rl | rk rg | rg | | rv | | |
| **sub. r** | vr dr | grā pr | vr gr | kr gr | śr | bhr śr | | tr | tr | |
| **rth sth** | | | | | | | | | | |
| **ṣth ṣth** | | | | | | | | | | |
| **sub. y** | dhy sy | ḍyo | khy | my | my ṣy | my | | śy | ky | |
| **Misc.** | | | kṣm smy | hm | str hl | thl cch | hn | str | | |

## TABLE 9
## NUMERALS OF THE ṬĀKARĪ ALPHABET

# APPENDIX

## DEVĀŚEṢA

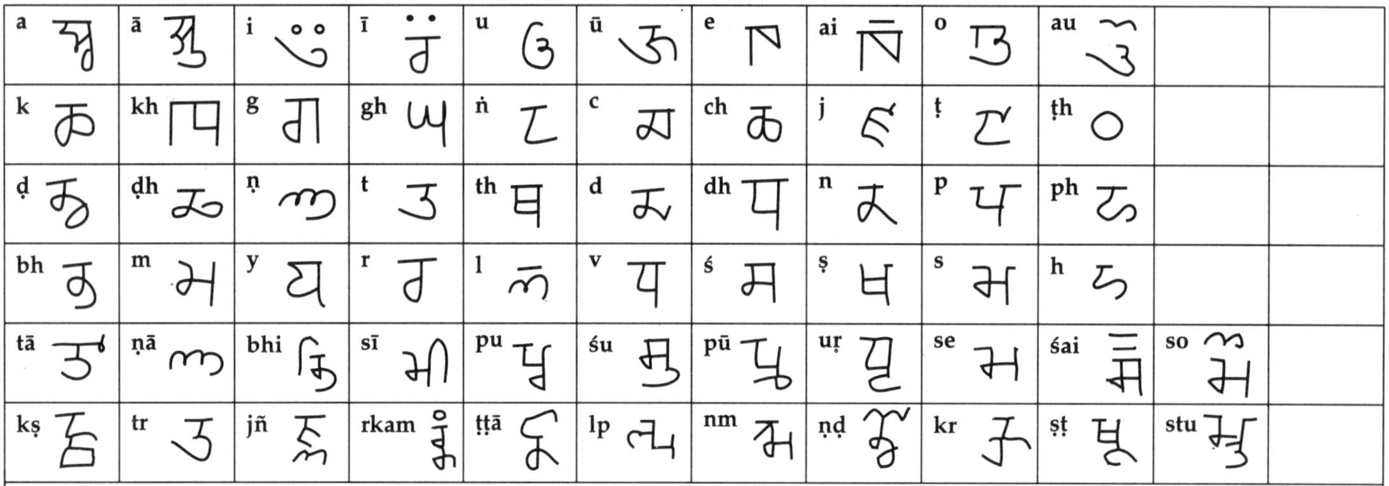


## ṬĀKARĪ

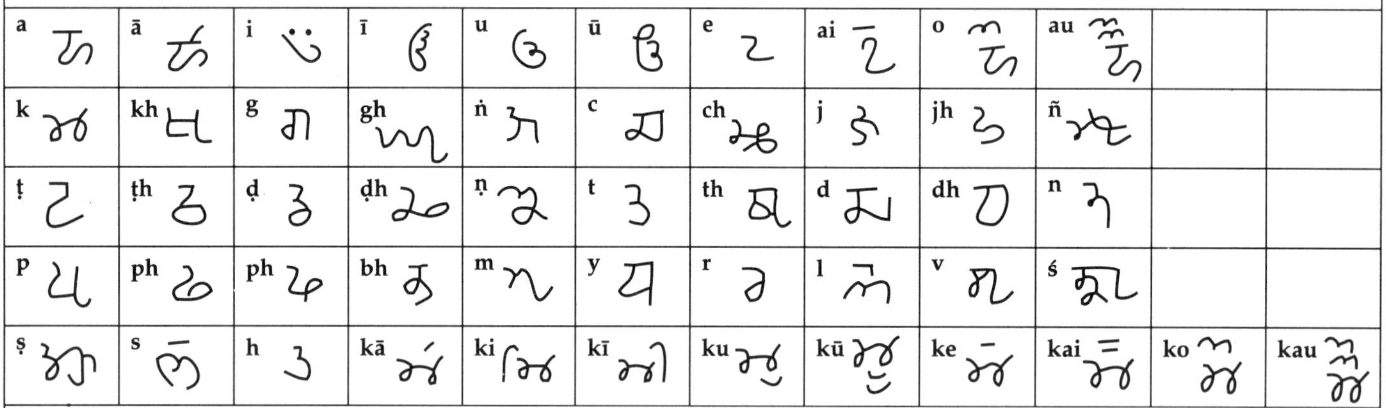


## GURUMUKHĪ

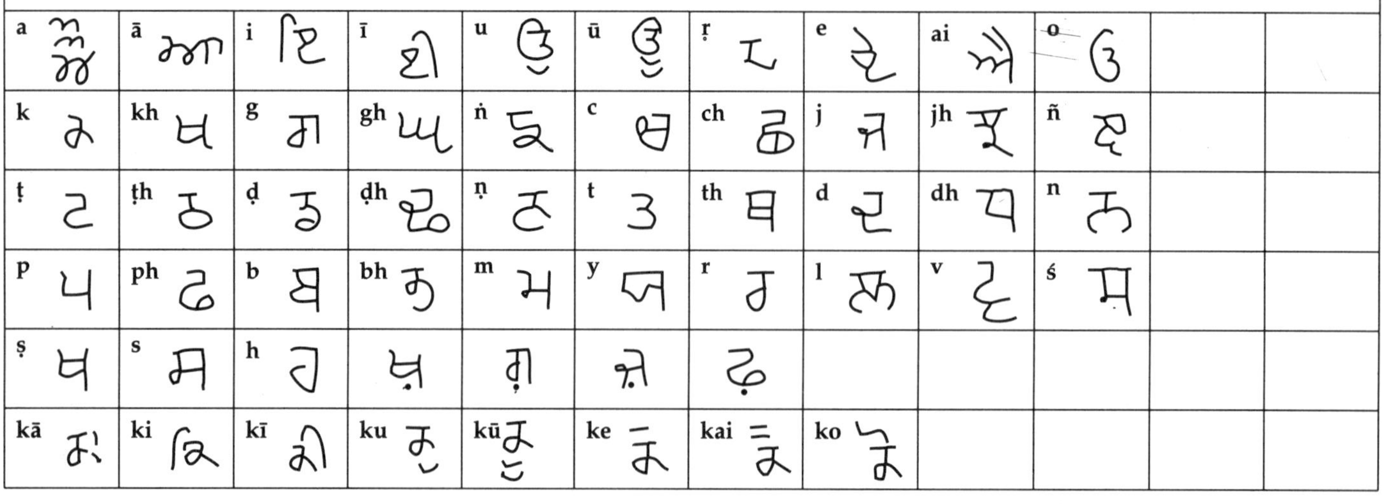

# MODERN ALPHABETS OF NORTH-WESTERN INDIA

| I | II | III | IV | V | VI | VII | VIII |
|---|---|---|---|---|---|---|---|
| DEVANĀGARĪ (National) | ŚĀRADĀ (Kashmir) | GURUMUKHĪ (Punjab) | ṬĀKARĪ (Himachal Pradesh) | DEVANĀGARĪ (National) | ŚĀRADĀ (Kashmir) | GURUMUKHĪ (Punjab) | ṬĀKARĪ (Himachal Pradesh) |
| अ | 𑆃 𑆃 | ਅ | 𑚀 | ञ | 𑆚 | ਞ | 𑚓 𑚓 |
| आ | 𑆄 | ਆ | 𑚁 | ट | 𑆛 | ਟ | 𑚔 |
| इ | 𑆅 | ਇ | 𑚂 | ठ | 𑆜 | ਠ | 𑚕 |
| ई | 𑆆 | ਈ | 𑚃 | ड | 𑆝 | ਡ | 𑚖 |
| उ | 𑆇 | ਉ | 𑚄 | ढ | 𑆞 | ਢ | 𑚗 |
| ऊ | 𑆈 | ਊ | 𑚅 | ण | 𑆟 | ਣ | 𑚘 |
| ए | 𑆍 | ਏ | 𑚆 | त | 𑆠 | ਤ | 𑚙 |
| ऐ | 𑆎 | ਐ | 𑚇 | थ | 𑆡 | ਥ | 𑚚 |
| ओ | 𑆏 | ਓ | 𑚈 | द | 𑆢 | ਦ | 𑚛 |
| क | 𑆑 | ਕ | 𑚊 | ध | 𑆣 | ਧ | 𑚜 |
| ख | 𑆒 | ਖ | 𑚋 | न | 𑆤 | ਨ | 𑚝 |
| ग | 𑆓 | ਗ | 𑚌 | प | 𑆥 | ਪ | 𑚞 |
| घ | 𑆔 | ਘ | 𑚍 | फ | 𑆦 | ਫ | 𑚟 |
| ङ | 𑆕 | ਙ | 𑚎 | ब | 𑆧 | ਬ | 𑚠 |
| च | 𑆖 | ਚ | 𑚏 | भ | 𑆨 | ਭ | 𑚡 |
| छ | 𑆗 | ਛ | 𑚐 | म | 𑆩 | ਮ | 𑚢 |
| ज | 𑆘 | ਜ | 𑚑 | य | 𑆪 | ਯ | 𑚣 |
| झ | 𑆙 | ਝ | 𑚒 | र | 𑆫 | ਰ | 𑚤 |

## MODERN ALPHABETS OF NORTH-WESTERN INDIA

| I | II | III | IV |
|---|---|---|---|
| DEVANĀGARĪ (National) | ŚĀRADĀ (Kashmir) | GURUMUKHĪ (Punjab) | ṬĀKARĪ (Himachal Pradesh) |
| ल | 𑆬 | ਲ | 𑚥 |
| व | 𑆮 | ਵ | 𑚦 |
| श | 𑆯 | ਸ਼ | 𑚧 |
| ष | 𑆰 | ਖ | 𑚋 |
| स | 𑆱 | ਸ | 𑚨 |
| ह | 𑆲 | ਹ | 𑚩 |
| का | 𑆑𑆳 | ਕਾ | 𑚊𑚭 |
| कि | 𑆑𑆴 | ਕਿ | 𑚊𑚮 |
| की | 𑆑𑆵 | ਕੀ | 𑚊𑚯 |
| कु | 𑆑𑆶 𑆑𑆶 | ਕੁ | 𑚊𑚰 |
| कू | 𑆑𑆷 𑆑𑆷 | ਕੂ | 𑚊𑚱 |
| के | 𑆑𑆼 | ਕੇ ਕੇ | 𑚊𑚲 |
| कै | 𑆑𑆽 | ਕੈ | 𑚊𑚳 |
| को | 𑆑𑆾 | ਕੋ | 𑚊𑚴 |
| कौ | 𑆑𑆿 |  | 𑚊𑚵 |

# Plates

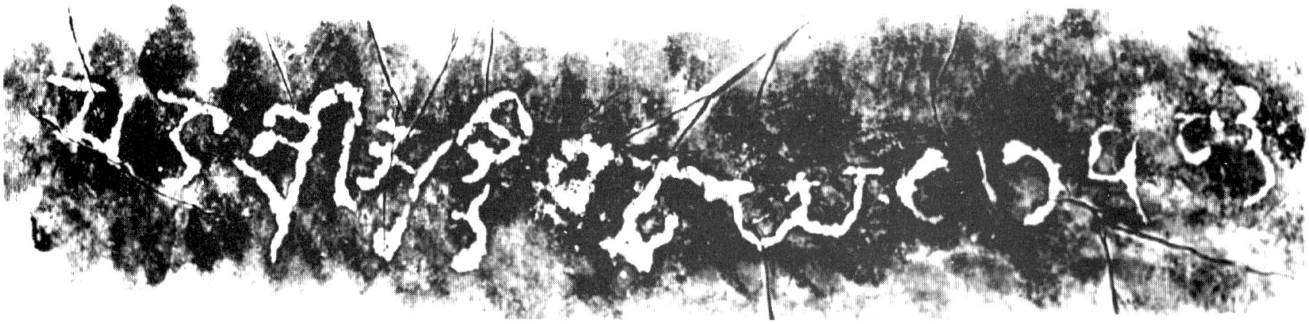

*Pl. 1*: Avantipur, Kashmir, storage vessel (*ghaṭa*) inscription, 9th Century.

*Pl. 2*: Stūpa and later inscription of Sura royal family (Proto-Nāgarī type of developed writing).

*Pl. 3*: Stūpa and later inscription of Śūra royal family.

*Pl. 4*: Sarahan Praśasti, 9th Century CE.

*Pl. 5*: Dewai inscription of Shāhī King Bhīmadeva, 9th-10th Century.

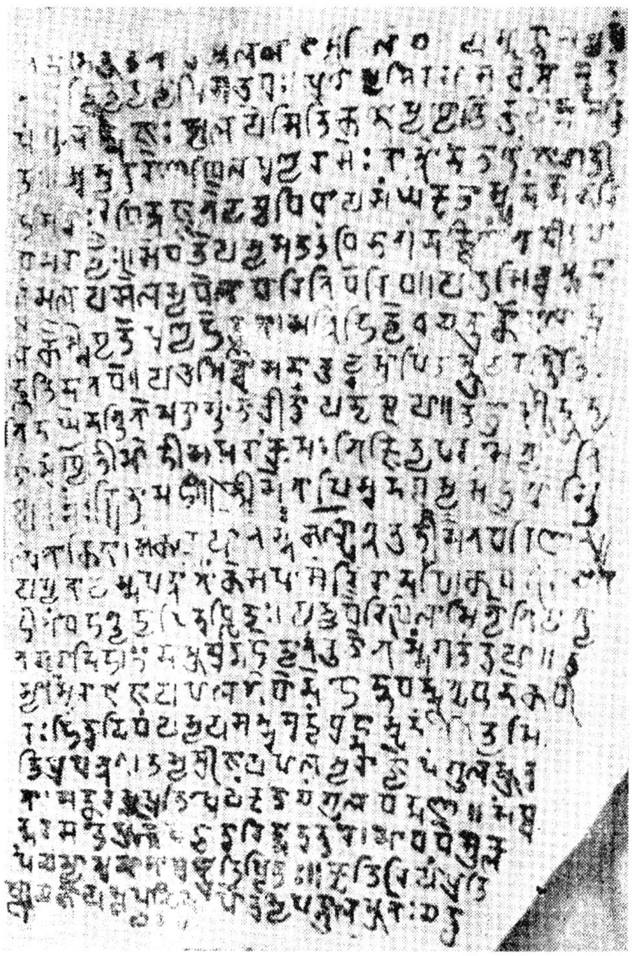

*Pl. 6*: Barikot inscription of Shāhī King Jayapāla, 9th-10th Century.

*Pl. 7*: The S.P.S. Museum, Srinagar, bronze image inscription of the reign of queen Diddā (*Laukika* '65) CE 1089.

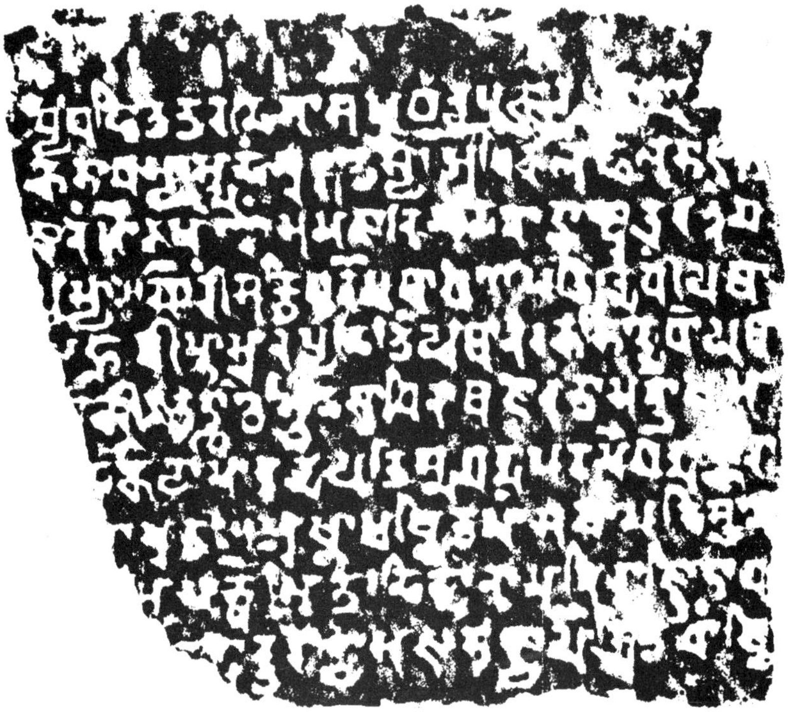

*Pl. 8*: Srinagar inscriptions of queen Diddā (*Laukika* '68) CE 1092.

*Pl. 9*: Brahmor, copper plate grant of Yugākaravarman, 10th Century.

Suṅgal Copper-plate Grant

SCALE 0·50

*Pl. 10*: Sungal copper plate grant of Vidagdhadeva, 10th Century.

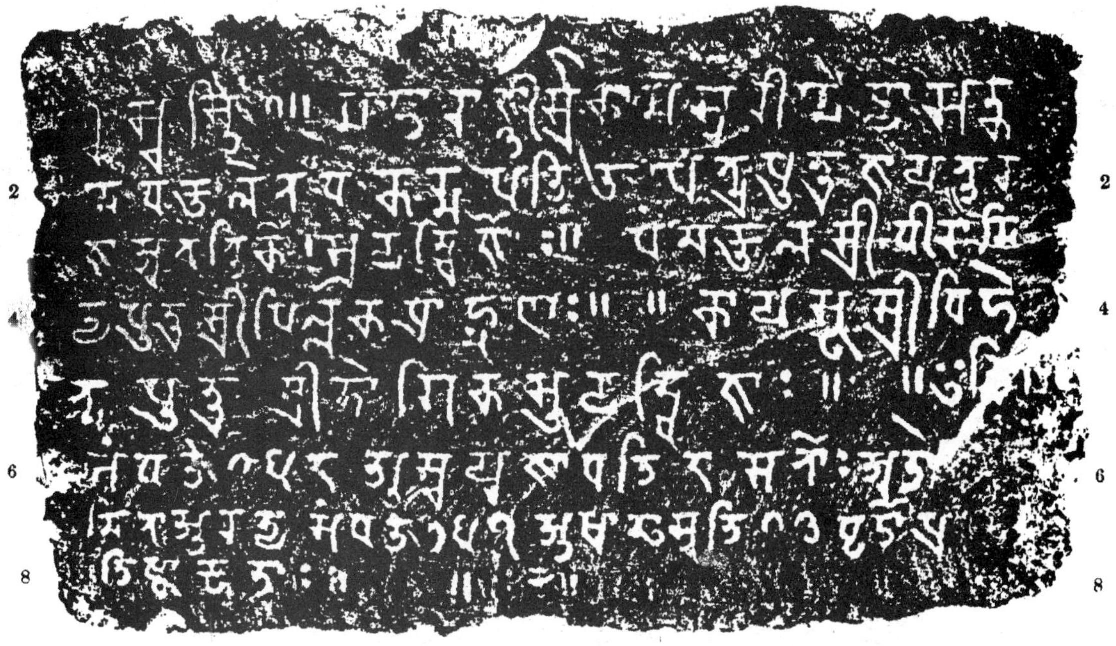

N. P. CHAKRAVARTI.
Reg. No. 3370 E'34-445.

SCALE: ONE-HALF.

SURVEY OF INDIA, CALCUTTA.

*Pl. 11*: A Śāradā inscription from Hund, Pakistan, 11th Century.

*Pl. 12*: Ḍaḍvār fountain inscription, 11th Century.

SCALE 0·20

*Pl. 13*: Bhakhūnd inscription, 11th Century.

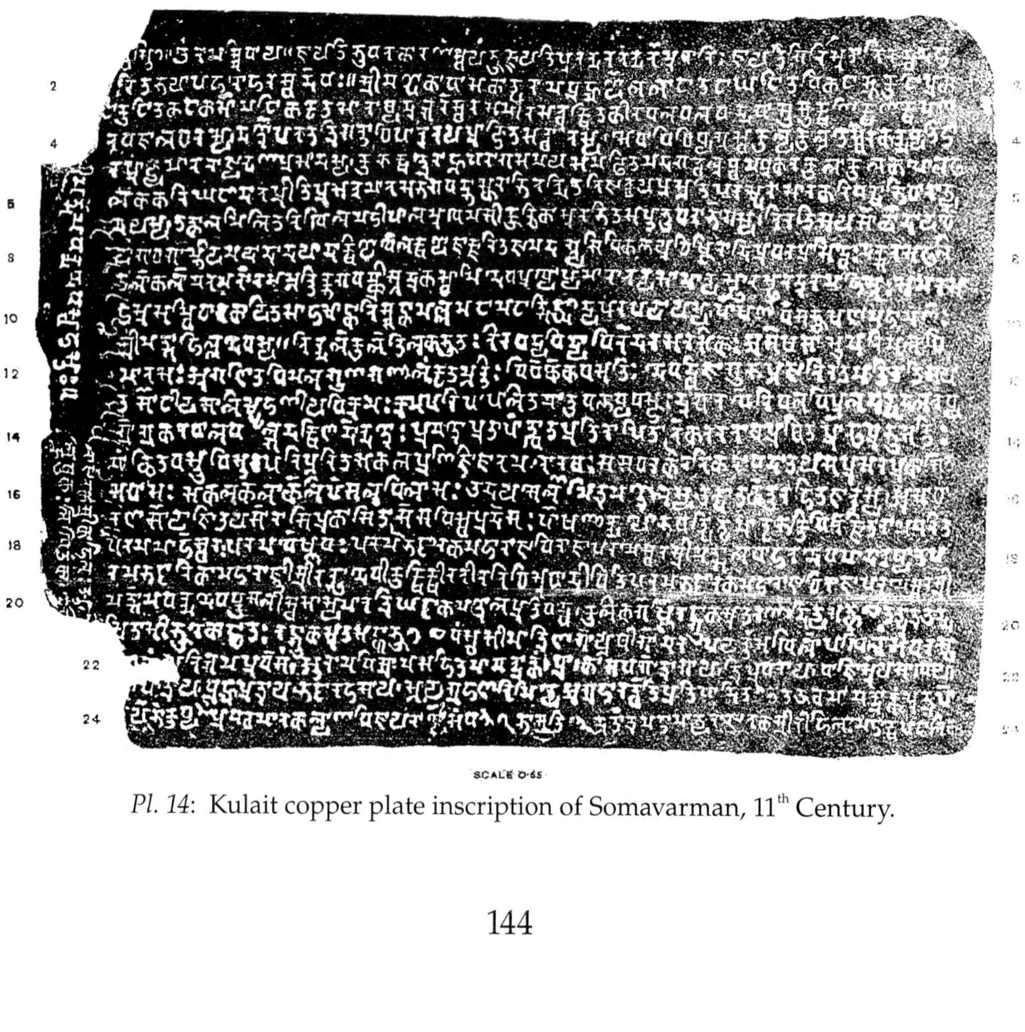

SCALE 0·65

*Pl. 14*: Kulait copper plate inscription of Somavarman, 11th Century.

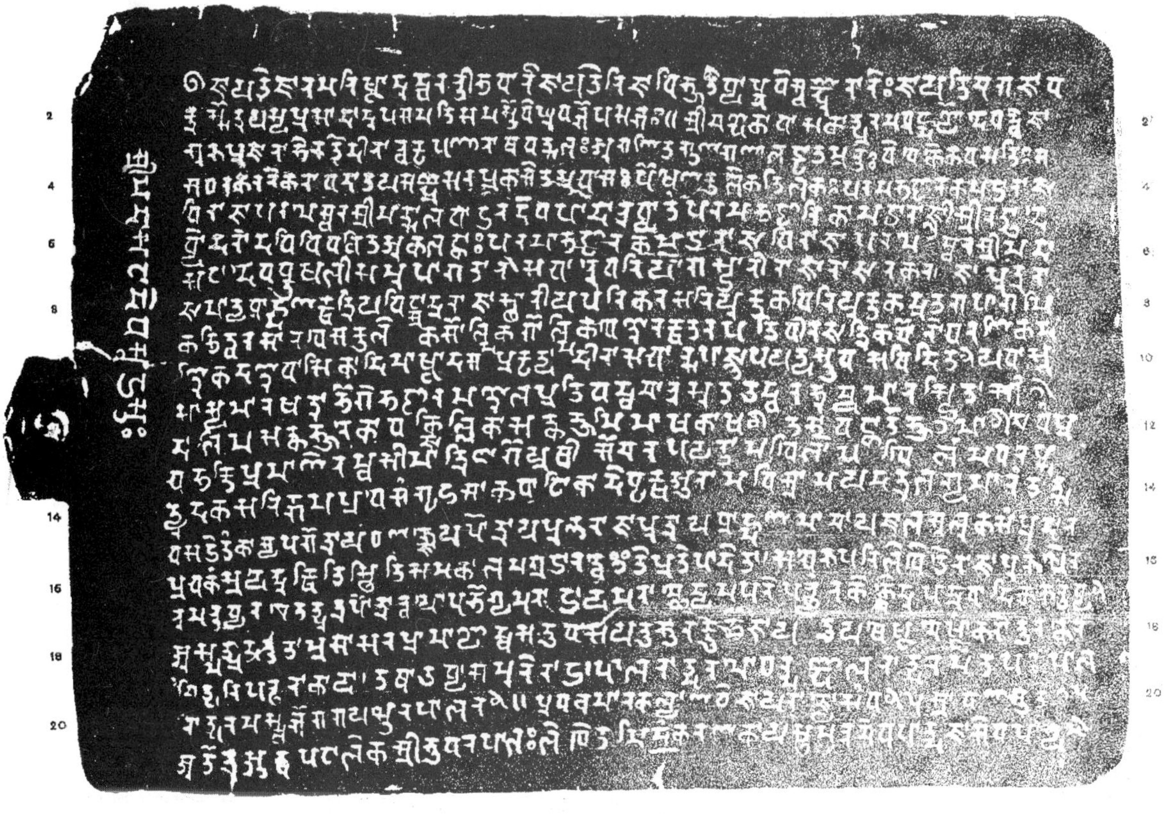

*Pl. 15*: Thunḍhu copper plate inscription of Āsaṭavarman, Chamba, H.P., 11th Century.

*Pl. 16*: The S. P. S. Museum, Srinagar, stone slab inscription of the reign of Jayasimha (*Laukika* '25) CE 1149.

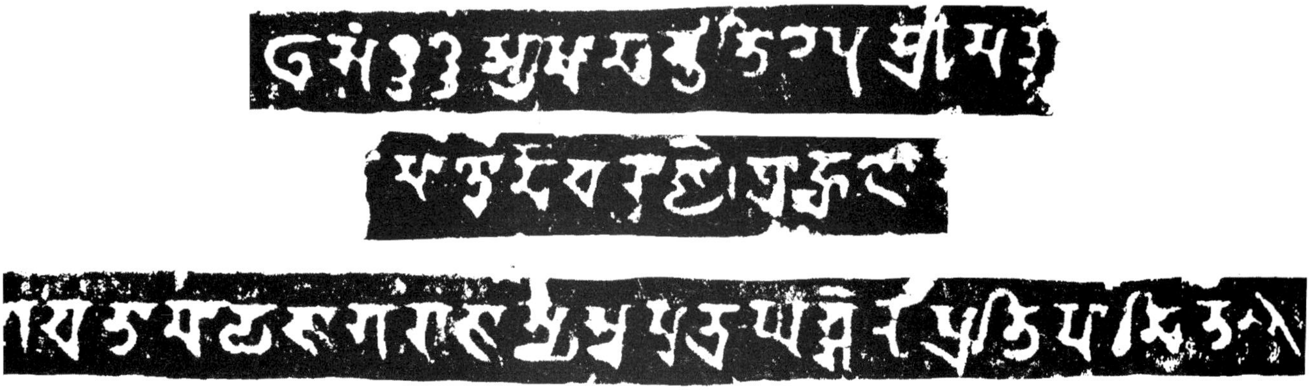

*Pl. 17*: Tapar, Kashmir, stone lintel inscription of Parmāṇḍadeva, 12th Century.

*Pl. 18*: Devi-ri-kothi, Chamba, H.P., fountain inscription of Rājānaka Nāgapāla and Nānapāla, 12th Century.

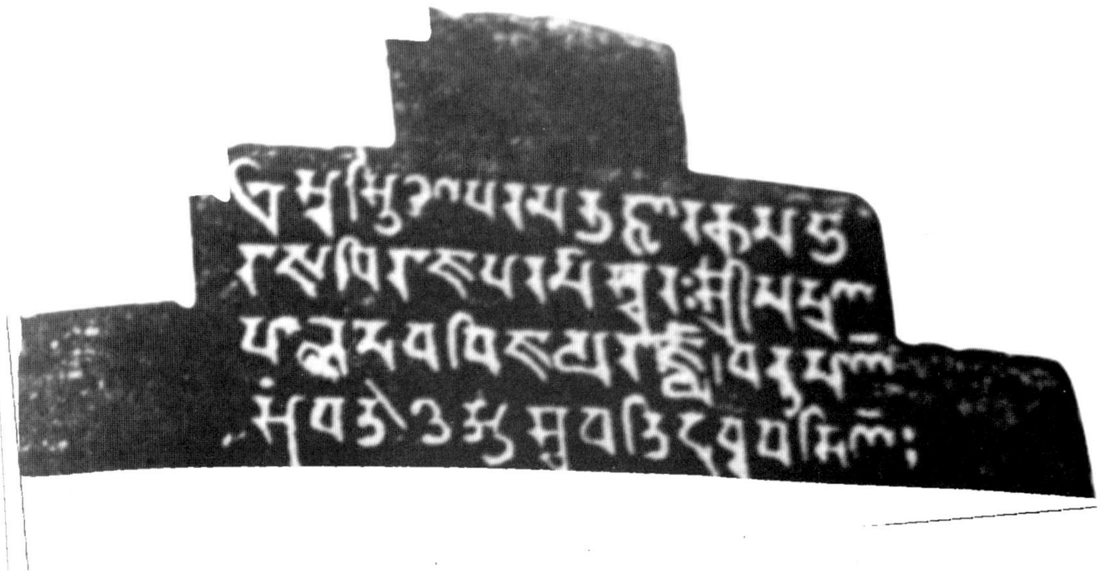

*Pl. 19*: Devi-rī-kothi, Chamba, H.P., fountain inscription of Sri Raṇapāladeva, 12th Century.

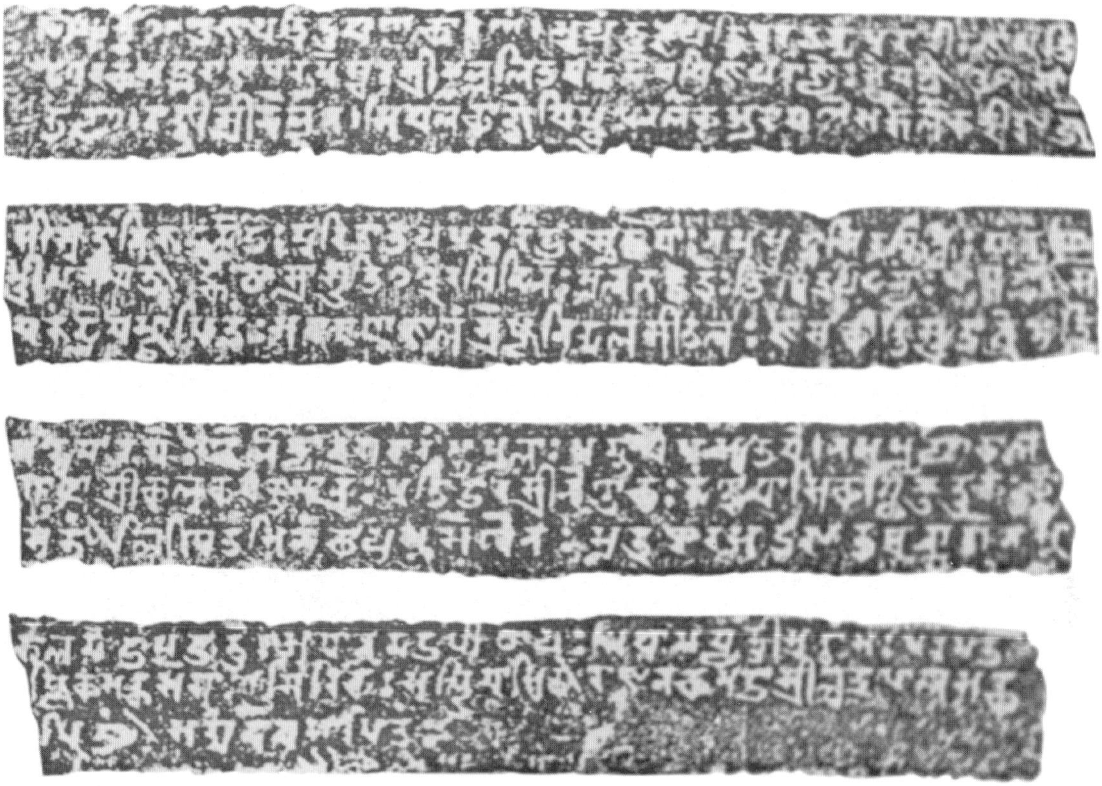

*Pl. 20*: Salhi, Chamba, H.P., fountain inscription of Rājānaka Ludrapāla, 12th Century.

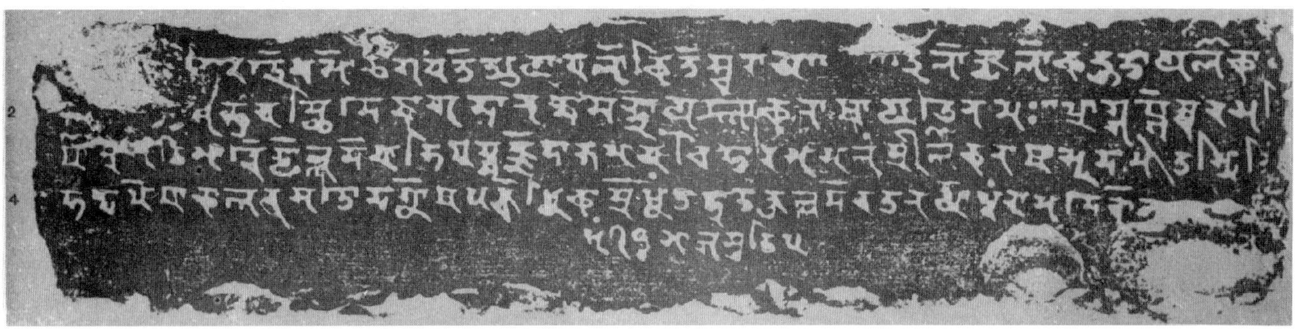

*Pl. 21*: Arigom, Kashmir, stone slab inscription (*Laukika* '73) CE 1197.

*Pl. 22*: Baijnāth, Kangra, H.P., Śiva Temple inscriptions, *Praśasti*, 1204 CE.

*Pl. 23*: Bijbehara (Vejebror), Kashmir, stone inscription of the reign of Rājadeva (*Śaka* 58 ?), CE 1235-36 (?).

*Pl. 24*: Bijbehara, Kashmir, stone inscription of the reign of Yaskaradeva, 13th Century.

*Pl. 25*: Kotiher, Kashmir, stone slab inscription of the reign of Shāhabadena (Shihabuddin) dated CE 1369 (*Laukika* '44 or 45).

*Pl. 26*: The Bhuvaneshvarī, Khonamuh, Kashmir, stone inscription of the reign of Jayanolabadena (Zain-ul-ābidin) dated *Kali* 4530 (CE 1428).

*Pl. 27*: Peshawar, NWFP Pakistan, Musuem inscription of Vaṇhaḍaka (*Laukika saṁ* (4) 538), CE 1462.

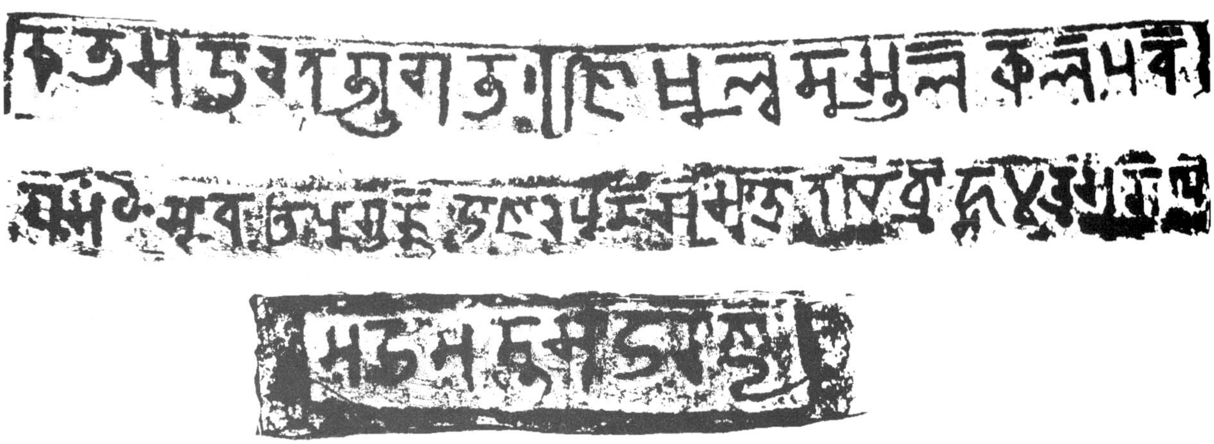

*Pl. 28*: Hariparbat, Srinagar, Kashmir, grave stone inscription of the reign of Mohammad Shāh (*Laukika saṁ* (45) 60), CE 1484.

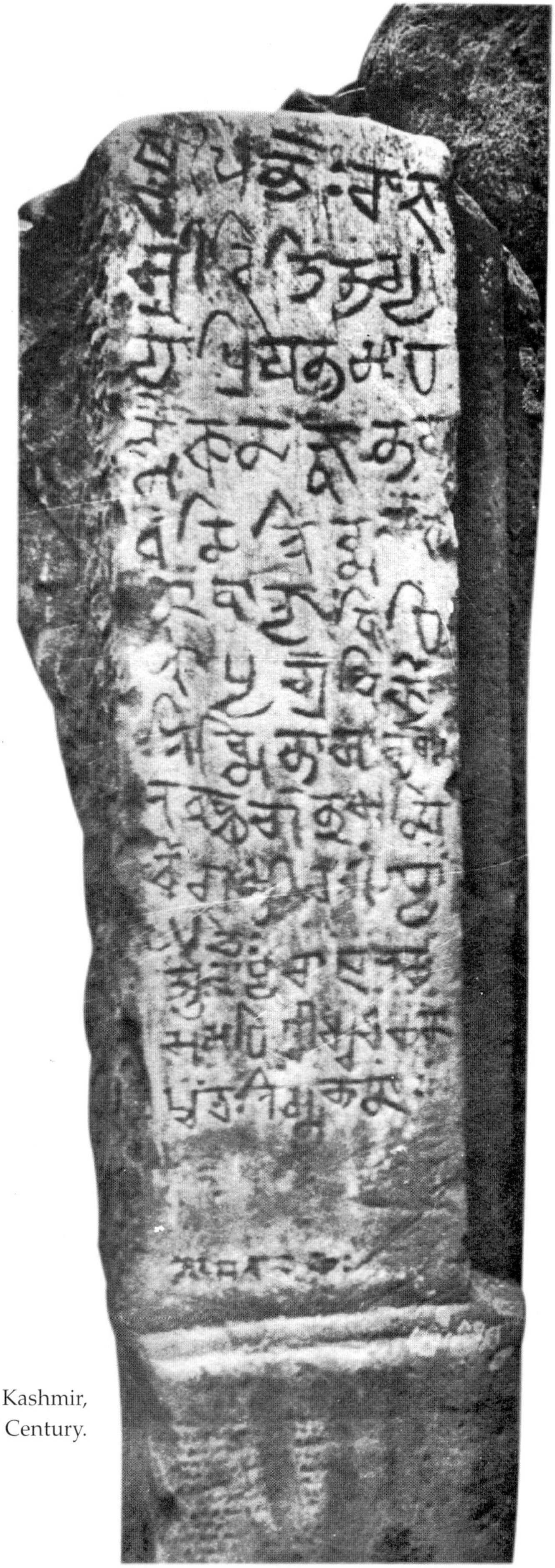

*Pl. 29*: Wularhama Bijbehara, Kashmir, bathroom gate inscription, 15th-16th Century.

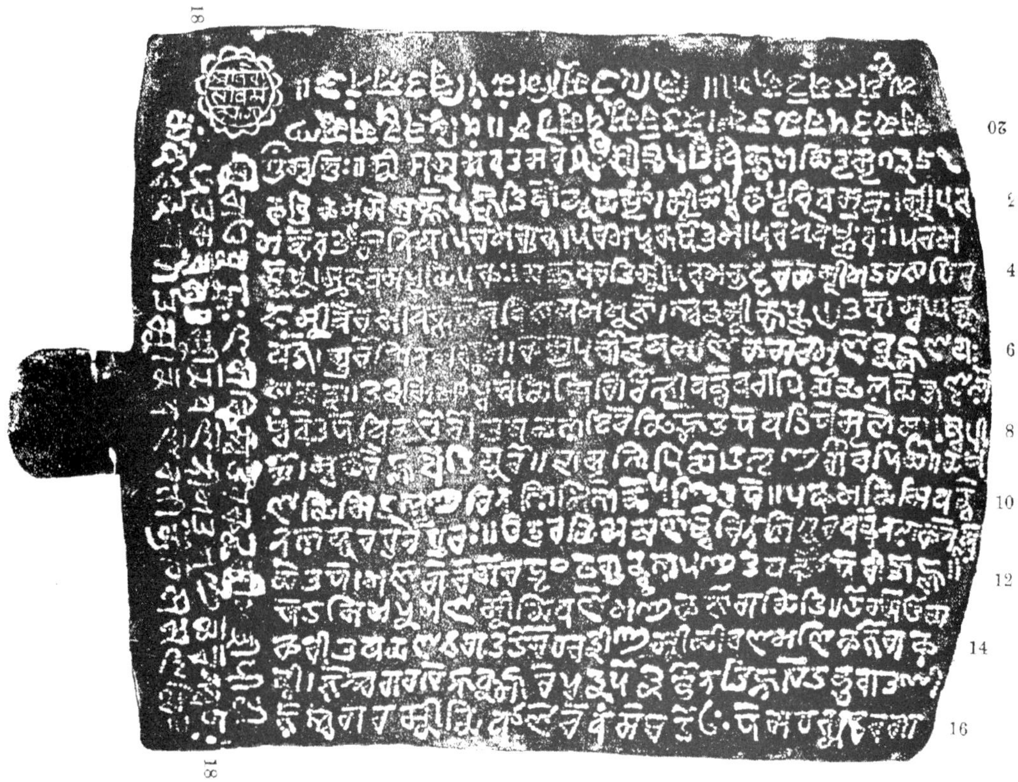

*Pl. 30*: Guroli plate of Vairaśivarman, *vs* 1387.

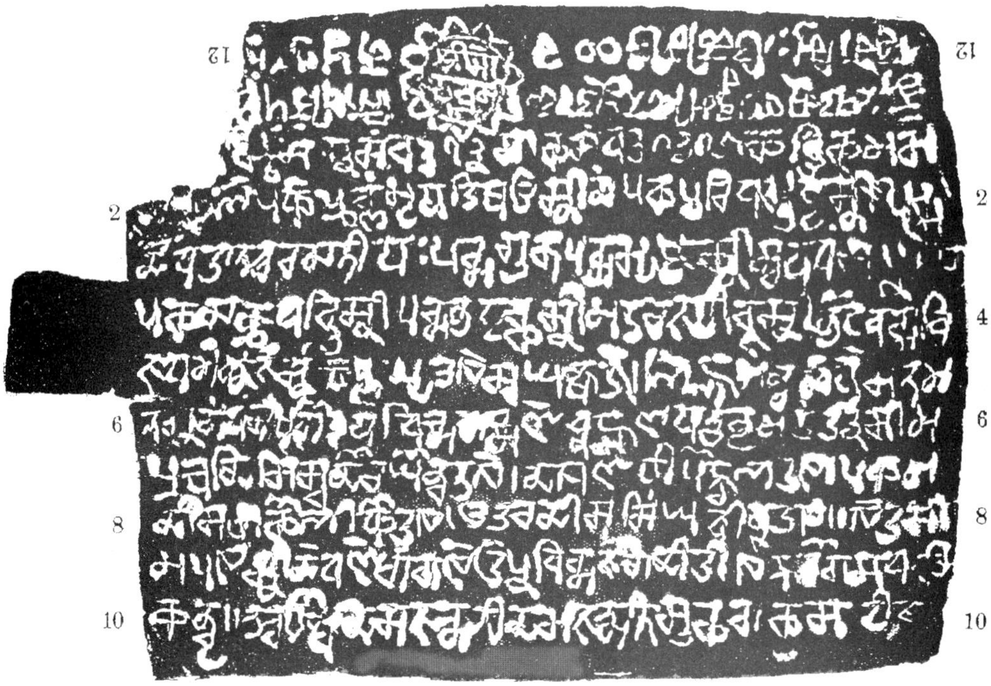

B. CH. CHHABRA. SCALE: THREE-FOURTHS. SURVEY OF INDIA, CALCUTTA.
REG. No. 3977 E'36-500'53.

*Pl. 31*: Mhesa plate of Bhoṭavarman, *Śaka* 1318.

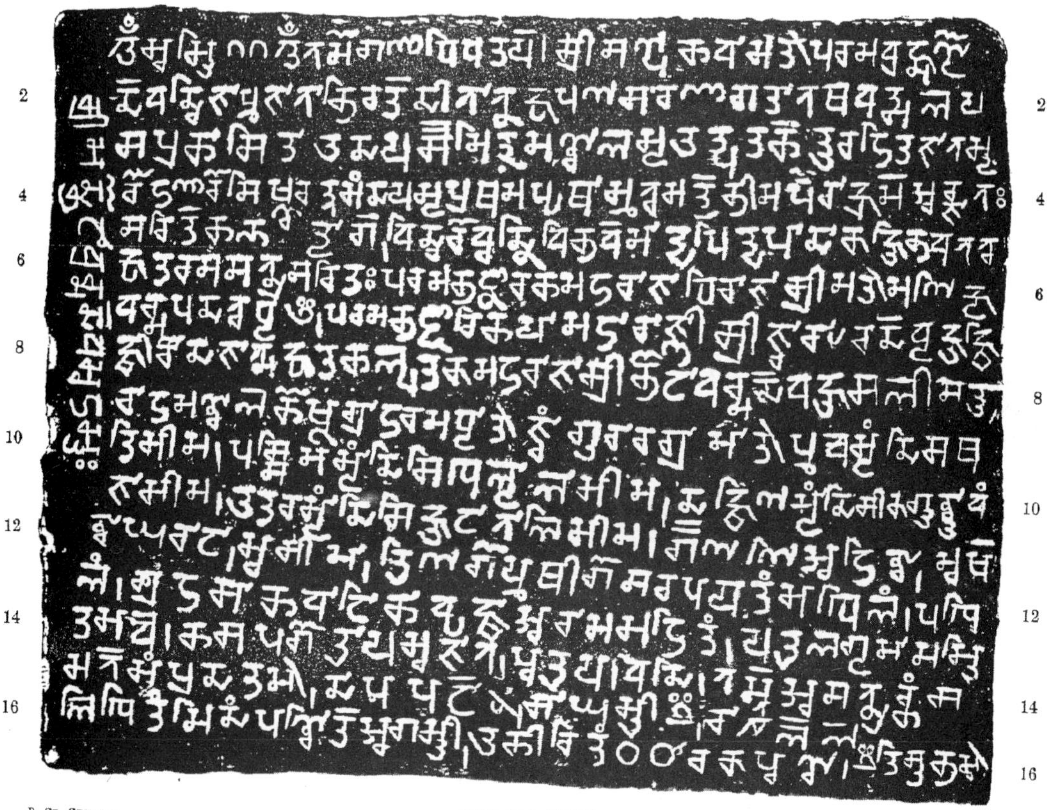


*Pl. 32*: Jungrar plate of Bhoṭavarman.

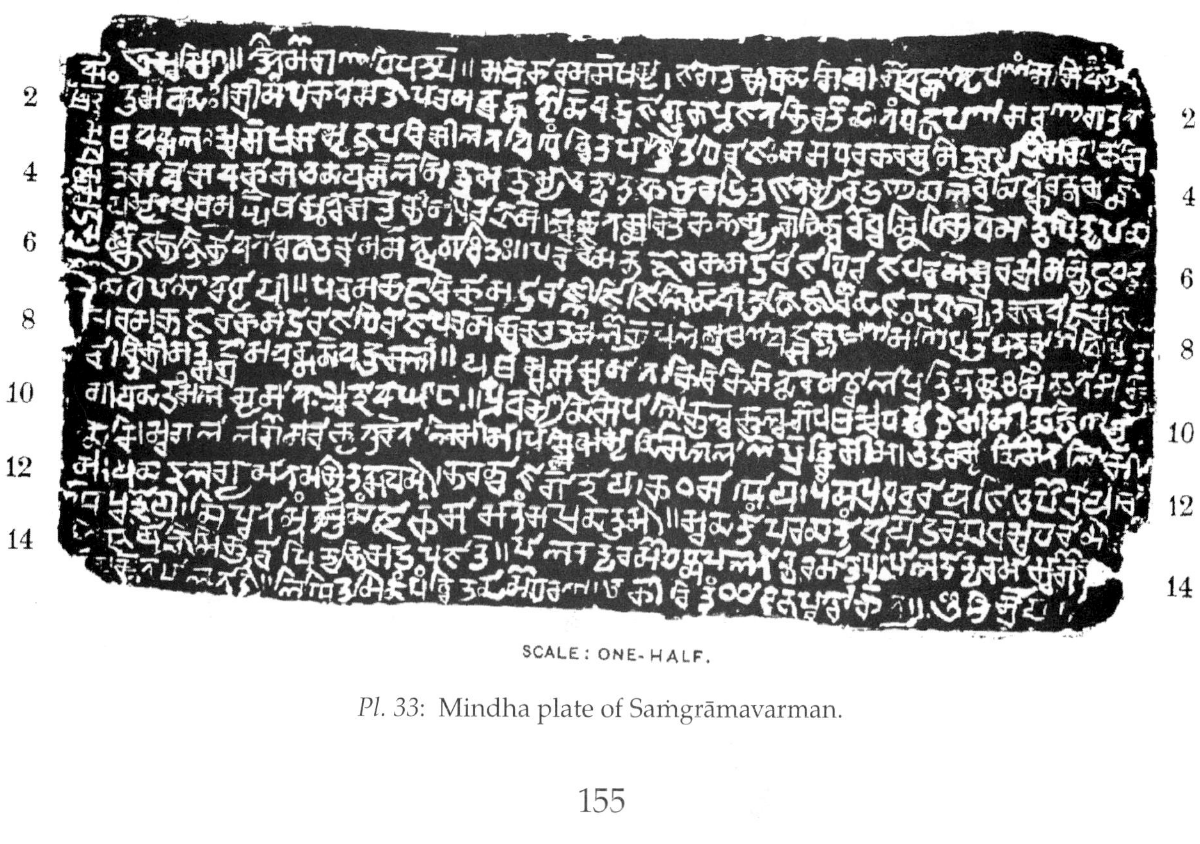


*Pl. 33*: Mindha plate of Saṁgrāmavarman.

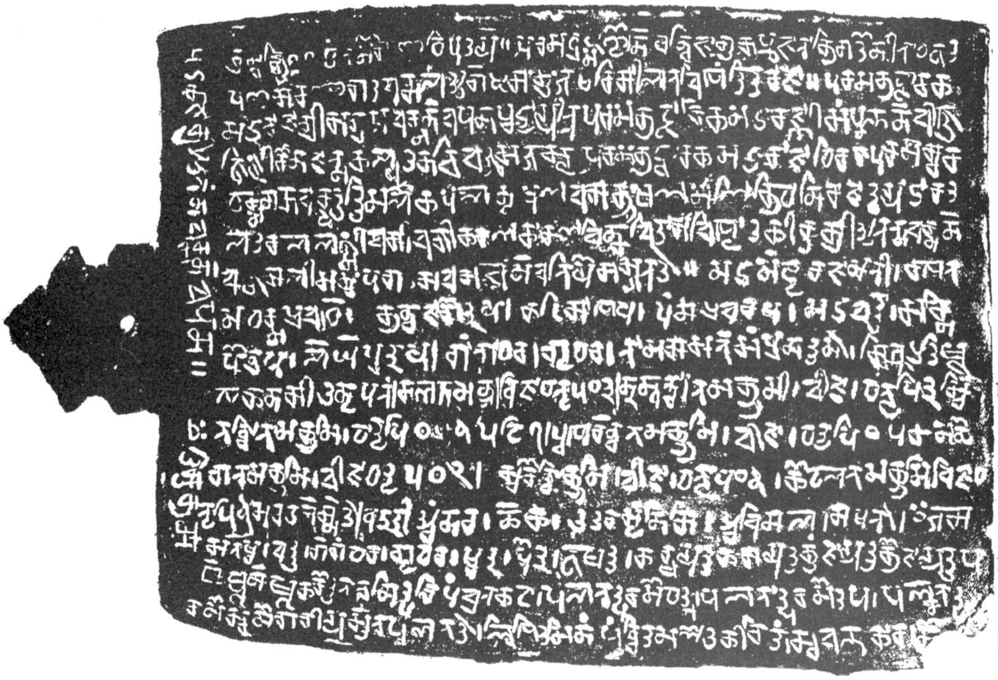

SCALE: THREE-FOURTHS.

*Pl. 34*: Chamba plate of Ānandavarman.

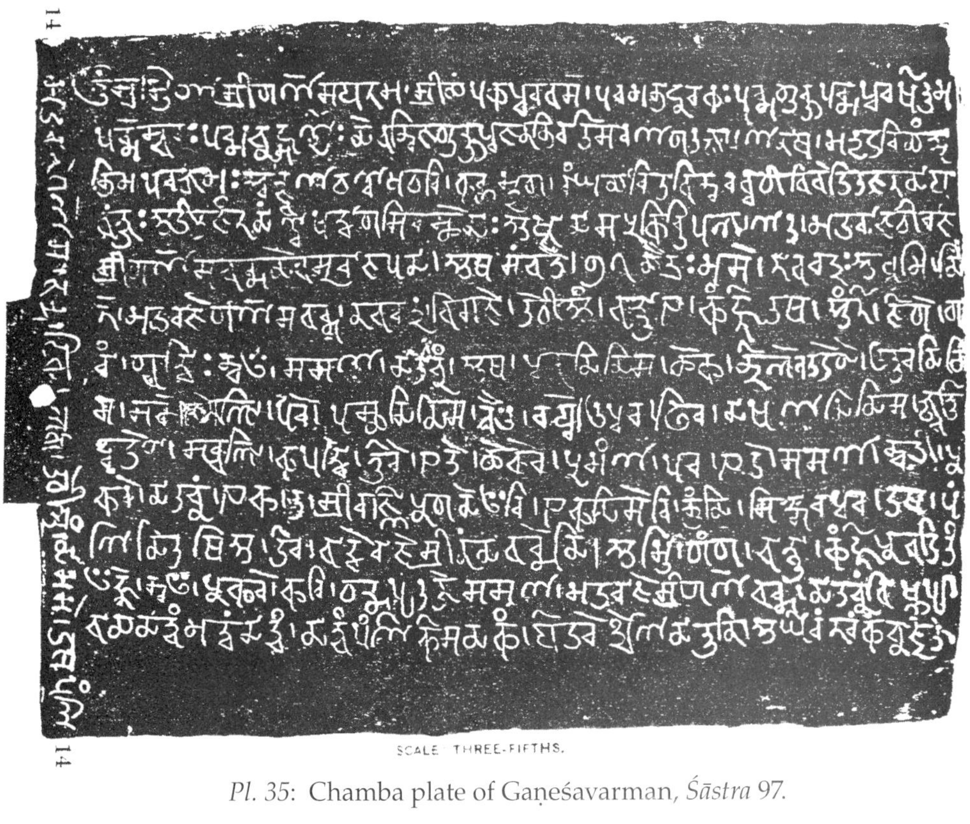

SCALE: THREE-FIFTHS.

*Pl. 35*: Chamba plate of Gaṇeśavarman, *Śāstra* 97.

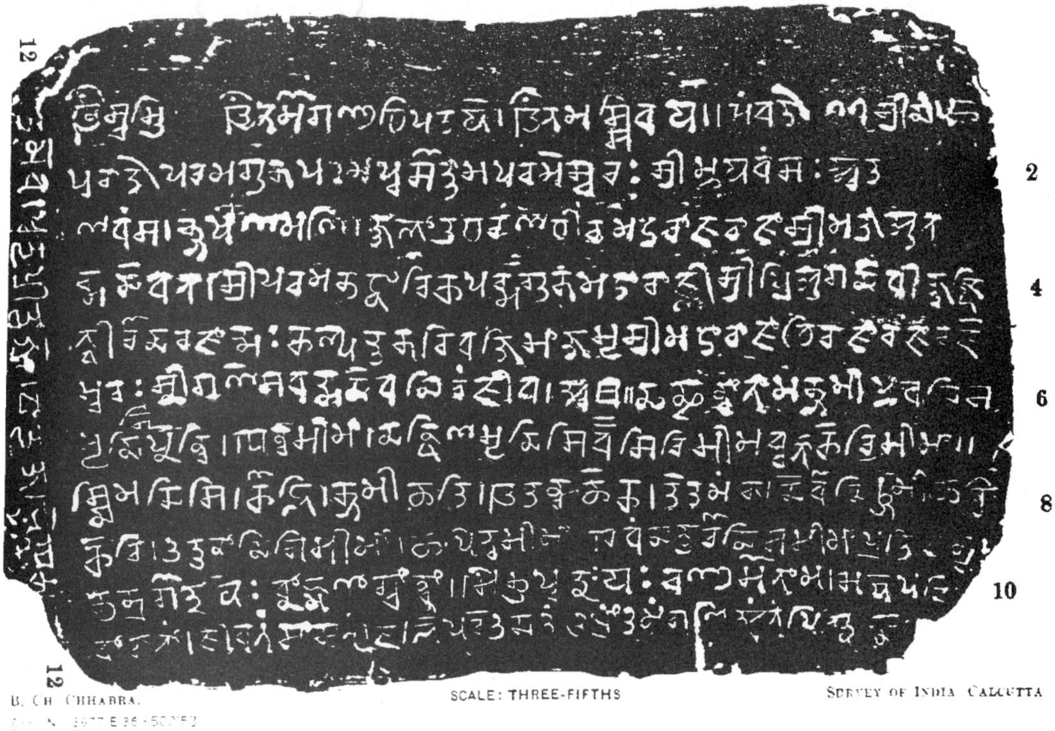


*Pl. 36*: Dhadhyada plate of Gaṇeśavarman, *Śāstra* 17.

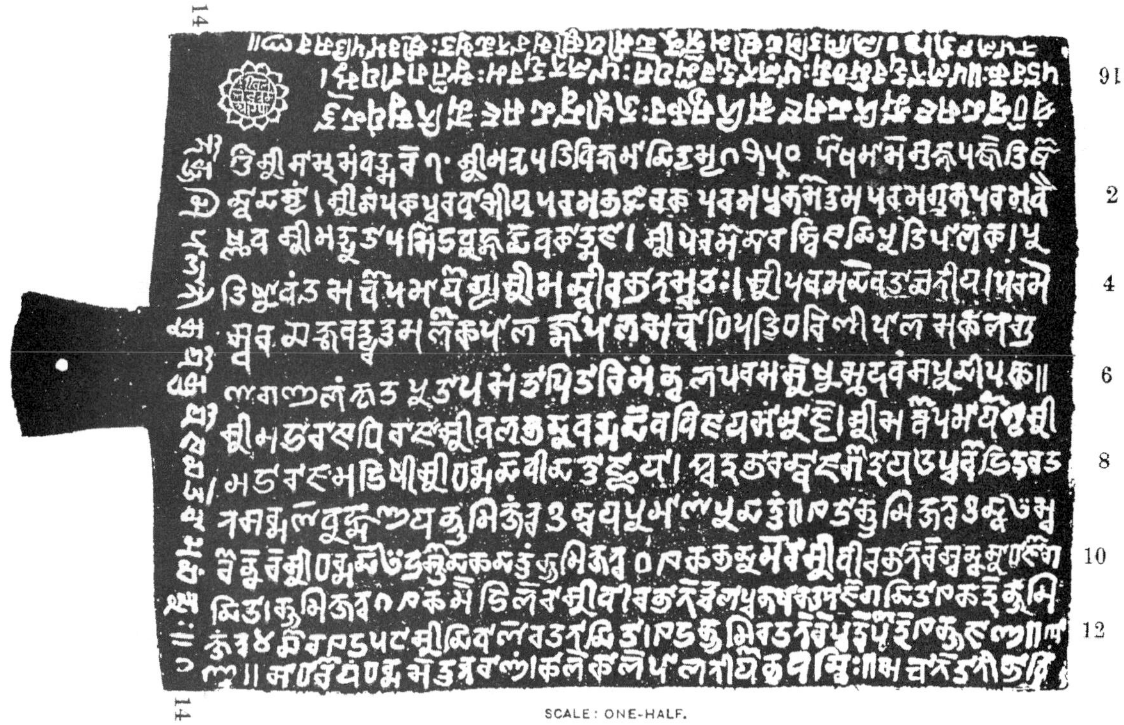


*Pl. 37*: Chamba plate of Balabhadra, *vs* 1651.

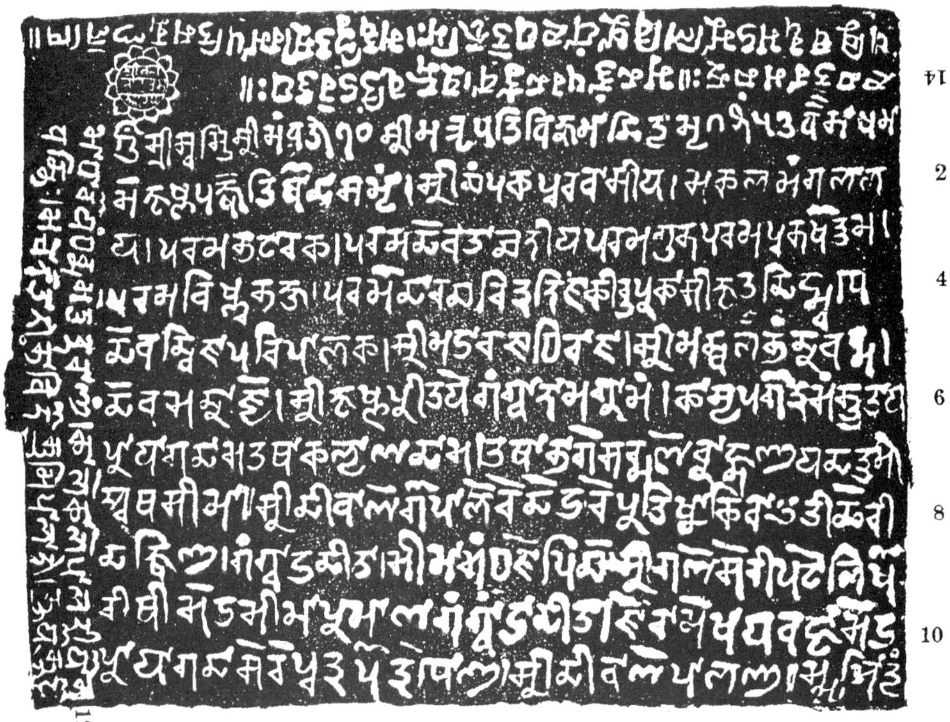

B. CH. CHHABRA. SCALE: THREE-FIFTHS. SURVEY OF INDIA, CALCUTTA.
REG. No. 3977 E'36-500'53.

*Pl. 38*: Chamba plate of Balabhadra, *vs* 1652.

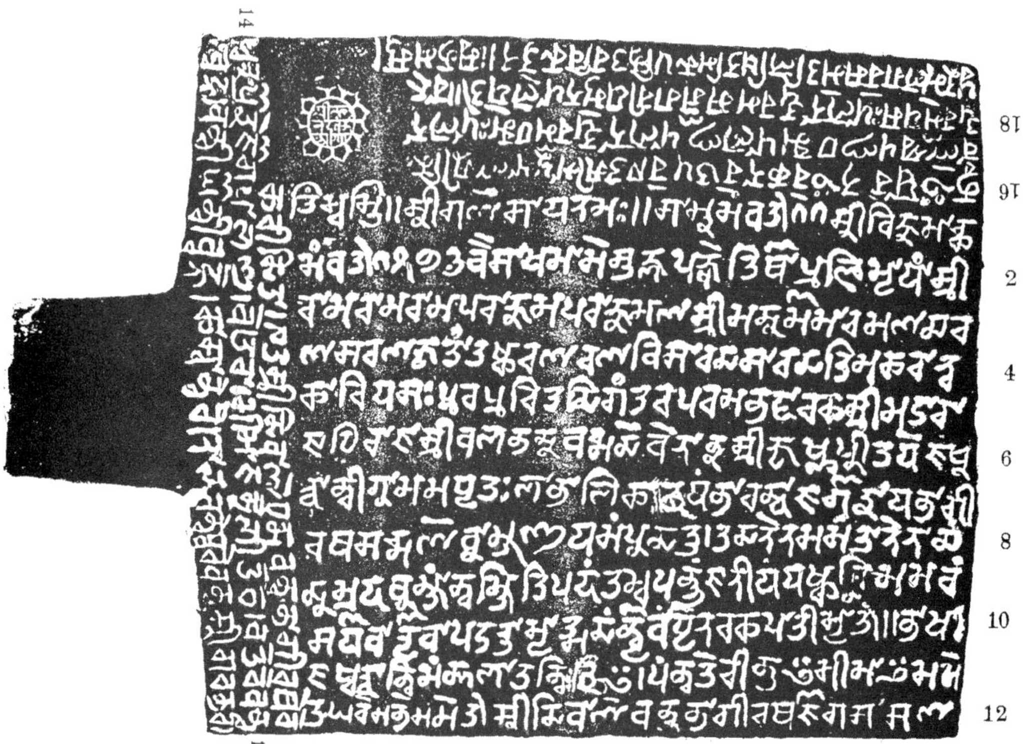

SCALE: TWO-THIRDS.

*Pl. 39*: Chamba plate of Balabhadra, *vs* 1692.

*Pl. 40*: Chamba plate of Balabhadra, *vs* 1693.

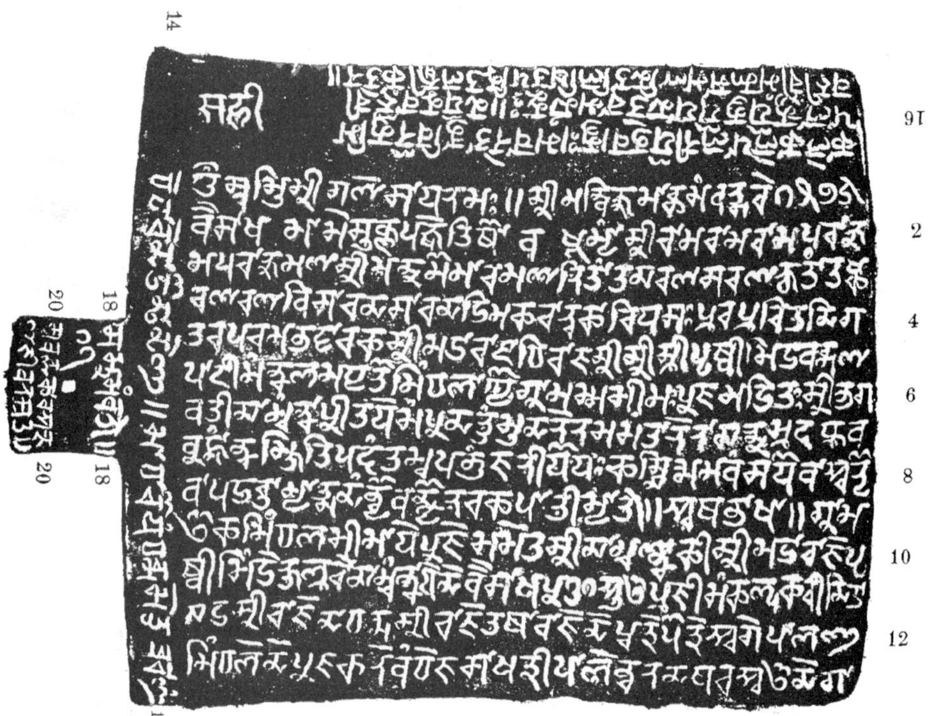


*Pl. 41*: Chamba plate of Pṛthvīsiṁha, *vs* 1698.

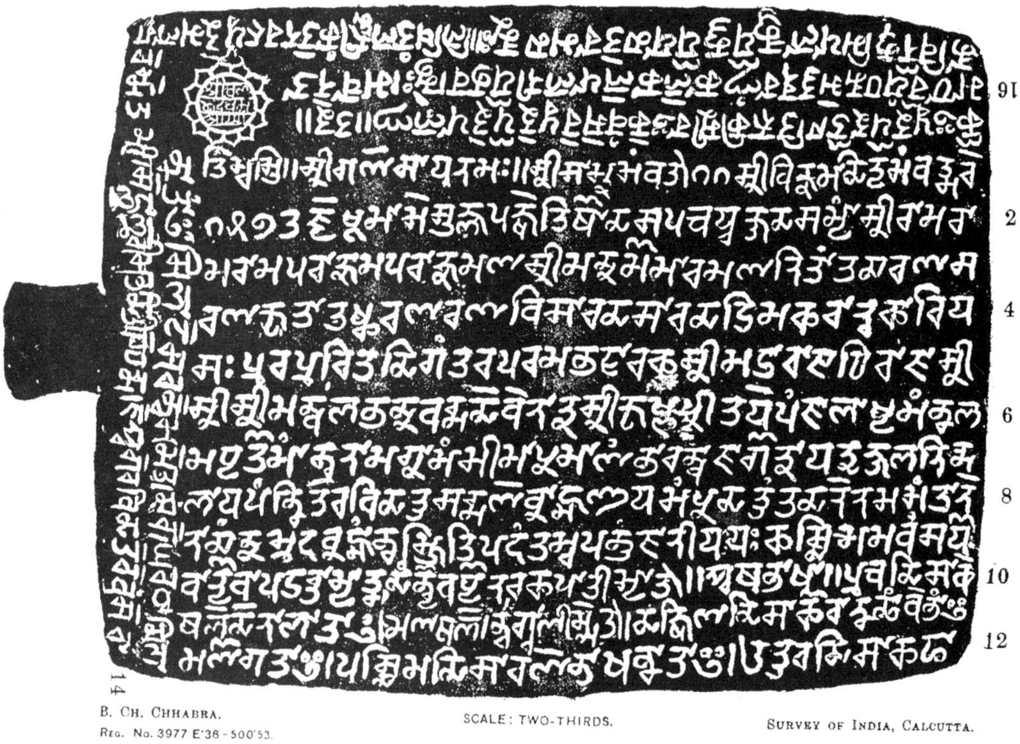

*Pl. 42*: Mindhal plate of Pṛthvīsiṁha, *vs* 1702.

*Pl. 43*: Chamba plate of Pṛthvisiṁha, *vs* 1692.

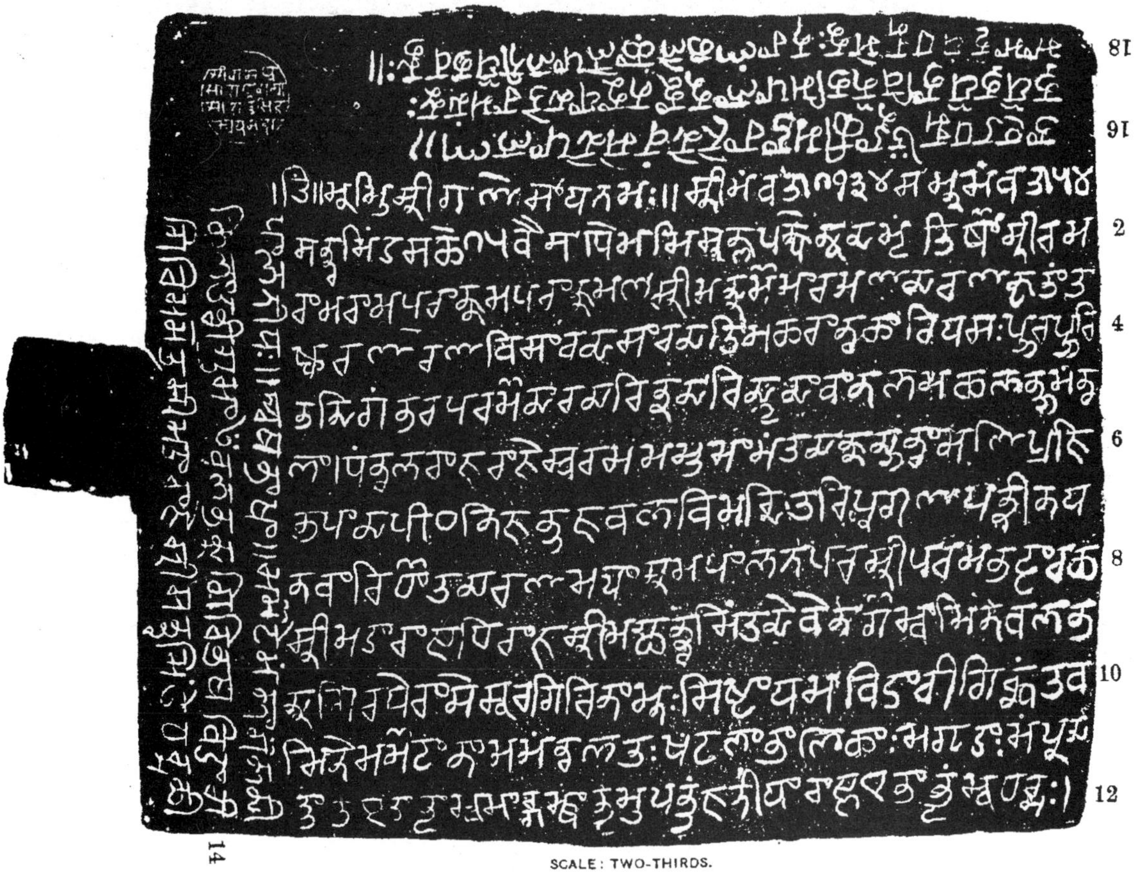

SCALE : TWO-THIRDS.

*Pl. 44*: Lakṣmī-Nārāyaṇa temple plate of Śatrusiṁha, *vs* 1734.

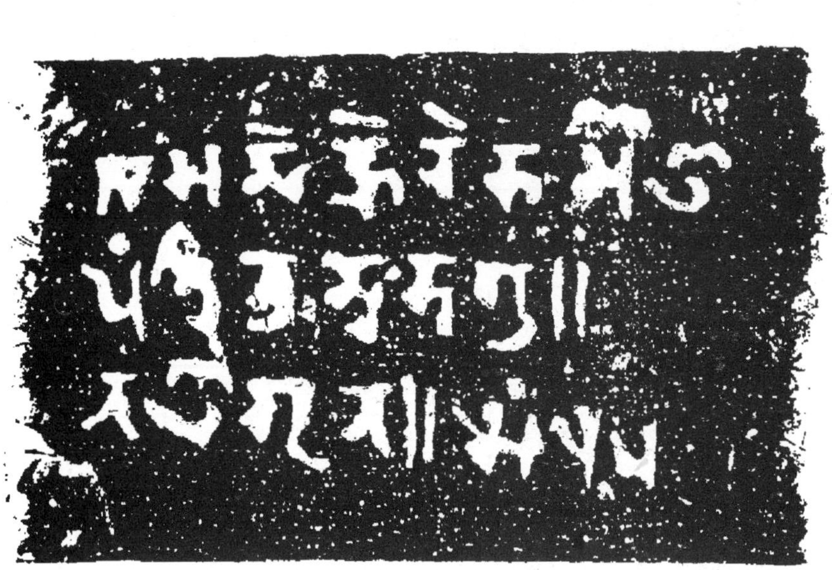

SCALE : FIVE-TWELFTHS.

*Pl. 45*: Lakṣmī Nārāyaṇa temple niche inscription, *Śāstra* 55.

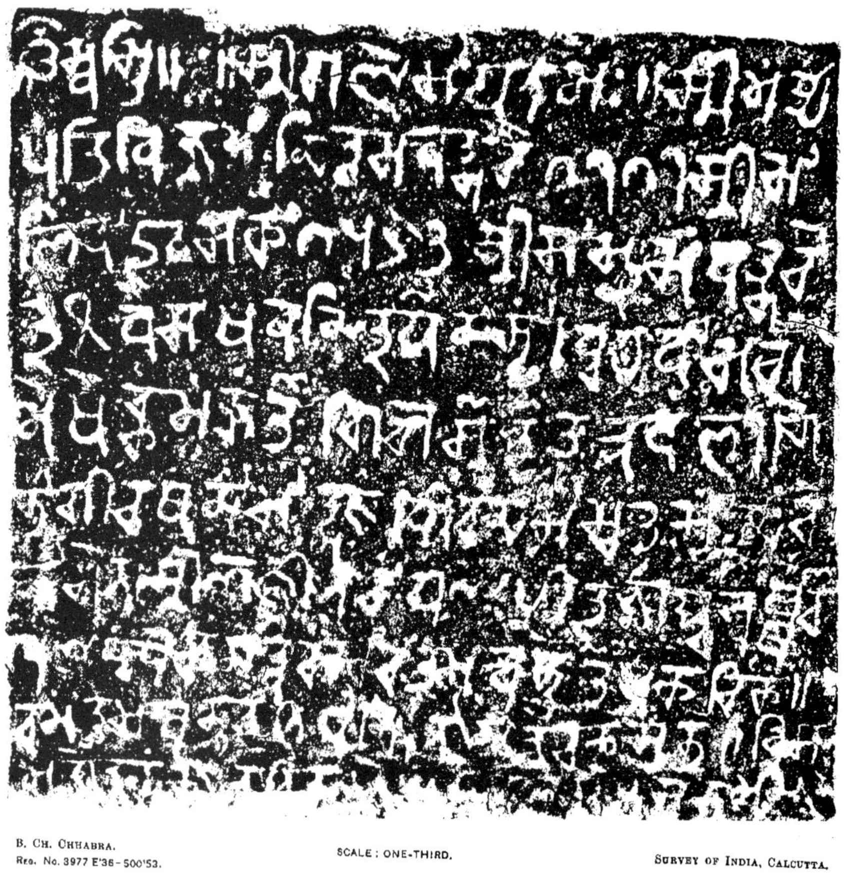


*Pl. 46*: Cabūtrā stone inscription, *vs* 1717.

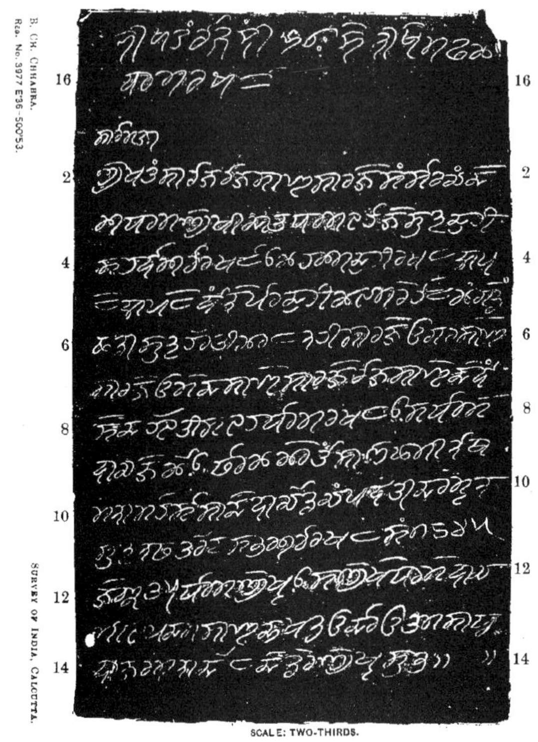


*Pl. 47*: Treaty between Rajasiṁha and Saṁsāracanda.

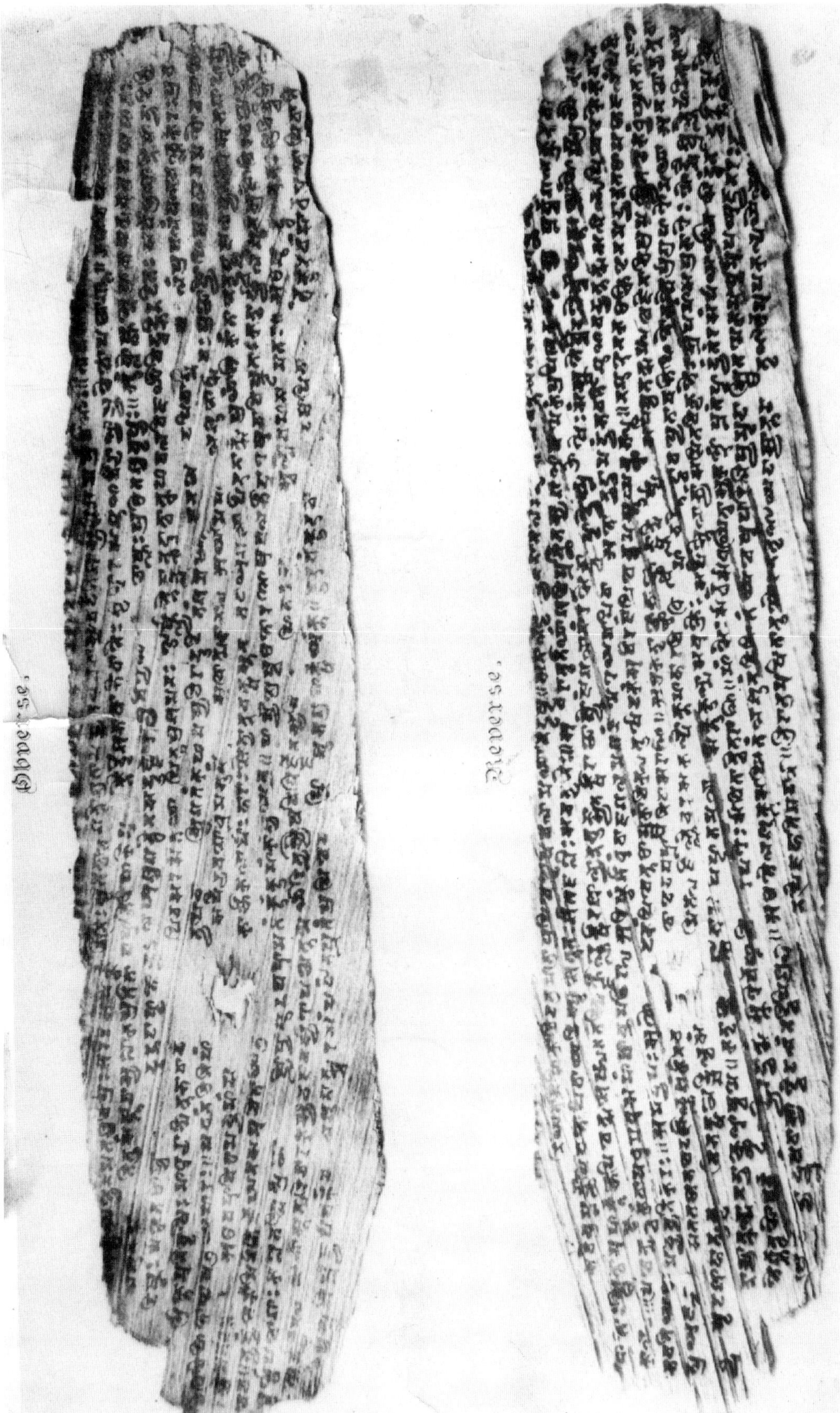


*Pl. 48:* The Bower Manuscript Part-I, vol.-22 plate-II, 4th-5th Century CE.

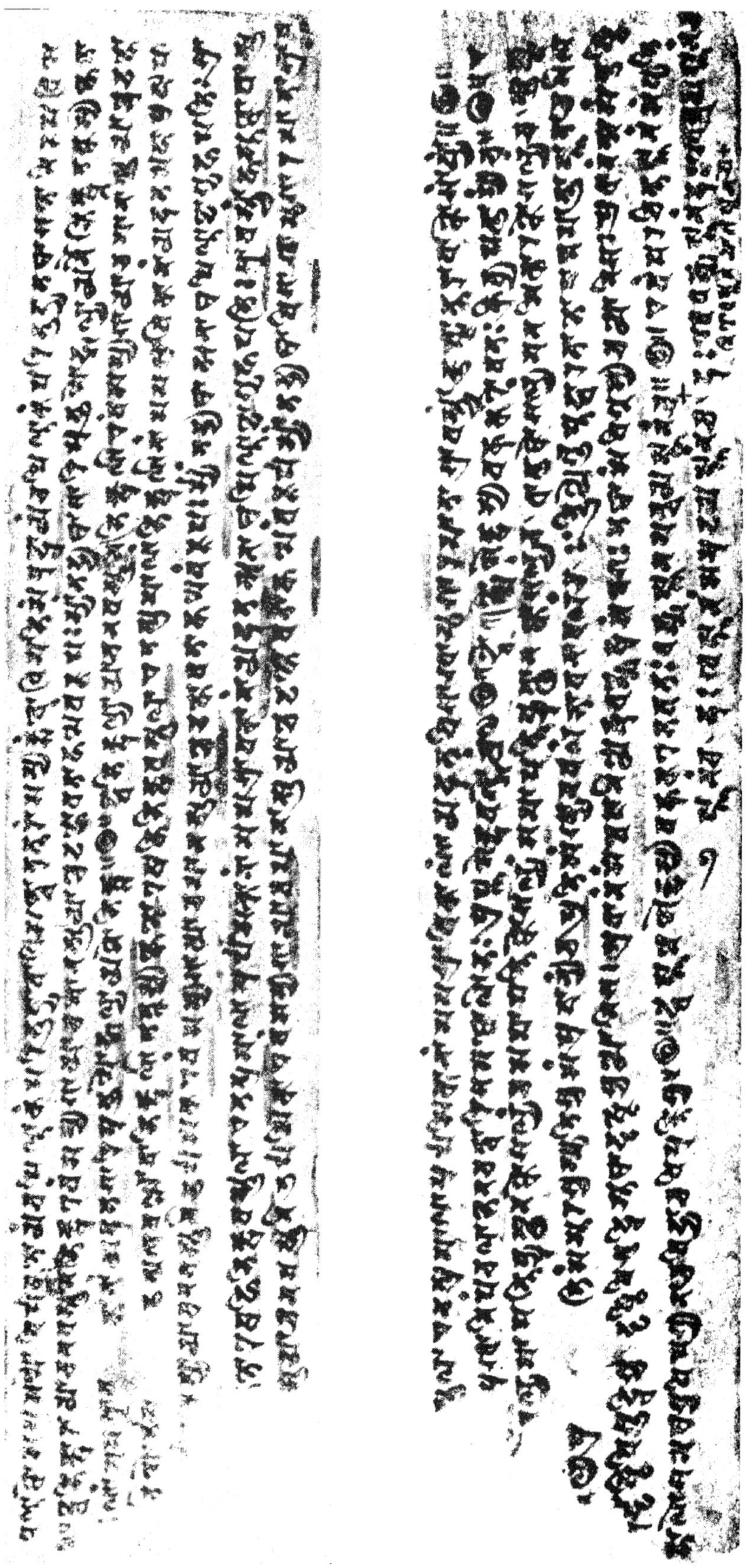

*Pl. 49*: Gilgit Manuscripts, 6th Century CE.

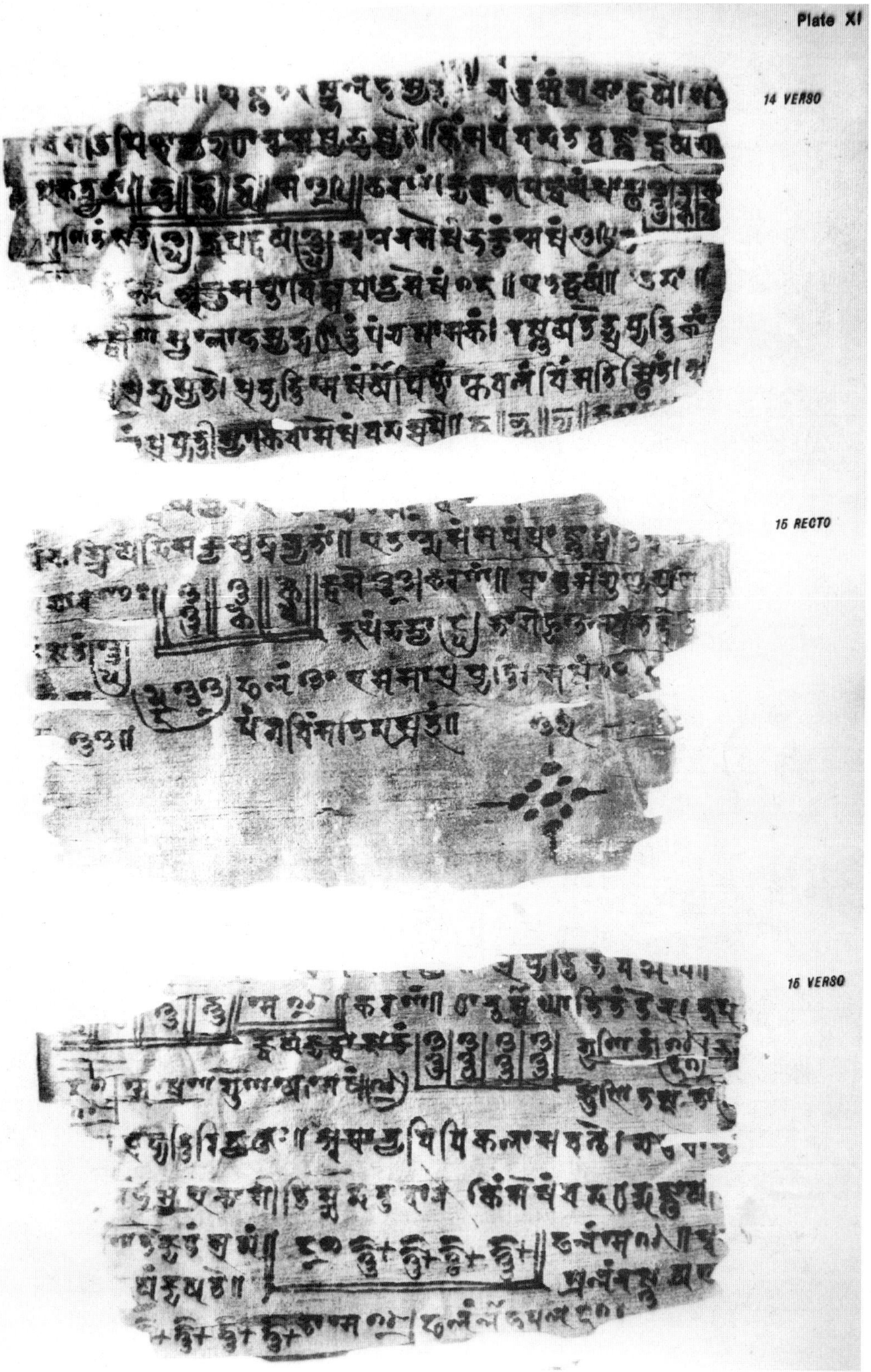


*Pl. 50*: Bakhshali Manuscript, 12[th] Century CE.

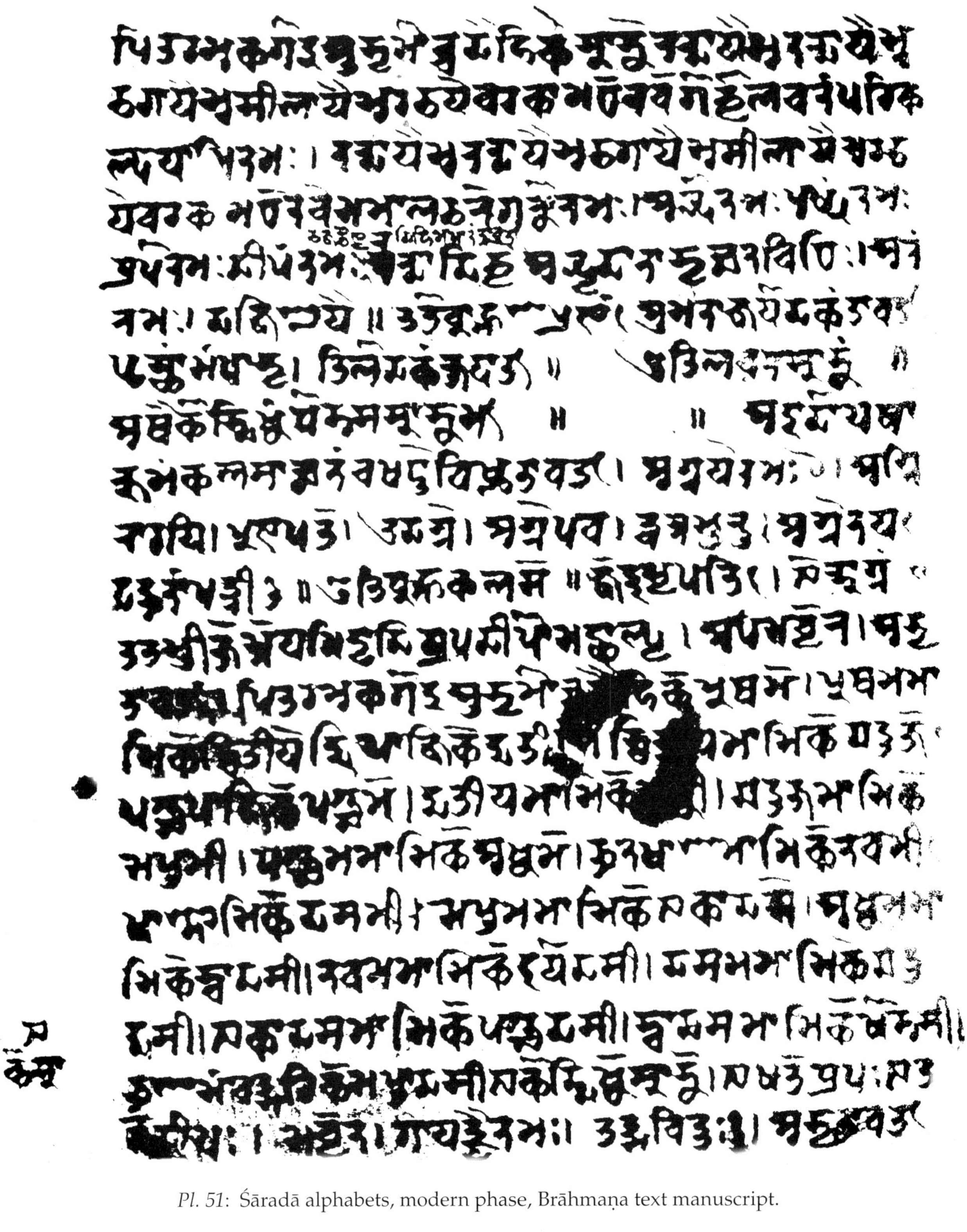

*Pl. 51*: Śāradā alphabets, modern phase, Brāhmaṇa text manuscript.

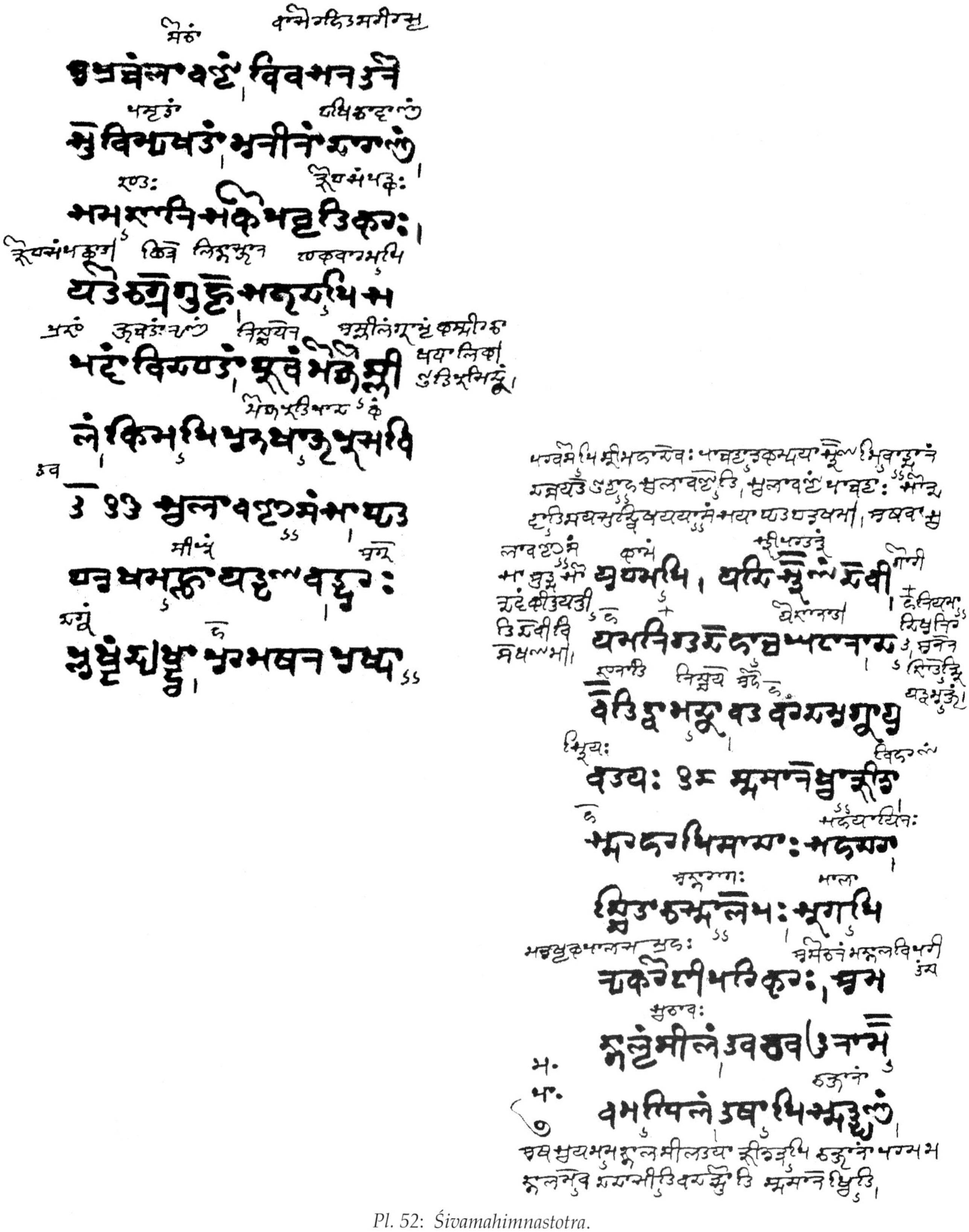

*Pl. 52: Śivamahimnastotra.*

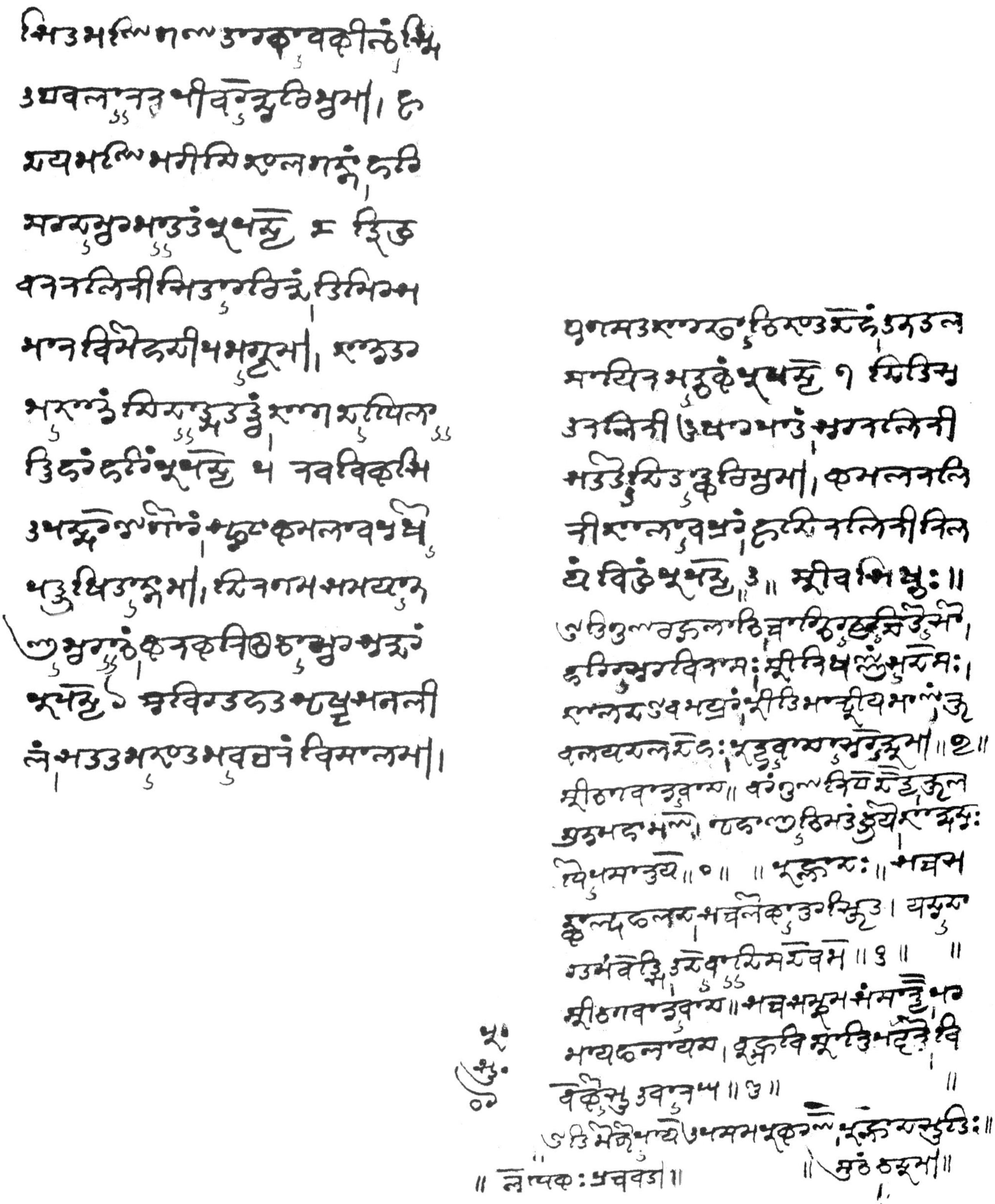

*Pl. 53: Prahlāda stuti.*

# Bibliography

## I. Original Sources


*Alberuni's India*, Eng. ed. by E.C. Sachau, London, 1910.

*Bakshali Manuscript*, ed. by G.R. Kaye, Archaeological Survey of India, New Imperial Series, vol. XLIII, Calcutta, 1927.

Birch Bark Manuscript of Ādi and Sabhā Parvan of *Mahābhārata*, Bhandarkar Oriental Research Institute, No. 159 of 1875-76.

Birch Bark Manuscript of *Muni-mata-maṇi-mālā*, MS. No. 201, Department of Research and Museums, J & K Government.

Birch Bark Manuscript of *Śākuntalam*, Bandarkar Oriental Research Institute, Poona, No. 192 of 1875-76.

Facsimiles of *Paippalāda Saṁhitā*, published in Roth and Whitney's edition of Atharvaveda.

*Gilgit Manuscripts*, ed. by N. Dutt, Srinagar, 1939; facsimilies of Sutapiṭaka, ed. by Dr. Raghubir, Dr. Lokesh Chandra, New Delhi, 1963.

*Hasan, Tarikh-i-Kashmir.*

*Hiuen-Tsang*, Eng. Trans by Samuel Beal (Buddhist Records of the Western World), London, 1884.

Jonaraja, *Dvitīya Rājataraṅgiṇī*, ed. by S.K. Kaul, VVRI, Hoshiarpur, 1968.

Kalhaṇa's *Rājataraṅgiṇī*, ed. by M.A. Stein, Bombay, 1892, Eng. Trans. M.A. Stein, Delhi, 1961.

——— Trans. by R.S. Pandit, Allahabad, 1935.

*Mahābhārata*, Bhandarkar Oriental Research Institute, Poona.

*Nīlamata Purāṇa*, ed. by Ved Kumari Ghai, J & K State Cultural Academy, Srinagar.

Srivara's *Jaina-Rājataraṅgiṇī*, ed. by S.K. Kaul, VVRI, Hoshiarpur, 1968.

*Tārikhi-Firishtā*, Eng. Trans. Briggs, Calcutta, 1808-10.

The *Bower Manuscript*, ed. by Hoernle, Archaeological Survey of India (New Imperial Series), Vol. XXII, Calcutta, 1893–1912.

*Yuang Chwang*, Eng. Trans. by T. Watters, London, 1904-05.


## II. Modern Sources

### A. WORKS ON PALAEOGRAPHY, EPIGRAPHY, NUMISMATICS & ARCHAEOLOGY


Agrawal, J.N., *Inscriptions of Haryana, Himachal Pradesh, Kashmir, adjoining Hilly Tracts and Delhi.*

Allan, J., *Catalogue of the Coins of Ancient India*, British Museum, London, 1936.

Banerji, R.D., *The Origin of the Bengali Script*, Calcutta, 1919.

Bühler, George, *Indian Palaeography*, Eng. Trans. by J.F. Fleet, Indian Studies: Past and Present, Calcutta, 1959.

Bühler, George, *Report of a Tour in Search of Sanskrit Manuscripts made in Kashmir, Rajputana and Central India*, 1877.

Burnell, A.C., *Elements of South Indian Palaeography*, London, 1878.

Chabra, B.Ch., *Antiquities of Chamba State, Part II* (Inscriptions of Post Muhammadan Period).

Cunningham, A., *Coins of Ancient India.*

Cunningham, A., *Coins of Medieval India*, London, 1893.

Dani, A.H., *Indian Palaeography*, London.

Dani, A.H., *CHILAS*, Islamabad 1983.

Dasgupta, C.C., *The Development of Kharoṣṭhī Script*, Calcutta, 1958.

Deambi, B.K. Kaul, *Corpus of Śāradā Inscriptions of Kashmir* Delhi, 1982.

Deambi, B.K. Kaul, *History and Culture of Ancient Gandhāra and Western Himalayas.*

Direnger, David, *The Alphabet*, 2nd Ed., London, 1949.

Fleet, J.F., *Corpus Inscriptionum Indicarum*, vol. III (Inscriptions of Early Gupta Kings and Their Successors), Calcutta, 1888; Indological Book House, Varanasi, 1963.

Gardener, Percy, *The Coins of the Greek and Scythic Kings of Bactria and India*, London, 1886.

Handa, Devender, *Studies in Indian Coins and Seals*, 1985.

Hulzsch, E., *Corpus Inscriptionum Indicarum*, vol. I (Inscriptions of Aśoka), Oxford, 1925.

Kak, R.C., *Ancient Monuments of Kashmir*, London, 1933.

Kak, R.C., *Antiquities of Marew Wadwan* (Memoirs of the Archaeological Survey of Kashmir No. 1), Srinagar, 1933.

Kak, R.C., *Handbook of the Archaeological and Numismatic Sections of Sri Pratap Singh Museum*, Calcutta, 1923.

Konow, Sten, *Notes on a Tour in Kashmir*, 1908.

Maity, S.K., & R.R. Mukherjee, *Corpus of Bengal Inscriptions*, Calcutta, 1967.

Marshall, John, *Note on Archaeological Work in Kashmir*, 1903.

Ojha, Gauri Shankar Hira Chand, *Bhāratīya Prācina Lipimālā* (*Indian Palaeography*), Third Ed., Delhi, 1959.

Pandey, R.B., *Indian Palaeography*, Varanasi, Second Ed. 1957.

Rapson, E.J., *Indian Coins.*

Sharma, Rita Devi, Tākarī Primer Part I & II, Shimla 1987.

Sircar, D.C., *Indian Epigraphical Glossary*, Delhi, 1966.

Sircar, D.C., *Indian Epigraphy*, Delhi, 1965.

Sircar, D.C., *Select Inscriptions*, Calcutta, 1965.

Smith, V.A., *Catalogue of Coins in the Indian Museum*, Calcutta.

Upasak, C., *History and Palaeography of Maurya Brahmi Alphabet.*

Vogel, J.Ph., *Antiquities of Chamba State*, Part I (Inscriptions of Pre-Muhammadan Period).

B. MISCELLANEOUS WORKS

Bannerjee, S.N., *Cultural Heritage of Kashmir*, Calcutta, 1965.

Cunningham, A., *Ancient Geography of India*, ed. by S. N. Majumdar, Calcutta, 1924.

Cunningham, A., *Book of Indian Eras*, Calcutta, 1883.

Cunningham, A., *Ladak-Physical, Statistical and Historical*, London, 1854.

Datta, B., and A.N. Singh, *History of Hindu Mathematics*, Parts 1-2, Lahore, 1935.

Drew, F., *The Jammu and Kashmir Territories*, London, 1875.

Francke, A.H., *History of Western Tibet*, London, 1907.

Grierson, G., *Linguistic Survey of India*, vol. VIII.

Macdonnel, A., and A. B. Keith (eds.), *Vedic Index of Names and Subjects*, in 2 vols.

Stein, M.A., *Memoir of the Ancient Geography of Kashmir*.

Vigne, G.T., *Travels in Kashmir, Ladak Iskardo*, 2 vols., London, 1842.

Vogel, J.Ph., *Catalogue of Bhuri Singh Museum*, Calcutta, 1909.

**III. Journals**

*Epigraphia Indica*

*Indian Antiquary*

*Journal of the Royal Asiatic Society*

*Journal of the Bombay Branch of the Royal Asiatic Society*

*Journal of the Asiatic Society of Bengal*

*Journal of the Numismatic Society of India*

*Journal of Central Asia, Peshawar*

**IV. Catalogues of Manuscripts**

Aufrecht., Th., *Catalogus Catalogorum*, Leipzig, 1891.

*Catalogue of the Sanskrit Manuscripts* in the Library of India Office, ed. by J. Eggeling, London, 1887-1891.

*Descriptive Catalogue of Sanskrit Manuscripts*, Sanskrit College, Calcutta.

*Descriptive Catalogue of Manuscripts* in Govt. Manuscript Library, Bhandarkar Oriental Research Institute, Pune.

*Hand List of Sanskrit Manuscripts*, in the Sanskrit Manuscripts, Research and Publications Department, vol. 1 (A-K), Centre for Centeral Asian Studies, University of Kashmir, 1989.

Mitra, Rajendra Lal, *Notices of Sanskrit Manuscripts*, Sanskrit College, Calcutta.

Stein, M.A., *Catalogue of Sanskrit Manuscripts* in the Raghunath Temple Library, Jammu.

# Index

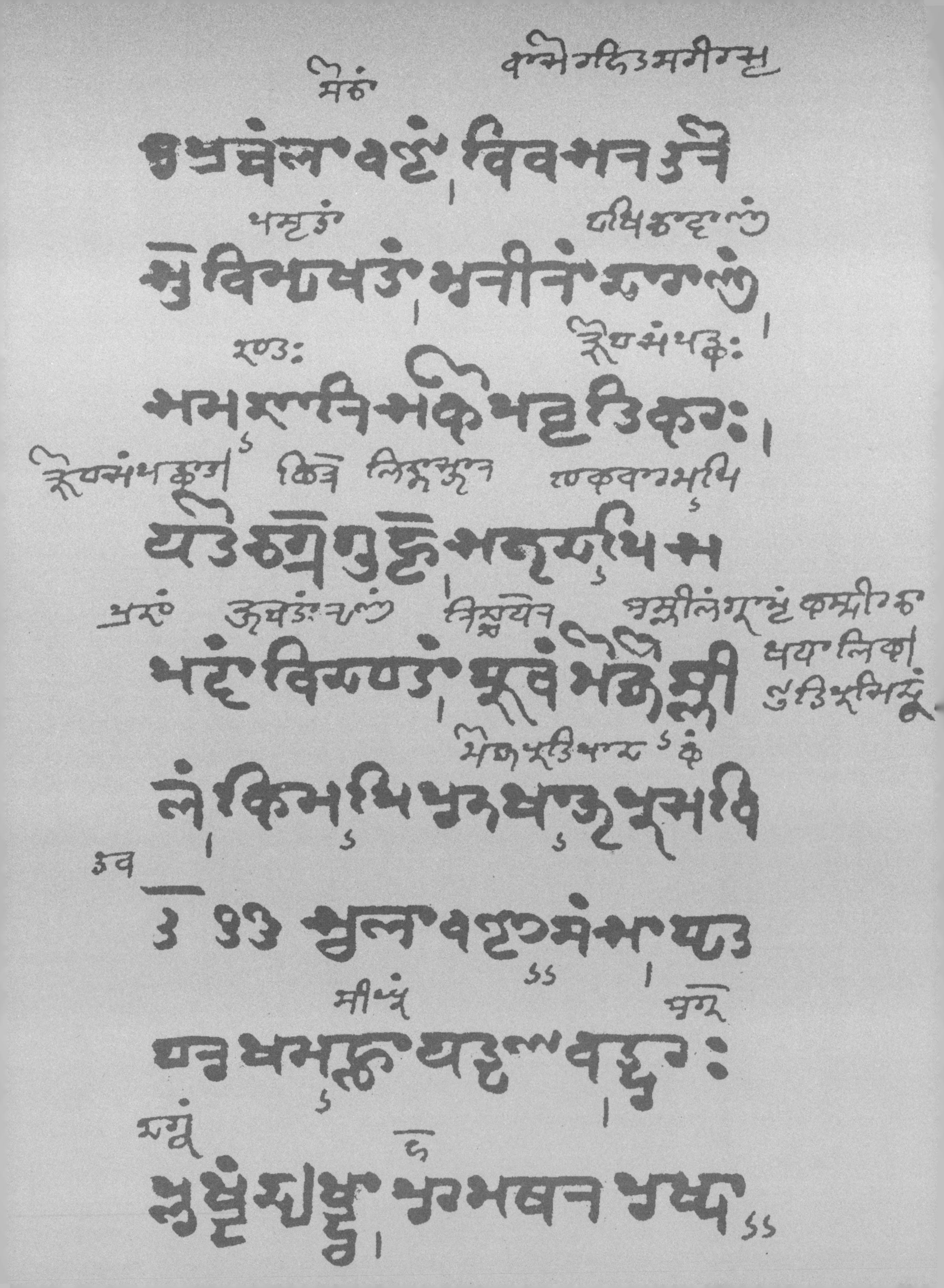